DATE DUE

GAYLORD   PRINTED IN U.S.A.

BOOKS ON TRIAL

BOOKS ON TRIAL

Red Scare in the Heartland

Shirley A. Wiegand
and Wayne A. Wiegand

UNIVERSITY OF OKLAHOMA PRESS : NORMAN

Library of Congress Cataloging-in-Publication Data

Wiegand, Shirley A.
Books on trial : red scare in the Heartland / Shirley A. Wiegand and Wayne A. Wiegand.
p. cm.
Includes bibliographical references and index.
ISBN 978-0-8061-3868-8 (hardcover : alk. paper)
1. Trials (Sedition) — Oklahoma. 2. Communists — Oklahoma.
3. Censorship — United States. I. Wiegand, Wayne A., 1946–   II. Title.
KF221.P6W54 2007
345.766'0231 — dc22   2007004141

345,766
WIE
9.07

For our son, Scott

Contents

Illustrations

Acknowledgments

I t's been a great experience. In the fall of 1999, I came across a short article in a 1940 issue of *Wilson Library Bulletin* that reported the conviction of an Oklahoma City bookseller for violating a state criminal syndicalism law. The defendant in the trial had been brought to "justice" not for anything he did, but for the content of the books he sold. Because I was much interested in censorship issues in American library and book history, I copied the two-paragraph piece for future reference, thinking it had the makings of a good article. But as I puzzled over what a "criminal syndicalism" law was on the way home that night, it occurred to me the incident might provide an opportunity to work on a project with my wife, Shirl, a law school professor. Certainly, I thought, she would know a whole lot more about criminal syndicalism than I. So I dropped the copy on her desk with a note that read: "Interesting article. What do you think of this as a joint research project?"

Fortunately for me, she considered it carefully for a few days, then agreed to discuss it. We had been married for thirty-five years, but this would be the first time we ever attempted to work together professionally on a scholarly project. Shirl knew how fussy I was in my research and writing; I knew the same about her. We had spent the vast majority of our professional lives working on single-authored articles and books. Although we were both a bit nervous, we none-theless decided to try. Scholarly articles didn't command that much effort, we thought, and it might be nice to show our children, rela-tives, and friends that we could actually work together professionally. Little did we know that the story hinted at in the *Wilson Library Bulletin* piece would quickly lead us in subsequent months (and ultimately years) to so much primary source data that was so incredi-bly rich in detail that the "Books on Trial" article we initially envi-sioned would have to become the *Books on Trial* you currently hold in your hands.

The project we began in the fall of 1999 has rewarded us in so many ways. Data gathering led to intellectually stimulating research full of exciting discoveries that we shared with one another at the end of many workdays, even though we were often thousands of miles apart. It allowed us to renew old friendships with people we had come to know while Shirl was on the law faculty at the Univer-sity of Oklahoma between 1988 and 1995. It also enabled us to form new friendships with people who were present at the 1940s events we set out to describe, or who were relatives or friends of the sub-jects we were studying and who had their own stories to tell. Finally, it reaffirmed our conviction that librarians and archivists in general (and particularly those responsible for the special collections rele-vant to our project) are among the most motivated, committed, and client-centered people in the world of professions.

While the actual writing has been as rewarding as the research, it was also a bit more taxing on our relationship. We quickly agreed I would draft the acknowledgments, and that Shirl would draft the chapter describing her interviewing experiences. Both of us, how-ever, also wanted to write the first draft of the main part of the manuscript. After considerable negotiation, I managed to convince Shirl to permit me to take a stab at it. From previous experience I knew that the first draft would function as the blueprint for subse-quent revisions; I worried Shirl might not know enough about the historical background of our story. She diplomatically and silently indulged me, then quickly exercised her relentlessly exacting pen to the first draft I laid on her desk. By the time I saw it again, Shirl had brought the manuscript into much better shape, and had rewritten much of my coverage of the trials. (And although I didn't tell her, I was surprised to find out how much she knew about history, and how little I knew about law.) Subsequent drafts were a process of give and take (I think I gave more than took; Shirl thinks it was the other way around). Despite the bumps along the way, however, the project begun in the fall of 1999 has been so much fun that when we finished it in late spring 2005, we decided to give it to each other as a fortieth wedding anniversary present.

We have many people and institutions to thank. While teaching at the University of Wisconsin–Madison through 2002, my part of the research benefited much from the services of librarians and materials in the collections amassed there over the generations, including those at the Wisconsin Historical Society. Anyone doing historical research on people whose voices were largely on the margins of dominant cultures almost inevitably comes into contact with the efforts of Jim Danky, now-retired newspaper/microtext/periodicals librarian at the Society, whose careful and diligent work over thirty-five years has resulted in collections of materials that have effectively preserved many of those voices. Much of the newspaper opinion on the book trials that we quote here was uncovered in the materials Jim collected for the Society.

We also want to thank University of Wisconsin–Madison School of Library and Information Studies Director Louise S. Robbins for her support and the school's librarian Michele Besant, who was especially helpful at a late date in uncovering an obscure periodical that yielded a very important detail. Since 2003, I have also benefited from the services and librarians at Florida State University, where students and colleagues helped test many ideas in this book. College of Information Dean Jane Robbins and her successor, Dean Larry Dennis, were supportive throughout.

Much of Shirl's research was assisted by the Marquette University Law School, where colleagues and students provided a welcome environment to discuss the project. Special thanks go to the librarians of the Marquette University Law School Library (especially Trish Cervenka, Robin Cork and Jim Mumm), the librarians of the

University Library, and especially to Dean Joseph Kearney. Joe was particularly supportive of this project and truly put his (or the school's) money where his mouth was, funding research trips, Freedom of Information Act charges, copying costs, and other expenses associated with this project.

The Oklahoma Department of Library and Archives housed the records and transcripts for the four trials that ultimately grounded our story. We spent many days there combing through these one-of-a-kind sources, gleaning valuable details that we were able to weave into our narrative. We owe much to the staff in the Archives Division for their ready assistance, and to staff members of the State Library and the Oklahoma Historical Society, both of which have rich state newspaper collections. Because the *Daily Oklahoman,* the Sooner State's major newspaper, was keyword searchable online from its origins, it was relatively easy to uncover every relevant detail contained in its pages. And once we nailed down the chronology of events, it was also relatively easy to exploit the files of other unindexed newspapers, in Oklahoma and elsewhere. We would also like to thank the staff at the Oklahoma County Courthouse.

The library and archives professionals, staff, and collections at the University of Oklahoma greatly helped this study along. University of Oklahoma Provost Nancy Mergler graciously gave permission to screen the old personnel files housed in an administration building basement room. Many thanks to University of Oklahoma David Ross Boyd Professor of History David W. Levy, author of a forthcoming multivolume history of the university, who guided me to these files and showed me how to use them. Staff members of the University of Oklahoma library system, especially its main library (Bizzell), its law library, and its Western Historical Collections, were equally helpful. Special thanks to former law library director, Nickie Singleton. And every time we returned to the Oklahoma City area to conduct research, we made sure to connect with good friends Pat and Bob Richardson of Norman, and Nina Rowland and Sandy Ingraham of McLoud. Often they put us up for the night, sometimes for the week, and Nina performed some valuable Oklahoma City research for us. All are lifelong friendships.

Thanks also to Cheryl Baker, of the Tulsa Public Library, who chased down a hard-to-find obituary; Debbie Dalton, of the Sacramento Public Library, who performed a similar service; and Ron Cohen, of Indiana University Northwest, who not only opened up his files of materials on Woody Guthrie, Pete Seeger, Sis Cunningham, and the Red Dust and Almanac Singers, but also shared his knowledge of them all with me at a delightful lunch in Gary.

On a trip to New York City in January 2004, Shirl met Mark Rosenzweig, who helped her explore the collections at the Reference Center for Marxist Studies he manages. These unique collections pointed us in directions we might not have taken, and to materials that greatly enriched our story. While in the Big Apple, she also used the Special Collections of Brooklyn College, alma mater to two of our subjects, and materials at the New York Public Library. She interviewed Timothy Wood, son of Robert and Ina Wood, two of the chief characters in our story. Materials he provided were invaluable in filling in detail; several of the photos and other materials he had saved are included elsewhere in this book. Timothy also demonstrated dignity, an impressive sense of fairness, and great care and patience as he answered countless questions about his father via e-mail and correspondence. He also agreed to meet with us a second time in early 2005.

From New York, Shirl drove to Hyde Park, where she spent several days interviewing Wilma Jaffe, wife of Eli (another chief character) and witness to many of the events we describe here. For three days Wilma willingly answered all questions honestly, openly, and to the best of her recollection, and (Shirl tells me) served up some delicious homemade meals as well. Our research proved she has an excellent memory. Wilma also accompanied Shirl to visit Sis Cunningham in a nearby nursing home, likely the last interview Sis gave; she died just months thereafter. Finally, Wilma put us in contact with her brother, Orval, whom we visited on our last research trip to Oklahoma City. Because Orval had different experiences of the events we describe, his contributions deepened our understanding even more. Orval died in 2006.

Two-thirds of the way through our project we discovered that

Alan Shaw (the fourth of the major subjects in our study) and his family had moved to Milwaukee at mid-century, and lived there the rest of their lives. Shirl spent many valuable hours interviewing Jo Biddle, partner to Toni Shaw (Alan's daughter); John Eklund (Toni's former husband); and Peggy Rose (Alan's longtime close friend). She also communicated via e-mail with Alan's daughter Judith Wheeldon, residing in Australia. Each gave unselfishly of his or her time; all supplied details we never would have been able to discover without their help.

Right at the end of the project, when we finally discovered the real name of Robert Wood, we also managed to identify and contact his nephew, Ed Sherin, who was most gracious and forthcoming in a telephone interview and in subsequent correspondence. From him we learned details about his uncle's family before and after the 1940s Oklahoma incidents that we would otherwise not have been able to discover. And once we had Robert Wood's original name, Lesley Schoenfeld of the Harvard Law School Special Collections Department responded quickly to requests for information and photocopies of materials on this HLS graduate.

We were also fortunate to find children of the two Sooner State lawyers who defended our Oklahoma Four. Candy Wilcott, Stanley Belden's daughter, spent much time with Shirl on the telephone, providing us with a wealth of details about her father's life after he left Oklahoma. She also sent written materials and copies of newspaper clippings we incorporated into our story. Bob Croom, son of George E. Croom, and Margaret Gandy, George's daughter, shared important details with me about their father's involvement in the cases in several telephone interviews.

Collections in the Library of Congress, the University of California–Berkeley, Southern Illinois University, the University of Wisconsin–Milwaukee, the University of Chicago, and the Seeley G. Mudd Manuscript Library at Princeton University were all very helpful. Other sources we found extremely informative were the U.S. Department of Justice files. In response to multiple requests under the Freedom of Information Act, the department provided over three thousand pages of material on our Oklahoma Four.

At our request, two people read the manuscript in its entirety, and we owe them special thanks. My former University of Wisconsin–Madison colleague Paul S. Boyer, Merle Curti Professor of History Emeritus, provided early and helpful feedback. Shirl's former University of Oklahoma colleague David Levy not only read the entire manuscript, but also provided detailed, perceptive, and oftentimes witty suggestions for change. We accepted most. We have benefited much from their careful commentary. Working with our University of Oklahoma Press editors, Kirk Bjornsgaard and Jay Dew, and our copyeditor, Mary Rodarte, has been a delight. Thanks also to Vitrude DeSpain, who prepared the index.

Once the Press expressed interest in the manuscript, editors sent it out to five anonymous readers. Their commentary was thorough and perceptive, and we much appreciate their critiques.

One final note. Although we give this book to each other as a fortieth anniversary present, we dedicate it to our son, Scott. His courage and commitment to truth during his own struggle against an oppressive and irresponsible exercise of governmental power has inspired and made us proud. And to his wife, Erin, his sister, Cori Sheets, and his brother, Andy, and wife, Jenelle Welling, all of whom immediately and without question offered support to Scott during his struggle, we extend our deepest and sincerest thanks.

Wayne A. Wiegand
Tallahassee, Florida
January 5, 2007

BOOKS ON TRIAL

CHAPTER ONE

Raids and Arrests, August 1940

Shortly after lunch on July 24, 1940, Oklahoma City Detective John Wade Webb unstrapped his gun and took off his street clothes. He then donned an oil-stained shirt, an oil-soaked hat and overalls, and some greasy, oil-soaked boots. He had not shaved for two days. "Now I look like a Communist," he thought as he checked himself in the mirror. Without his gun, he walked from police head-quarters to 129 West Grand, a two-story brick office building. Upon arrival, he opened a door marked 129½, and climbed the narrow stairs to a second floor, which had ten rooms, five on either side of the corridor. Several tenants occupied these rooms, but Webb was particularly interested in the two doors at the back of the building. Above one a sign read "Communist Party." The second read "Progressive Book Store," with an arrow pointing (appropriately enough) to the left.

Webb turned left and went in. The room he entered was neat, clean, and colorful, unlike the neighborhood in which it was located. On surrounding walls (including above the bookshelves) were pictures of Vladimir Lenin, Joseph Stalin, Karl Marx, and General Secretary of the Communist Party of the United States of America (CPUSA) Earl Browder. On the south and west walls he saw bookshelves made of packing crates that held several thousand books and pamphlets, including copies of the U.S. Constitution, autobiographies of famous Americans, and the Declaration of Independence. On the north wall stood a small stand with copies of the American Communist Party's *Daily Worker* and several other newspapers, and on the east side Webb spotted a staircase-shelf full of pamphlets and a partition that separated open floor space from a desk and typewriter.[1]

Working behind the partition was the bookstore's proprietor, thirty-three-year-old state Communist Party Secretary Bob Wood, a handsome man with a round, kindly face, who stood just under six feet tall and weighed about 180 pounds. The men nodded at each other and briefly chatted. Because people working in the oil fields near Oklahoma City regularly frequented the store during their lunch hours (Communist Party magazine *New Masses* noted later that "the shop is considered something of a palace" to neighborhood visitors), Bob assumed Webb might be interested in trade union pamphlets and pointed to several. Webb demurred, instead asking for works by Lenin and Stalin. After browsing the shelves for the next half hour, Webb selected two recent copies of the *Daily Worker* and thirteen pamphlets, including Lenin's *State and Revolution,* Stalin's *Foundations of Leninism,* and Marx's *The Communist Manifesto.* He then paid Bob fifty-five cents for the materials, left the store, and descended to the street. Back at police headquarters, Webb handed his purchases to Captain Dan Hollingsworth, head of the Intelligence Division of the Oklahoma City Police Department, on whose orders he had visited the Progressive Book Store that day to buy the materials.[2]

Shortly after noon on August 17 — a hot, sunny Saturday three weeks after Webb's visit — the Oklahoma City Police initiated a series of raids on the Progressive Book Store, the local office of the Communist Party, and five private homes. Deputy Sheriff Ross Biggers supervised the bookstore and Party office raids, and with other officers arrested everyone in the store, including Ina Wood, Bob's thirty-two-year-old, attractive but rather quiet wife, along with Elizabeth Green (a thin, stylishly dressed social worker from New York who had stopped in to use a typewriter), Herb Brausch (a big, blue-eyed bricklayer who was doing some carpentry work), and at least eight other customers.

As the police escorted this motley group down the stairs and into police cars, the Clarence Lewis family pulled up in their vege-table-delivery truck, as they often did during regular Saturday trips to town. Officers quickly surrounded sixteen-year-old Wilma (a small, brown-eyed brunette with a round, dimpled face), her lanky seventeen-year-old brother Orval, and their parents. Police ordered them into cars, but as they pushed the Lewises into the back seats, they debated what to do with Wilma. They worried about how arrest-ing a sixteen-year-old female would look in the newspapers. Al-though her mother urged her to join them in the back seat, Wilma resisted. To the police Wilma brazenly cited her rights under the Constitution. "Hell," said one of the officers, "out here we make our own Constitution!" "Aw, let her go," another snipped. "She's only a kid. When she grows up she'll get married and forget all about this stuff." While police temporarily turned their attention to other matters, Clarence reached into his pocket for the only money he had, and slipped Wilma three dollars. When the police drove off with her family and others they had arrested, Wilma stood alone on the street with no idea why her family had been taken, or where police had taken them. And all she had to sustain her was the three dollars her father had sneaked into her hand.[3] The raids had lasted fifteen minutes.

Simultaneous with the raid on the bookstore, Captain Dan Hol-lingsworth drove to 508 NW Fifth Street, where Elizabeth Green rented two rooms; he was unaware she had been arrested at the bookstore. Four miles from the bookstore four "burly" officers broke into the home of Ina and Bob Wood at 2331 SW 20th Street and arrested him, Alan Shaw, and Eli Jaffe. Alan and Eli were visiting Bob, who was sick in bed. "Somebody downtown wants to see you," one officer said. Police searched all three. Unlike the arresting of-ficers, Alan and Eli had heavy New York accents. Eli stood five feet five inches tall, weighed 135 pounds, and was energetic, quick-tempered and quick-moving. Alan was pale-skinned, slightly built (five feet nine inches, 150 pounds), and walked and spoke slowly. From Eli, officers took an automobile license, an application for automobile registration, and cards stating he was a member of the Oklahoma Young Communist League and a journalist representing Communist newspapers *Midwest Daily Record* and the *Daily Worker*. They hustled Bob, Eli, and Alan into the back seats of three different police cars. "What's this all about? Where are you taking me?" Eli asked. Neither of the two officers in the car answered. Instead, one said to the other, "Say Ross, you know you broke the jaw of that guy who tried to get away?" Eli realized they were trying to intimidate him.[4]

Armed with liquor search warrants authorized by Justice of the Peace Paul Powers (Oklahoma was a dry state at the time), other authorities returned to the bookstore, the Communist Party office, and the residences later that afternoon. The warrant to search 129½ West Grand resembled the others. Based on a deputy sheriff's affidavit, it stated that Robert and Ina Wood, Alan Shaw, "and members of the Communist Party" at the "two story brick building at 129½ West Grand" were in the business of selling intoxicating liquors. The warrant authorized a search but failed to specify which rooms on the second floor. And added to the preprinted official form that authorized a search for liquor was new typewritten language that authorized authorities to seek out "books, records, papers and articles which are used in and are evidence of the commission of criminal syndicalism or any other crime against the laws of the State of Oklahoma and of the United States."[5]

At the bookstore police seized thousands of books and pamphlets, including fifteen copies of the U.S. Constitution; novels by Jack London, Leo Tolstoy, and Andre Malraux; works of classical political economy by Karl Marx and Friedrich Engels; biographies of Thomas Jefferson and Charles Dickens; and pamphlets by Earl Browder. From the Party office they confiscated work calendars; rubber stamps with inscriptions such as "Dues, Communist Party, U.S.A." and "International Solidarity;" letterhead stationery; several press releases; maps; and documents labeled "Plans for Oklahoma City Anti-War Work," "Distribution of 4,000 anti-war leaflets on east side on 'Negro and the War,' " and "Sale of Anti-war Literature in Unions." Officers were particularly excited about the maps — certain proof the group was dangerous, they thought. Police also took pictures from the walls and seized typewriters and mimeograph machines. At the time, they made no inventory of confiscated materials.[6]

From Elizabeth Green's residence police took a "trunk full" of books, papers, records, pictures, and letters; a "bankbook registering the balance of a legacy from her grandfather; and an expired unused passport."[7] From Bob and Ina's house and outbuildings police took personal property, including a "battery and bell set," and a projector and film. They also searched and confiscated the contents of a safe deposit box Bob had rented at an Oklahoma City bank. In it they found a $2,000 certificate for a defense fund (likely the International Labor Defense), signed by prominent Communist Party officials. When police searched the apartments of Alan and Eli at 2320 SW 19th (they had apartments in the same building, across an alley that backed up to the Woods's home), they found a variety of books and pamphlets, including copies of *A Short History of the Y.C.I.: Young Communist Internationale* and *Communist Party: A Manual on Organization* with Eli's name handwritten on the flyleaf. They also took Alan's Communist Party membership card and a picture of Alan with Earl Browder. Because they lacked a search warrant for the home of Herbert Brausch, police got creative; they instead had the County Relief investigator go to the house, from which he took Herb's hod carriers labor union book.[8] By the end of the day, police had arrested around twenty people (the exact number is unclear because of the veil of secrecy surrounding the arrests), including five women and a boy of seventeen. They had also confiscated 7,000 pieces of evidence, all of which they took to a county jail cell. Although they found no liquor, they were not disappointed. The liquor warrants had been only a pretext to justify the raids.

Between the time of the arrests around noon and the search of the bookstore, Communist Party offices, and residences several

hours later, officials stationed plainclothes policemen at each location to detain and possibly arrest anyone else who appeared at the
sites. During this interim, Alan Shaw's sister and brother-in-law, Joyce
and Max Sparer, who were visiting for a couple of days, returned to
Bob and Ina Wood's residence from a walk with their eighteen-
month-old daughter. Assuming the stranger was a friend of Alan's,
Max fixed his daughter's lunch while discussing with him the relative
merits of canned spinach for babies and similar mundane topics. Six
other people arrived soon thereafter and announced themselves as
police and county officials. One was Assistant County Attorney John
Eberle, a short but imperious man who gave orders easily. He and the
others accused Max of being a "commissar" from New York who was
transporting "Moscow gold" for local Communists. The baby he
held was probably a "front," someone commented. She ought to
be taken to an orphan asylum because she "probably wasn't even
theirs," and Max should be charged with kidnapping, commented
another. Police then put Max in the back seat of a police car and
drove away.[9] They also pushed Joyce into a corner with the baby; one
officer stayed behind to watch them.

In the meantime, Wilma Lewis spent some of her three dollars
on public transportation that took her to Bob and Ina Wood's
house. She worried that people were watching her. When she
walked onto the porch, a man she did not recognize came to the
door and grabbed her arm. Remembering what had just happened
to her family, Wilma told the man she sold vegetables to the Wood
family and that she had come to collect her money. The man did not
believe her. For the next three hours she was questioned by "at least
a dozen different men who came and went." At one point she asked
permission to go to the bathroom, where she swallowed her membership card to the Oklahoma Youth Legislature (OYL).[10]

In the corner Wilma noticed a frightened young woman and a
baby also being detained by police. Only later did she realize it was
Alan Shaw's sister. Finally, after Wilma cried that she had to milk the
cow at home, the men released her. After a night alone there she
took an interurban trolley to the outskirts of town, then walked the
remaining distance to the home of friend Sis Cunningham. Fearful

of being followed, she ducked into roadside cornfields when cars approached. Sis had been a fellow traveler with Wilma's parents in activism on behalf of poor people. In the late 1930s Sis was an organizer for the Southern Tenants Farmers' Union. In 1939 she had formed a musical group called the Red Dust Players to raise morale among farmers and oil-field workers. Wilma stayed with Sis for a few days, but because Sis feared for her own safety, she called upon friends to house Wilma a few more evenings. Several days later Wilma returned home to tend the animals and crops on the one-acre homestead that kept her family alive.[11]

For all these people, August 17 had been a harrowing day; for those arrested, especially so. Within five hours they had been carted off to jail without being told the charges against them. All were held incommunicado and under false names supplied by the police so relatives could not trace them to the jail. (The *Daily Oklahoman*, Oklahoma City's major morning newspaper, looked at it differently. Most of them, it reported on August 20, "gave fictitious names.") When one worried wife called the jail to find out if her husband was there she was told: "We don't know, and even if we did we wouldn't tell you." She immediately knew where he was. She then asked how long he would be held. "We'll let him out when the war is over," was the response. Over the entire weekend Oklahoma county and city officials kept the Saturday noon raids secret.[12]

Ina Wood, Elizabeth Green, and two other female prisoners were placed in a "holding tank" with prostitutes and drug addicts, permitted no change of clothes, and denied basic facilities for feminine hygiene. Upstairs the men were placed in another holding tank, a large room "that stank of urine" and held more than fifty steel jail bunks. In both the men's and women's sections, the phrases "Jew-bastards" and "Christ-killers" echoed down the corridors, clearly a reference to the fact that some of those arrested were Jews. "We could kill you like we would rattlesnakes," one jailer remarked. "Where do you want your body shipped?" another asked. Several "nasty acting" jailers proudly and deliberately wore American Legion caps.[13]

First to be questioned was Eli Jaffe; Assistant County Attorney

Eberle was one of his interrogators. Are you a member of the Communist Party? Yes. Where did you originally join? New York City. How long have you been a member? About three or four years. Was the general headquarters for the Party in Oklahoma at the bookshop? That is right. After returning to his cell, Eli asked the guard who brought him dinner, "What's the charge against me? How long are you going to keep me here?" Initially the guard said nothing; when he returned to pick up the dishes he mumbled: "72 hours."[14]

On Monday afternoon, August 19, the *Oklahoma Times,* Oklahoma City's major afternoon paper owned by the same person as the morning *Oklahoman,* finally picked up the story and began piecing it together. "Officials did not identify the 16 persons held," the *Times* said, "nor were the prisoners permitted to contact relatives and friends." Next morning the *Daily Oklahoman* noticed "an atmosphere of deepest mystery cloaked the seventh floor jail," where authorities questioned the suspects throughout the day. "We're still in the midst of an investigation," prosecutor Eberle told the *Oklahoman* that afternoon. "At least six will be charged under the criminal syndicalism statute, and the remainder will be held as material witnesses." When asked to define "criminal syndicalism," Eberle responded: "teaching, preaching, publishing or distributing anything, or doing anything, that calls for overthrow of our government."[15]

The *Times* article prompted local attorney Moman Pruiett to visit the jail and file a petition for a writ of habeas corpus to free all the people being held. Sixty-eight-year-old Pruiett had had a long and colorful law career in Oklahoma, but in August 1940, chronic alcoholism left him nearly destitute and desperate for cases. At the time, however, he was all the defendants had, and they welcomed his help. Although he was not allowed to talk to them, Pruiett did get a list of their names for the petition, and asked for a hearing the next morning. And from that petition local newspapers obtained at least some of the names of those to be charged: Robert and Ina Wood; C. A. and Hulda Lewis and their son, Orval; Elizabeth Green; Eli Jaffe; Alan Shaw; and Alan's brother-in-law, Max Sparer.[16]

Tuesday afternoon, three days after the arrests, the defendants were arraigned. By that time prosecutor Eberle had arranged to gather the accused into the same holding cell for transfer to Justice of the Peace Paul Powers's courtroom. It was the first time they had a chance to piece together what had happened to friends and relatives during the previous seventy-two hours. Bob, Eli, Alan, and four other male prisoners were herded into a wide corridor, enclosed by two big steel doors, that, Eli later recalled, was immaculately white and reeked of disinfectant. "Deep grooves under our eyes, bewildered-looking, dressed in ill-fitting grey jail coveralls, we sure were a ragged group of builders of the brave new world." Eli moved slowly over to Bob and muttered, "What's it all about, Bob? What the hell are we in for?" Because of their Communist Party membership and activities, he understood why he, Alan, and Bob might be there, but he could not fathom why the others were there too. It did not occur to him that they had merely been in the wrong place at the wrong time when the authorities made their sweeps, and that they had been given no opportunity to explain.

After a short time in the corridor they were greeted by "Floyd," a six-foot two-inch, 235-pound jailer. Eli had been warned about Floyd by a trustee who brought his food: "He's big 'n blonde 'n German and one mean son-of-a-bitch." In the corridor Floyd rattled his big ring of keys to get everyone's attention. "You may think you're hot shit with all your books 'n such," he roared, "but to me, you're just a bunch of goddamn furrin' agitators. Well, this is my jail and I don't want no grief out of any of you."[17]

In their grey prison garb, the men were manacled together, taken down the elevator, and marched across the street to Judge Powers's courtroom for arraignment. There they heard Eberle give an animated speech in which he charged many of the defendants with violating a 1919 state criminal syndicalism law by being members of the Communist Party, which advocated "doing acts of physical violence, and unlawful acts, as a means of accomplishing and effecting industrial and political change and revolution." As members, Eberle further argued, the defendants sought recruits, collected dues, held meetings, and "by writings, books, pamphlets and papers," advocated criminal syndicalism and unlawful acts.[18]

It was the first time the defendants learned of the charges

against them and the law they were accused of violating. They were not being charged for anything they did, but for being Communist Party members and/or for selling printed materials that, Eberle argued, advocated the violent overthrow of the government. Judge Powers followed Eberle's recommendation and set bail at $50,000 for each defendant, and for each charge. Some defendants thus faced bail of $100,000. Bond was set at $2,000 for material witnesses, including young Orval Lewis; two other unnamed suspects were released. Since none of the defendants could post bond, they were marched back to their cells. Before leaving the courtroom, however, Bob Wood hinted that three defendants were contemplating civil suits against the county attorney's office for their wrongful arrest and prosecution.

Outside the courtroom Eberle explained to reporters that high bail was necessary to make sure the defendants remained in Oklahoma City to face charges. "All have several aliases, and we can't find out where they came from, what they do, or how long they will be here." When asked why the county attorney's office had decided to move now, Eberle responded, "Communists have increased their activity here a great deal recently. They have brought in outside workers, have been making a large number of contacts and have had a lot of money to spend in their work here." He noted that two of the defendants had recently arrived in Oklahoma from New York.

Attorney Pruiett, who was finally allowed to confer with his clients on Tuesday afternoon, asked that a hearing on his habeas corpus writ be rescheduled for 9 A.M. the next morning before District Judge George H. Giddings when, he told reporters, he would ask that bail be reduced. The next morning, without explanation Giddings dismissed Pruiett's application; the defendants would remain in jail. Pruiett promised to file another before Judge Powers the next morning.[19]

But getting access to his clients continued to be difficult. On Wednesday the county jailer refused to let Pruiett see them. It was "Visiting Day," the jailer claimed, and his employees were too busy to arrange for "private consultation." At the same time a deputy jailer announced that officials were taking special precautions to safeguard the jail against potential retaliation for the arrests. "Jail Guarded Against Moves to Free Reds," the *Daily Oklahoman* reported. American Legion Post 35 adopted a resolution at its Tuesday evening meeting commending the county attorney, city police, and county sheriff for prosecuting Communists. In its August 21 issue the *Oklahoman* ran an article interviewing Luther Harrison, its own editorial writer, who explained that as a member of the Oklahoma Legislature in 1919, he had authored the criminal syndicalism law. That same day the paper ran an editorial elaborating on Harrison's explanation under the heading, "To Prevent Violence."[20]

In jail, several defendants were in danger. Some received threatening letters. The men were deliberately separated from each other. Floyd put Alan Shaw into one holding tank, Bob Wood in another. Eli Jaffe was paired with two of his fellow prisoners, one of them a "frail composer from Tulsa," and all three were taken to a forty-person cell. After locking them in, Floyd reminded everyone to behave. "Remember this — you take one step out of line and I'd just as soon stomp on your head as I would a rattlesnake," he shouted. Then he looked directly at Eli. "And that goes double for you — you goddamn Christ-killer."[21]

Floyd's words suggested Eli was in for a hard time. He soon realized he had been housed with the "hard-ass gang," a group of men who had spent a large amount of time in penitentiaries and jails developing "hard asses" by sleeping on institutional benches. After a while, he noticed a group of men gathered around a prisoner called Johnny, who poured a liquid into a tin cup (Eli later learned it was rubbing alcohol mixed with orange juice), to which he added yellow pills and then heated with a homemade torch. After mixing up a couple of batches, he and his friends began to drink the brew and in a short time, they became boisterous. Eli was sure they were drunk. One of the group approached Eli's frail companion and growled: "Listen, fresh meat, there's a price for invadin' this jail without Johnny's permission" and then slapped him "hard and provocatively." "Hey, cut it out!" Eli yelled. At that moment, he was blindsided with a blow to the jaw and lost consciousness. When he came to several minutes later, he thought he saw Johnny and three of his friends talking to Floyd, all of them "yocking it up." Eli later surmised Floyd had given Johnny rubbing alcohol; Johnny knew how to thank him for the favor. That night, Eli leaned against the wall separating his cell area from Bob Wood and told him of the day's events. "We're not alone," Bob responded, and said that the next day they would finally be seeing their lawyers about bail as everyone prepared for their preliminary hearing.[22]

By this time, the Associated Press had circulated news of the arrests and treatment of prisoners.[23] The *Oklahoman* reported a "strong possibility" that the American Civil Liberties Union (ACLU) would send a representative from New York, and that ACLU General Counsel Arthur Garfield Hays had written a letter to Oklahoma Governor Leon "Red" Phillips (nicknamed for his hair color, not his political ideology) deploring action against the defendants as "a direct violation of freedom of speech." The paper did not report the full content of the protest, in which Hays noted: "We believe the use of such laws against members of an unpopular minority party at this time can be interpreted only as repression rather than any justified action for the protection of the citizens of your state from any real or present danger."[24]

The newspaper did report that the city's mayor had received a telegram from a Long Island, New York, couple. "Vehemently protest arrest of Wood and others," the telegram said. "Your action fully in accord with Hitler's methods which no decent American will tolerate." The newspaper also quoted Bob Wood, who said Communists "are doing nothing they have not been doing for years." Finally, the newspaper noted that Eberle's immediate superior, Lewis R. Morris, had just returned from a vacation. Seeming somewhat surprised at (and uninformed about) the raids and arrests conducted by his subordinate, he told reporters he would "study the charges and see what it is all about."[25]

In an August 24 editorial, the *Oklahoman* chose to ignore the question of whether Oklahoma City Communists were justifiably incarcerated or not and instead focus on Bob Wood's claim that Communists were the first Americans to warn of Hitlerism. Three days later the *Oklahoman* carried an Associated Press story reporting that Texas congressman Martin Dies, chairman of the House ad hoc Committee on Un-American Activities, estimated there were six million sympathizers of Communist, Fascist, and Nazi organizations in the United States.[26]

At the Friday morning hearing, the judge reduced bonds for a number of defendants to $10,000 and released one elderly prisoner who had been sick for several days. Two other suspects held as material witnesses were allowed to sign their own bonds and were released from jail. At the time of the raid, one of them — a young woman — was recovering from an operation on her leg. Denied medical treatment while in jail, she left that morning with a serious infection. On Saturday, police released on their own recognizance two bookstore customers and seventeen-year-old Orval Lewis. All had been in jail for one week; all promised to appear before the hearing the following Wednesday.[27] That left eleven defendants in jail.

When Orval returned home that night, four boys confronted him. Tell us the names of other Communists, they demanded. As a material witness to the court, Orval responded, he was under order not to talk. They then pummeled him with their fists, leaving him with a sore body, a black eye, and a swollen cheek. Neighbors took him in and made a sleeping pallet for him on their floor, where he stayed overnight. The next morning he returned home. Wilma was already there. "Don't look at me," he said as he walked in the door. "I have to tell you something first." Later that day Orval returned to police headquarters and told them he knew his attackers. They advised him to sign a complaint charging assault and battery, but he declined. First he wanted to confer with his parents, he said, and they were still in jail. He never filed charges.[28]

A preliminary hearing took place on Wednesday, August 28, eleven days after the raids. As people entered the county courthouse to attend the hearing, they walked under an inscription by Thomas Jefferson: "Equal and exact justice to all men, of whatever state or persuasion, religious or political." Because it attracted more than fifty spectators, Judge Powers moved the hearing to a larger courtroom. Except for attorney Pruiett, the defendants had difficulty finding other attorneys in Oklahoma City willing to represent them. The day before, one defendant had written the ACLU, "We are handled like a hot potato and everyone afraid to touch it."[29]

By the 28th, however, the six defendants facing the most serious charges (Eli Jaffe, Alan Shaw, Elizabeth Green, Herb Brausch, and Bob and Ina Wood) were represented by Pruiett and George Croom, a thirty-eight-year-old pipe-smoking Tulsa lawyer, who, radicalized by previous experiences defending civil liberties in Oklahoma, now came to assist Pruiett. All afternoon they engaged in heated debate with Eberle, who introduced as evidence a number of pamphlets lauding Communism, the rule of the proletariat, the abolition of capitalism, and what Eberle called "the creation of a separate Negro government." Eberle had Dan Hollingsworth testify that as head of the city's police intelligence squad he was on the mailing list of many Communist front organizations. After regular prompts by Eberle, Hollingsworth read excerpts from a number of printed works confiscated in the raids, including the *Communist Manifesto, Strategy and Tactics* (which argued that "the time to strike is when the crisis is at its highest pitch"), Stalin's *Leninism: Dictatorship of the Proletariat,* and *Reds in Dixie* (which proposed a separate government for Negroes after the workers take over the government). When permitted to respond, Pruiett argued that many of the books confiscated by authorities could be bought in other downtown stores.

But Eberle ignored Pruiett's point. Instead, he touted "Americanism" and the need to suppress Communist activities. "It is the duty of every American to hate these Communists," he said, "and fight them to the last ditch." Everyone knew Communists stood for the violent overthrow of the government, he argued. "I say a jury ought to give them the maximum sentence of ten years and a $5,000 fine. . . . Then they can go back where they came from, and tell the people who sent them 'Oklahoma's too hot.' " He then returned to his call-and-response routine with Hollingsworth. The *Daily Oklahoman* noticed that during this time Bob and Ina Wood looked up cases in law books brought to court. What drew most of the paper's attention, however, was a $9,000 account Elizabeth Green had in a New Haven, Connecticut, bank, from which $6,000 had recently been withdrawn. Eberle argued that this evidence suggested the money was being used to fund Communist Party work in the Sooner State. The hearing had to be carried over until the next morning because Eberle and Hollingsworth had taken so much time.[30]

On August 29 the courtroom was again packed, this time with several American Legion members, all donning their familiar caps. Eberle announced that state testimony would be the same for trials of Bob and Ina, Eli, Alan, and Elizabeth Green. Judge Powers bound all five over and set their bonds at $10,000 per charge. Eberle and Pruiett agreed that state testimony already introduced would apply to Herbert Brausch, who was also bound over to district court with bond fixed at $5,000. Thus, Brausch became the sixth person charged for being a member of the Communist Party. Pruiett told the judge he would soon file a writ of habeas corpus in district court to dismiss the charges "on grounds there has been no crime committed and there is no legal testimony to justify the court in holding" his clients. When Judge Powers commented, "According to the testimony the Communist Party advocates violence," Pruiett replied, "I beg you not to become a party to oppression. Why don't you hold the ones you think are guilty and responsible and let the others go on their own recognizance?" Powers did not respond.[31]

Next day matters took a new twist when the Oklahoma Bar Association informed Judge Powers that Pruiett was "not a member of the Bar in good standing" and "has no right to practice law" in a court of record. What the Association official failed to say was that Pruiett had been suspended in February for nonpayment of dues, but that he was part of a group of attorneys testing the fairness of a new set of Bar rules assessing attorneys for dues. Jailers immediately seized upon the news, and denied Pruiett access to his clients. "It's true I am delinquent in my dues like thousands of others," Pruiett told the *Daily Oklahoman*, "but I'm going ahead and practice law." In a conference with prosecutors on Friday afternoon, he agreed that Clarence and Hulda Lewis would waive preliminary hearing and be bound over for trial in district court. Their bonds would be reduced to $2,000.[32]

But the Bar Association was not the only organization that had problems with Pruiett. Shortly after he heard about the arrests, New York City attorney Abe Unger contacted the ACLU about proper representation for the defendants. He "did not have much confidence in Moman Pruiett," he said, and urged the ACLU to approach Cushing, Oklahoma, attorney Stanley Belden instead. Unger knew Belden was fearless when acting on principle; Belden had been a defiant conscientious objector in World War I and had worked for the NAACP with attorney Thurgood Marshall on an Oklahoma civil rights case in which a murder confession had been beaten out of an African American tenant farmer. Belden had also recently represented Jehovah's Witnesses in the state. "A member of the Police," Belden wrote the ACLU on September 3, had warned him "they had an organization that was going to save America, that my every move was being watched and that if I got outside of my county (where I was known) that my life was in danger." When Unger contacted Belden about the Oklahoma City situation, he agreed to take the case, but only if Pruiett was dismissed. Belden told the ACLU that Pruiett "is known throughout the State as a broken-down, drunken, renegade lawyer" who "appears in the court room always more or less under the influence of liquor. There is no way of controling [sic] him." The ACLU promised to ease Pruiett out in the coming weeks.[33]

On September 4 Judge Powers dismissed charges against one defendant, released another on $1,000 bond, and bound a third over to district court. On September 5 six defendants appeared before District Judge Clarence Mills for arraignment, but because they asked for "constitutional time" to prepare pleas, Mills agreed to delay arraignment for twenty-four hours. On September 6 Dan Hollingsworth obtained another liquor search warrant, and with it directed one of his officers to confiscate the remaining contents of the bookstore. That pushed the total number of items confiscated from the store and five residences to over 10,000, all of which were then boxed and located in an Oklahoma County jail cell. There a deputy sheriff ultimately marked the materials according to his memory of their point of origin. Items he believed were seized from the bookstore he marked "A," from Bob and Ina Wood's home "B," from Elizabeth Green's home "C," and from Alan Shaw's home "D." Others were marked "E."[34]

All of the principal parties — Bob and Ina Wood, Alan Shaw, Eli Jaffe, Elizabeth Green, and Herbert Brausch — were required to be present for arraignment in Judge Clarence Mills's courtroom on Friday, September 6, an easy-enough task since all were still confined to the county jail. "Send out the goddamn Christ-killers," Floyd yelled that morning as defendants were collected from their cells for the trip downstairs. Eli still sported bruises from his altercation with Johnny. "Slip on the soap?" Floyd teased. "Fuck you, you Nazi bastard," Eli muttered under his breath. As they gathered in an anteroom, defendants met with their lawyers. By that time the International Labor Defense (ILD), a New York–based legal services agency controlled by the Communist Party, had agreed to retain George Croom. He would be one of several attorneys representing the ILD throughout the proceedings. For the first time defendants also met Stanley Belden, now representing the ACLU.

Once in the courtroom, Pruiett and his colleagues, Croom and Belden, complained about the treatment they had received, and especially noted they had routinely been denied access to their clients and to details of their arrests, which were in possession of the assistant county attorney. Croom also complained that Eli had been beaten in jail without the jailers' intervention. Judge Mills promised to refer the latter to the sheriff's office for investigation. "This is asking the fox to guard the henhouse," Croom said. The judge angrily responded, "Let's get down to legal matters."

Through their lawyers, all six defendants pleaded not guilty. "This is no time for intolerance and prejudice," Pruiett argued. "This is the time for every man on the bench to look into the constitution and see that every man gets his rights. I may not agree with these clients, but the issue is to protect the rights given them by the constitution." Croom and Belden attacked the constitutionality of the criminal syndicalism act. "It was passed right after the last war," Croom said. "There have been periods in history when the world has lost its moorings and gone far afield from established precedents." When Belden also began talking about the Constitution, Mills cut him short. "Less rhetoric," he said, "more law!" Belden was undeterred. He argued that the evidence was obtained by the use of illegal search warrants, that the warrants authorized the officers to seize only "intoxicating liquors," and that they "contained indefinite descriptions of the premises to be searched and the evidence to be seized." Mills rustled through a pile of papers on his desk and replied: "I'll take this under advisement." All three defense attorneys then recommended against an early trial date, arguing they needed more time to prepare. Looking at Eberle, Pruiett shook his finger and shouted: "You have hijackers, thieves, and murderers to try on the docket," then turned back to the judge: "but for political purposes the county attorney is asking to set these cases down within ten days after arraignment." The defendants' lawyers also called for a reduction in bail.

Angry at accusations he was politically motivated, Eberle argued vociferously against their request for reduced bail — so vociferously he broke the glass covering the courtroom tabletop when he pounded his fist. "Nobody knows their true names, nobody knows where they're going," he argued, and "unless they are held under high bail, they'll make bond and won't be here when their trial comes up. These are subversive people, your Honor." That remark incensed Eli, who rose from his seat and said in a muted voice: "That's a lie!" Eberle heard it. "Don't you call me a liar!" At this exchange Judge Mills flushed. "What was that? Did you call him a liar?" While Eli and Eberle glared angrily at each other, deputy sheriffs jumped to their feet, Eli's attorneys began shouting objections, and for a moment it appeared the courtroom was going to erupt in a fight.

Quickly, the judge regained his composure and called Eli before the bench. "Did you call him a liar?" Mills asked. "The county attorney inferred we wouldn't be here," Eli responded. "I inferred he was wrong." When the judge pressed him, however, Eli admitted he had called Eberle a liar, but at the same time indicated he was merely muttering to himself. "Sit back down there and keep still," Mills fumed, "or you'll get a trial without a jury and get it quick." Belden immediately jumped to his feet, but before he could open his mouth Mills gaveled him down. At the end of the hearing Mills upheld the criminal syndicalism law and ruled that bond would remain unchanged at $10,000 per charge. He set a trial date of September 17 for all six defendants, exactly one month after their arrests. As all parties left the courtroom, Eberle told reporters he had not yet decided who would be tried first.[35]

Back in the conference room, the defense attorneys explained to their clients that this was a tough case, but not because of legal matters. Eberle was ambitious for the county attorney's position, they said, and his boss, Lewis Morris, was preparing to run for governor. "Eberle inspired this whole farce," Belden said. "We've learned that before the arrests an investigator from the Dies Committee in Washington came to Oklahoma City to confer with him. Eberle decided to take advantage of the anti-communist feeling throughout the country and invoked the criminal syndicalism statute of 1919 for the first time in the history of Oklahoma County." Croom handed Bob Wood a clipping from the August 22 *Daily Oklahoman* with the "Jail Guarded Against Moves to Free Reds" headline. Shaking his head in disgust, Bob read it aloud to all the defendants. Croom said it was likely Eberle would use selected titles seized from the bookstore as evidence to convict them under the criminal syndicalism law. "We're going to make him prove that each of you committed a criminal act, not just selling books or belonging to a political party he doesn't like," Croom said. "We've got a strong case. And the ILD will raise bail money. But you can be sure the press is going to tilt this whole thing so that you couldn't possibly get a fair trial in this county." Belden added, "We'll try to get a change of venue, but I don't think we've got a chance of a snowball in hell." Belden later wrote the ACLU that he had heard a rumor that Eberle wanted to impress the American Legion at its state convention so he could garner support for a run for public office.[36]

After arraignment, Croom filed a writ of habeas corpus with the Oklahoma Criminal Court of Appeals on September 7. On September 13, Pruiett filed a motion to disqualify Judge Mills from presiding, arguing that "the judge had conferred with Eberle in regard to setting of the trial date, arraignment, and other related matters outside the presence of the defendants" and that Mills had previously "prepared a brief and orally argued a case for disbarment against" Pruiett. On September 15, Criminal Court of Appeals Judge Thomas Doyle ordered all parties to appear before his court for a hearing on defense motions. The next day Doyle announced that he refused to consider Croom's writ, but he would disqualify Clarence Mills from trying the cases and instead assigned them to the district court of Judge Ben Arnold. The first trial would begin September 30. He also granted Bob Wood a severance on the charge of distributing Communist literature so he could be tried separately on that charge, and agreed to allow Pruiett to withdraw as defense attorney because of a "dispute over legal procedure." Thus, Bob would be tried first, but without Moman Pruiett to defend him. Stanley Belden got his way.[37]

On September 18 the ACLU formally announced it had hired Belden to defend the six Oklahoma defendants. But "hired" may not be the most accurate descriptor. In a letter dated September 6, the ACLU advised Belden, "We wish that we could pay you a fee, but unfortunately we are not in a position to do so." The ACLU did, however, offer to pay his out-of-pocket expenses. Reluctantly, Belden agreed to join the defense team, but he also noted that "to represent Communists will mean the ruin of my law practice; but I believe in the Constitution and civil liberties and am willing to uphold them — even at that price."[38] Belden fully understood what he was getting into. Shortly after setting up office in Oklahoma City, he was approached by a Legionnaire lawyer who "told me that he could shoot them [the defendants] just as he could a rattlesnake and that they had no rights in this country."[39]

When Belden and Croom went to the county jail on the 17th to interview their clients, they were again refused permission — visiting day, they were told, private consultations were not allowed. When they asked when they could talk to their clients privately, Jailer J. C. Farrand said "there had been enough consultations" and that he "would not grant any further private consultations." Belden protested, saying he had just been hired as counsel. Farrand insisted Belden show him his Bar membership card and prove his dues were current. Belden first complained to Eberle, who sent him to the sheriff's office. There he was assured he could see his clients the next day. When he and Croom arrived, however, they were again denied. Again Farrand demanded proof Belden was a member of the state Bar and that he had paid his dues. Belden called the Oklahoma Bar Association office, then handed Farrand the phone so officials there could assure him Belden was a member in good standing. Farrand yielded, but still refused to grant him and Croom a private consultation. Instead, they were allowed to interview the defendants through a "screen . . . a device," Belden later described, "whereby talking loudly in the presence of many other prisoners and officers, one may be heard, during which time one cannot see the defendant." That afternoon Belden and Croom filed a motion to force jailers to respect their right of private consultation with their clients. Judge Arnold granted their motion. "The jailer was certainly different after the hearing as to the courtesies extended to Mr. Croom and me," Belden later wrote.[40]

On September 16, a second ILD-funded defense attorney, Sam Neuberger, arrived in Oklahoma City from New York. First he checked into a local hotel, then went to the jail to see his clients. Again the jailer refused. "I don't think I'll even bring them down for Croom now," he said. Back at his hotel, Neuberger noticed he was under "constant surveillance." Two men who knocked on his door said they were after "Mr. George Dickinson," and when he let them in, he noticed how closely they analyzed his appearance and luggage. He suspected it was "for the purpose of future identification." He also took note of individuals at court hearings he was sure were FBI agents.[41]

On September 20, young Orval Lewis was arrested for a second time. Sharp-eyed policemen had seen him use a screwdriver to get into the Progressive Book Store in order to retrieve additional paper supplies for the defense attorneys. They charged him with entering a building "under circumstances not amounting to burglary." Before again being tossed in the county jail, however, Police Captain Dan Hollingsworth interrogated him. "If you tell us what we want to know and the people we want to know about, you'll walk out of here as free as anybody. But if you don't—you can go to the State Reformatory for 25 years. Your folks are going for 10 years anyway." Orval said nothing. Instead, he was arraigned the next morning, pled not guilty, and was held under $250 bond. At that point, he gave up any hope of enrolling as an engineering student at the University of Oklahoma that fall.[42]

By this time defendants and their lawyers fully recognized they faced a tightly knit network of local, state, and federal officials determined to force a case against Oklahoma Communists. But in response an opposition also began to mobilize outside the Sooner State. On September 25 president of the ILD and New York City congressman Vito Marcantonio ("the closest thing the United States ever had to a Communist member of Congress," historian Michael J. Ybarra called him) sent an open letter to U.S. Attorney General Robert Jackson outlining violations already committed against the Oklahoma defendants. "Certain manifestations of hostility towards them in the community in which they are to be tried are so shocking," Marcantonio wrote, "as to make us feel that only immediate intervention by your office can guarantee them any semblance of a fair and impartial trial." He told Jackson he was also sending copies of his letters to justices of the Supreme Court, federal authorities in the state of Oklahoma, the governor and state attorney general, the mayor of Oklahoma City, the Oklahoma Bar Association, the American Bar Association's Civil Liberties Committee, the National Lawyer's Guild, and the National Federation for Constitutional Liberties. Marcantonio had obviously decided Oklahoma was going to be a battleground for a fight on civil liberties and the forthcoming trials the occasion to engage the fight. An ILD press release issued three days later paraphrased the open letter to Jackson and announced the ILD's decision to intervene on the defendants' behalf with a fund-raising effort to pay their legal expenses.[43]

Although Marcantonio had put Oklahoma officials on notice that the book trials would be closely watched outside the Sooner State, Oklahoma officials did not seem intimidated. On September 29, the *Daily Oklahoman* reported that the Oklahoma county attorney's office had consulted with U.S. Representative Martin Dies about the most effective way to combat Communism. "It may be the Dies Committee will have an observer here during the criminal syndicalism trials," Eberle told the *Daily Oklahoman*. A Dies Committee member added, "The Committee might start an investigation" there.[44] By the end of September, all parties associated with the case were gearing up for Bob Wood's trial, set for September 30. Nine of those arrested in the August 17 raids remained in jail.

Ironically, Bob Wood's trial was scheduled to begin the day before the first annual National Newspaper Week, October 1–8. In its October 4 issue, the *Daily Oklahoman* ran a full page of quotes by local and national leaders speaking in appreciation of the free press enjoyed in the United States. "These expressions today take on an especially deep significance," the *Oklahoman* opined, "coming as they do when the rest of the world views its news through the eyes of tyrants, dictators, and censors."[45]

CHAPTER TWO

Communism Comes to Oklahoma, 1917–1940

The bookstore roundup did not come as a complete surprise to at least some of the defendants. In fact, the primary defendants — Bob and Ina Wood, Alan Shaw, and Eli Jaffe — were well aware that events taking place in Oklahoma, the United States, and Europe after war broke out there in September 1939 increasingly meant that they would be targeted. Patriotic fervor unleashed by national hysteria in the previous World War had prompted half the states to pass criminal syndicalism laws to fend off any activities perceived as un-American. During the 1930s officials in thirteen states dusted off these laws and relied upon them to arrest labor organizers and Communists.[1] And as the pressure increased in 1940 for U.S. involvement in another war, so too did a strain of super-patriotism and concern for national security, neither of which seemed willing to tolerate dissent.

The origins of the criminal syndicalism law used to arrest the Oklahoma City defendants can be found in the Sooner State's Green Corn Rebellion of 1917. Oklahoma had not been admitted to the Union as a state until 1907, and for the first ten years of its existence manifested a socialist more than a conservative profile. In 1915, for example, only Wisconsin outranked Oklahoma in number of socialists in state legislatures. World War I changed all that, however. In May 1917, President Woodrow Wilson signed the National Draft Act, forcing young men into the military. Some Sooner State residents resisted, including Stanley Belden, seventeen-year-old Pawnee County member of the Socialist Party of America and conscientious objector, who was tossed in jail for ten months. "I am proud to be a martyr," he told the judge who sentenced him. From his own jail cell, socialist leader Eugene Debs commended Belden for his courage. "In good time all will come right and you will stand forth vindicated."[2]

Other resistance was more organized, including that posed by the tattered remnants of a three-year-old ragtag regional organization called the Working Class Union. The group decided early on this was a "rich man's war and a poor man's fight," used it as a catalyst for action, and laid plans to resist. At best, they were naïve. Leaders hoped to assemble rebels at a central site on a predetermined date, recruit farmers to join them, contact similar rebellious groups from other Southern states, then merge with another "army" of protestors from the Northwest in a massive march on Washington, where they would overthrow the federal government and stop the war. On the way, rebels planned to subsist on barbecued steer donated by sympathetic farmers, and green corn not yet ripened in the fields.[3]

But before Oklahoma leaders of this Green Corn Rebellion could start their revolt, Seminole County officials launched an investigation. When the county sheriff and his deputies rode through a river bottom in search of subversive activity on August 3, 1917, they were ambushed by rebels. Although no lives were lost in the ambush, the "rebellion" had begun. Over the next two weeks local officials assembled posses of several hundred men and crushed it. Three men died (two were bystanders to a gunfight), eighteen were wounded, 450 arrested. "The mob in Pontotoc and Seminole Counties that raised the red flag must be dealt with promptly and sternly," the *Daily Oklahoman* demanded. Within months, fifty-one were sentenced to federal prison, thirty-four to state prison, and one to a local jail.[4]

Although the rebellion was a dismal failure, it functioned as a defining moment in different ways for each side. On the one hand, rebels often referred to themselves as Green Corn "veterans" and pointed proudly to their stand against oppressive government. On the other, it frightened a conservative, powerful alliance of Oklahoma politicians, industry (especially oil) leaders, newspaper owners and editors, government bureaucrats and civil servants, superpatriotic organizations, and middle-class professionals (including the vast majority of public educators at all levels) and upper-class elites who thought they best represented the "people," but whose economic, social, and political well-being depended on a stable social order. Frequently, the loose coalition of conservative interests also found that positions it took coincided with those of clandestine but marginal societies like the Ku Klux Klan, or with religious groups like Pentecostals, Baptists, and Roman Catholics.

Often, over time, members of this informal coalition migrated from group to group. For example, Wewoka *Capital-Democrat* editor Luther Harrison rode with one of the posses pursuing the rebels. "Every man who followed" the rebel leaders, he wrote on August 9, 1917, "should ascend a Federal scaffold or spend the remainder of his days in a Federal prison." During World War I Harrison also served as chairman of Seminole County's Council on National Defense, a pseudoofficial body that assumed responsibility for generating support for the war effort and closely monitoring (and often enforcing) a rigid patriotism. At the same time, Harrison served as state senator, a position he used to introduce Senate Bill No. 242 on February 10, 1919, a criminal syndicalism law that "will bar . . . from Oklahoma forever" any organization advocating the overthrow of the government by force and violence.[5]

Other events had alarmed Harrison and his colleagues in Oklahoma, including the Bolshevik takeover of Russia and labor organizing successes by the Industrial Workers of the World (IWW, or Wobblies) on the West Coast. In Harrison's mind, the two were connected; he and other conservative Oklahomans with a vested interest in social stability worried what would happen if Wobblies gained control of labor in the Oklahoma oil fields. Just two years earlier in Tulsa, seventeen alleged IWW members had been convicted on trumped-up charges. Local authorities dealt with this crisis by turning the seventeen over to a mob that stripped, beat, and tarred and feathered them.[6]

In other parts of the country in 1919, riots broke out in several major cities, and in late spring thirty bombs were mailed to the homes of industrial and political leaders, including one that destroyed part of the home of U.S. Attorney General A. Mitchell Palmer. He quickly ordered raids on offices of scores of radical organizations, and in almost every case seized printed materials as evidence of conspiracy to overthrow the government. Like much of the rest of the country, Oklahoma found itself in the midst of a post–World War I antiradical, antilabor hysteria. Harrison's bill was one response. "The law is so worded," Harrison said, "as to even preclude the distribution of I.W.W. pamphlets, songs, and literature."[7]

Harrison modeled his bill on a law Oregon had enacted two weeks earlier, defining criminal syndicalism as advocating "crime, physical violence, arson, destruction of property, sabotage, or other unlawful acts or methods, as a means of accomplishing or effecting industrial or political revolution, or for profit." His own bill punished with up to ten years in prison and a $5,000 fine "[a]ny person who . . . prints, publishes . . . or knowingly circulates, sells, distributes, or publicly displays any books, pamphlets . . . or printed matter . . . containing matter advocating, advising, affirmatively suggesting, or teaching criminal syndicalism," and like a driftnet promised to pick up and punish anyone "who organizes . . . or becomes a member of or voluntarily assembles with any society or assemblage of persons which teaches, advocates or affirmatively suggests the doctrine of criminal syndicalism." The bill met little opposition in the Senate, almost no opposition in the House, and on March 8, 1919, passed by a vote of 82–4. The governor signed it into law a week later.[8]

For several years the law remained unused and untested. In 1923, however, political conditions fostered its resurrection. The year before, Jack Walton had been elected governor of Oklahoma by a coalition of farmers and laborers who shared a hatred of the influential and increasingly militant state chapter of the Ku Klux

Klan. But the Klan refused to back away and managed to put together a coalition of its own that impeached Walton and removed him from office in late 1923.[9] In the midst of this political warfare, two criminal syndicalism trials occurred. In February, a Pittsburg County prosecutor used language in the IWW constitution's preamble to convict a labor organizer of violating the law. The presiding judge sentenced him to ten years in the penitentiary and a $5,000 fine. In September, an Ottawa County jury convicted another IWW organizer of distributing literature that advocated criminal syndicalism. He was sentenced to five years. Although both convictions were reversed within two years, in neither case did the appellate court hold that the criminal syndicalism law was unconstitutional.[10] By that time Luther Harrison had moved from Wewoka to Oklahoma City, where he became an editorial writer for the *Daily Oklahoman*.

The 1929 stock market crash ushered in the Great Depression, which gripped the nation for more than a decade and proved to be the worst in its history. In a short time the gross national product fell 30 percent, prices decreased 23 percent, and for much of the next decade the nation's unemployment rate hovered near 25 percent. To address this malaise, Americans overwhelmingly elected Franklin Roosevelt as president in 1932. His first hundred days in office produced a massive amount of legislation, much of which funded new agencies and programs that fundamentally altered the relationship between the federal government and the American people. By the end of the decade, Roosevelt's New Deal legislation enabled the federal government to create agricultural price supports; regulate securities, banking, and utilities; create public housing, Social Security, and unemployment insurance; protect collective bargaining for unions; and establish minimum wage and maximum hour benchmarks.[11] Although most powerful conservative Oklahomans were Democrats, many were displeased with this liberal, activist agenda.

During the Depression, Oklahoma suffered more than most states, in part because it had not shared in the nation's general prosperity a decade earlier. Between 1921 and 1932, the Sooner State suffered the third-largest decline in income of all states in the nation. Its population fell along with oil revenues. After the Depression hit, many laborers occupied two-room shacks, almost always without electricity or water. The coal industry was near collapse. In 1935, 93.5 percent of the population of one big coal county depended on some form of public assistance. The average miner worked only four months a year; many had no work for the entire decade. The oil industry fared better, but once the derricks were erected the industry required relatively few laborers.[12]

Those who were tied to the land lost their livelihoods to grasshopper plagues, untimely frosts, summer hailstorms, searing heat, and a seemingly constant wind that lifted topsoil into huge dust storms. For many, Black Sunday (April 14, 1935) was the worst. It started out sunny, but soon a huge cloud of dust rolled in from the north like a giant tidal wave that blackened the skies for days. "Wearing our shade hats, with handkerchiefs tied over our faces and vaseline in our nostrils, we have been trying to rescue our home from the accumulation of windblown dust which penetrates wherever the air can go," Caroline Henderson wrote in "Letters from the Dust Bowl" in the May 1936 issue of *Atlantic Monthly*. "[T]here is rarely a day when the dust clouds do not roll over. . . . We may have to leave." In 1939 the *Daily Oklahoman* reported the state had lost a fourth of its topsoil during the 1930s.[13] At the beginning of the decade more than half of Oklahoma's citizens were occupationally tied to agriculture. Between 1935 and 1940, however, one in six farmers was driven off the land. The rate was even higher for African Americans. And as they left their land, small farm operators could see over their shoulders the mortgage companies, insurance agencies, and big landlords taking over, bringing with them tractors small-farm operators could not afford.

Contributing to the problem was inequitable state taxation. Most fell on the consumer, the farmer, and the home owner, relatively little on oil and big business, whose property received low assessments. "Life in Oklahoma for the average man is woefully inadequate," wrote University of Oklahoma government professor Robert K. Carr in July 1937. "There can be little doubt but that the fundamental responsibility for Oklahoma's failure must be charged against its governments and public officials, state and local."[14]

Under these conditions, 80,000 Oklahomans fled the state between 1935 and 1940 (twice as many as the state with the next-highest total) for what they hoped were brighter prospects elsewhere, their plight and trek fictionalized and sympathetically described in John Steinbeck's *The Grapes of Wrath*. Most, however, stayed in Oklahoma, which offered no state relief for the able-bodied unemployed. The state did participate in the federal Social Security program for unemployment compensation, and in federal programs that benefited the elderly, dependent and crippled children, and the blind. It also maintained a general relief fund for the unemployable, who received one dollar a month in summer and two dollars in winter. In April 1940, one census showed 84,000 Oklahoma residents were unemployed and searching for employment, while another 57,000 were employed by the federal Work Projects Administration (WPA).[15] African American unemployment was twice the rate of whites. Applications for relief overwhelmed WPA offices. Half the population was on some form of relief, not including "the tens of thousands" of tenant farmers living below the subsistence level. But even these figures were misleading. "No authentic statistics with respect to unemployment in Oklahoma are available," the U.S. Commissioner of Labor noted in 1940. "[C]onflicting reports have been made, and little done to reduce unemployment or alleviate its hardship by counting and recounting agencies."[16]

Thousands gravitated to urban areas in a desperate attempt to find work, food, and shelter. In larger towns like Tulsa and Oklahoma City, they gathered in camps known as Hoovervilles, named after President Herbert Hoover, whom many blamed for the economic plight in which they found themselves. Oklahoma City had two Hoovervilles, one the May Avenue Camp, the other the much larger Community Camp, which took root in the Graybelt area (a dry riverbed) on the south side of the city in view of the oil derricks. It was bordered by an abandoned railroad, the Canadian River, and the city dump.

There 3,000 people, consisting mostly of the unemployed and their families, lived with no toilet facilities. They got their water from a common tap, scratched through the dump for food scraps and salvageable materials, and on plots they rented for a dollar a month built shacks from license plates, cardboard, rusty tinplate, and old plywood. Poorly clothed children ran barefoot through the "streets," shivered in the winter, and played with whatever junk they could find. "Death came calling every day," Sis Cunningham later recalled, "and there'd be a funeral, usually a double or triple one, in a hovel called the church house" (another shack slightly larger than others). On April 7, 1939, one Oklahoma City attorney complained to the mayor about this "human cesspool," then reminded him that the city had recently spent $285,000 for improvements at the Lincoln Park Zoo, but nothing for the Community Camp. The mayor asked the city manager to look into the matter, but nothing changed.[17]

Officials' nonresponse reflected the perspectives of their culture. Many officials and their supporters preferred to ignore the problem of poverty or shift the blame to the "individual." Wrapped in this mindset, they made little effort for all of the 1930s to address social and economic inequities or to foster cooperative movements. "If American character is not misjudged," the *Daily Oklahoman* said in an edition commemorating the fiftieth anniversary of the 1889 land run, "the old frontier spirit will show the way in the next fifty years as it did in the past fifty. This means we will not tamely submit to a paternalistic regime in which government does everything and the individual takes what government is willing to give."[18] Three days after celebrating "the frontier spirit," the *Daily Oklahoman* ran an article that lamented the Sooner State's top ranking for people on WPA rolls. "And apparently this unenviable record is due to the fact that Oklahoma has a sadly large number of people who are willing to take the government's money regardless of how they get it."[19]

Governor Phillips saw it only slightly differently. To the hundreds of letters he received begging for WPA work, he issued boilerplate responses claiming no jurisdiction over the federal program. "If you are in immediate need of food or other necessities, I suggest that you place your case fully before your County Welfare Board." Most had already done that, and received little or no relief. And although Phillips thought drought, federal farm subsidies, and discriminatory freight rates were mostly to blame for Oklahoma's problems, individuals also had to take responsibility. "There are some who are naturally shiftless, hate to work and will go to any length to avoid it. . . . the State that hands out the most money, food, and clothing free will find its population ever increased by the indolent and lazy," he told members of the federal Interstate Migration of Destitute Citizens Commission who met in Oklahoma City in September 1940. During his term in office, Phillips pocket vetoed a bill that would have provided $8 million in federal money for housing, but would have cost the state nothing — competition with private enterprise, he argued. Still, Oklahoma conservatives worried about this concentration of unemployed workers and their often malnourished families.[20]

For many, *The Grapes of Wrath* (the Pulitzer Prize–winning book was published in spring 1939; the Academy Award–winning movie opened in January 1940) became the narrative of the Depression. Its reception in Oklahoma perhaps best characterized the great divide between the downtrodden and oppressed people of the state and powerful Oklahoma conservatives (public officials and private citizens) who despised its popularity and often publicly bristled at the mention of the book or movie. Congressman Lyle Boren excoriated the book on the floor of the U.S. Congress, calling it a "dirty, lying, filthy manuscript" created by a "twisted, distorted mind." The book, he said, "exposes nothing but the total depravity, vulgarity, and degraded mentality of the author." The *Oklahoma City Times* argued: "Any reader who has his roots planted in the red soil will boil with indignation over the bedraggled, bestial characters that will give the ignorant east convincing confirmation of their ideas of the people of the southwest."

But Oklahoma officials did not reflect the attitude of all Sooner State citizens. Although most high school libraries chose not to buy copies (local school boards were often part of the loose coalition of conservative interests), in the absence of any active censorship campaign most Oklahoma public libraries (like public libraries in other states) did buy copies for their patrons, where the book ranked second in circulation only to *Gone with the Wind*. And patrons often commented that the novel accurately reflected conditions experienced by Oklahoma tenant farmers. When the movie version premiered in Oklahoma City and Tulsa in March 1940, people lined up at the ticket counters.[21]

Because of the social and economic hardships experienced by millions in the 1930s, many people questioned the viability of the American system, and among the groups whose memberships benefited most from this unease was the Communist Party of the United States of America (CPUSA), born in September 1919, and from the beginning a puppet of the Communist International, or Comintern. Early on, head of the Justice Department's Bureau of Investigation J. Edgar Hoover determined that the Party was a threat to the social order and the nation's security, and he committed his office to combating it, often by methods many deemed illegal. By the 1930s, those who agreed with his methods argued they were necessary to save the country. Those who disagreed argued that civil liberties must be protected. Hidden as subtexts in the arguments on both sides were issues of race, creed, class, ethnicity, anti-intellectualism, regionalism, and sometimes gender. And always, printed materials were at the center of the dispute, providing both sides with ready evidence to bolster their positions. The Oklahoma City book trials reflected all of this.

Among the many things Roosevelt accomplished in his first term was recognition of the Soviet Union in 1933, which the United States had withheld since the worker-based Bolsheviks had taken power in 1917. To gain recognition, the Soviet Union promised not to agitate for the overthrow of the American government, nor to engage in propaganda campaigns. It never kept either of those promises, but only chose its moments to increase or decrease the intensity of its efforts. Recognition allowed Moscow to expand its espionage activity on American soil, and within a few years hundreds of secret Party members found jobs in federal agencies that the New Deal had created. Moscow was also more easily able to fund and direct the activities of the CPUSA through its embassy and consulates, and although recognition had added legitimacy to the Party as a political entity, the Party nonetheless followed Moscow's dictates precisely.[22]

Roosevelt fully recognized all this, but rather than confront Moscow directly, in the summer of 1936 he authorized Federal Bureau of Investigation ("Federal" was added to the division's title in 1935) Director Hoover to investigate all suspected subversives. In 1938 Congress passed a Foreign Agents Registration Act, allowing the FBI to arrest unregistered spies, and in 1939 the Hatch Political Activity Act, preventing any federal employee from joining a political party that advocated the overthrow of the government. Following passage of these laws, Roosevelt consolidated investigations of domestic espionage and sabotage into three agencies—Hoover's FBI, and the intelligence divisions of the Army and Navy. Hoover finally had his mandate to pursue Communists and an open door to the Oval Office.

In part Hoover was motivated to act because the Great Depression provided a fertile environment for the CPUSA, which portrayed itself as defender of the unemployed, champion of the racially oppressed, and opponent of Fascism. In 1932, the Communist Party ticket of William Z. Foster and James W. Ford, the first African American nominated for national office, received 102,785 votes. Ford even made a campaign appearance at a union hall in Oklahoma City, surprisingly without incident. Three years later the Seventh Comintern Congress in Moscow directed Communist parties around the world to cooperate with left-wing politicians. In the United States, this meant generally supporting Roosevelt in 1936 (when the Party vote dropped to 80,159), establishing alliances with the newly formed Congress of Industrial Organizations, and infiltrating existing or organizing new left-leaning groups referred to by Party leaders as "Innocents' Clubs." So successful were they in working out alliances with other groups that historian Ted Morgan has called this "the Pink Decade."[23] By January 1, 1939, the Party had "enrolled" membership of 88,000, though just over half were "dues-paying" members.[24]

Already in 1931 a congressional committee accused the ACLU of being "closely affiliated with the Communist movement . . . and fully 90 percent of its efforts are on behalf of communists who have come into conflict with the law." An American Writers Congress organized in New York in 1935 had many Party members. Several advocated an increased need "to bring proletarian literature to the workers." Louis Adamic complained in a 1934 issue of the *Saturday Review of Literature* "that the overwhelming majority of the American working class does not read books and serious, purposeful magazines." One answer to the dilemma was to make "serious purposeful" reading more readily available. Another was to influence publishers. Party leaders were particularly successful with the New York publishing industry. "The Stalinists and their friends, under multiform disguises, have managed to penetrate into the offices of publishing houses, the editorial staffs of magazines, and the book-review sections of conservative newspapers," said a *New Leader* columnist in 1938. By 1936, members of the Young Communist League had taken control of the American Youth Congress — established two years earlier as a coalition of youth groups like the Boy Scouts and YMCA.[25]

Out of this milieu emerged the Special Committee on Un-American Activities (HUAC), authorized by the U.S. House of Representatives in May 1938, and chaired by Texas congressman Martin Dies, Jr. Armed with the power to subpoena and issue contempt citations, Dies led his committee into a high profile investigation of Communist front groups. Between them, HUAC and J. Edgar Hoover turned up enough evidence to strongly suggest the CPUSA was not the champion of the downtrodden it claimed but was determined to exploit social inequities for a Party agenda set in Moscow.

Although the thousands of Party members doing the organizational field work throughout the country did indeed follow the dictates of Moscow-controlled CPUSA leaders (particularly on foreign-policy issues), most appeared to draw their inspiration from social ideals rather than political ideology. Party leaders often referred to them derisively as "useful idiots." These idealists, mostly driven by a passionate desire to address social and economic inequities, found the Party a convenient and useful place to champion the downtrodden and oppose racism. The "people" they claimed to speak for generally did not include upper- and middle-class America but instead consisted of that very large fraction of the American population suffering most in the Great Depression. Their ideals and motives, in fact, brought them to the Party more than any allegiance to a political ideology calling for the overthrow of the American government by force. In many cases, their mindset was so provincial, so nationalistic, that they considered what was happening in the Soviet Union of secondary interest, something to be overlooked or explained away in order to keep a focus on local, state, and national social and economic issues. That was certainly obvious from the activities of Oklahoma Communists and their fellow travelers on the left in the last half of the decade. And for the most part, it was the former who attached their activism to the latter, rather than the other way around.[26]

The history of the Communist Party in Oklahoma was never a huge success story. Party members claimed to have organized a state chapter in 1930. But even a hint of Communist activity drew a quick reaction. Already in January 1932, Assistant County Attorney John Eberle was on the lookout. That month he charged a man "said by police and fire department inspectors to be a Communist leader" with setting a house on fire. A bill to bar Communists from the ballot passed in the state senate in 1935, but failed to become law.[27]

That was the year before Bob Wood moved to Tulsa from Birmingham, Alabama, and began organizing and recruiting for the Party in the Sooner State. But "Robert Wood" was not his original name. In 1917 Bob's mother, Ella Sherishevsky, brought her family of Russian Jews to the United States from Bialystok (at the time in Russia, now in Poland); her husband had died there two years earlier. Accompanying Ella were her five children, including the youngest and brightest, ten-year-old Charles. When Ella brought her family through Ellis Island, the Irish-American immigration officer there renamed them "Sherin" because, he said, it was easier to spell. For a while the Sherins were itinerant textile workers moving wherever they could find employment on the East Coast. "Charlie" himself worked in one of these mills. Later, while in law school, he would write an essay about the workers he saw, the factory's "din" and "clamor," "the symbol of drudgery and automaton futility."

Early on Charlie was singled out as the member of the family to be put through college. He entered the University of Pennsylvania in 1925, graduated four years later, and went to Harvard Law School. After receiving his LL.B. in 1932, he worked briefly at a New York publishing company, then at a law firm, but shortly thereafter he left law practice and joined the Communist Party. "My profession was wrong for me because it had a minimum of social usefulness," he later told his nephew, "and socially useful is what I wanted to be above all else." At that point, he changed his name to "Robert Wood" — in part to protect his family, in part because he feared that as "Charles Sherin," a naturalized U.S. citizen, he would more easily be subject to deportation for his Party membership and for the career of social activism he was about to launch.[28]

For several years after joining the Party, Bob served as ILD Southern District Secretary, based in Atlanta. Beginning September 1, 1933, he frequently traveled to Birmingham to assist in the Scottsboro trials. He was arrested there on March 11, 1935, and charged with possessing "communistic papers," but was found not guilty three months later. On May 1, 1935, as he walked along a busy Birmingham street, he was kidnapped by four members of the "White Legion" and taken to a remote wooded area, where he was badly beaten, tarred and feathered, and had barbed wire wrapped around his head. "Get the hell out of Birmingham, you damn Nigger-lover," they screamed at him after throwing him into a nearby creek, "and tell your people back North the same goes for them." Bob managed to crawl to a local African American sharecropper's home, where he received first aid. (When Eli Jaffe first met him in New York in 1937, his eyes were drawn to Bob's head, where he noticed gaps in Bob's hairline "as though chunks of it had been yanked out, revealing bare splotches of skull." Only later did Eli learn why.)

Because the Alabama vigilantes made it clear they intended to kill him, the Communist Party decided to reassign Bob to Oklahoma in 1936. For a Party organizer, Bob was unusual. He had a presence that commanded attention, both positive and negative, and an uncanny ability to adopt the accents and mannerisms of people and audiences to whom he was speaking. He seldom used the word "capitalism" in his speeches or writing and was more likely

to negotiate agendas with subordinates than issue Party directives.
For a while he and Ina lived in the economically depressed section
of Tulsa, where they frequently hosted fellow organizers. Bob often
came down for breakfast in the morning, armed with copies of the
Tulsa World, Daily Worker, and several other newspapers and magazines. He would then begin clipping articles, and editorialize on
content. Many of the clippings would go into his pockets, to be
pulled out later for quotation in public speeches. "As I became
aware he was a political leader," Eli later recalled, "Bob's style appeared . . . actually more concerned with people than with politics."

Several times a year Bob drove to New York, where he informed
Party leaders living there in relative comfort about the plight of
Oklahoma's unemployed. He generally returned with crates of contributions, including books, issues of left-wing publications, and
boxes of donated clothing. Little wonder he became a charismatic
leader for many left-leaning Oklahomans, whether they were members of the Communist Party or not. At the same time, however, Bob
made no mention of the ongoing purges Stalin had initiated in the
Soviet Union in the summer of 1936 to rid the country of potential
rivals to his power. Between 1936 and 1940, 750,000 Russians were
shot as traitors, and millions more were imprisoned.[29]

In 1938 Bob moved to Oklahoma City to organize, recruit, and
set up the Progressive Book Store, which (like other radical bookstores supported by the CPUSA about the same time in larger cities
across the country) sold books and pamphlets with a leftist perspective. Although much of what he sold was available in large public
and academic libraries in many states, most of the kind of "serious,
purposeful" reading Louis Adamic called for was not readily available elsewhere in Oklahoma. The few people in the Sooner State
who did share these political perspectives found the bookstore an
inviting gathering place to peruse printed materials and engage a
sympathetic listener or two. But like bookstores throughout American history, not only did it function as a site for adherents of a
particular political ideology, it also served as a convenient and
reachable target for opponents of that ideology. By 1938, this had
become apparent in Oklahoma City. In May, the bookstore's land-

lord made Bob remove the red hammer and sickle he had painted on the window because so many passersby complained.[30] Proprietors and many customers knew they were being watched. To enter the bookstore was in many respects a political statement and an act of defiance against Oklahoma's dominant culture.

International politics directly affected the Progressive Book Store. In 1937 Eugene Poling left his Kiowa County, Oklahoma, farm to fight in the Spanish Civil War on the side of Loyalists (supported by the Soviet Union) and against the Nationalists (supported by Hitler and Mussolini). For Poling (like hundreds of other Americans on the political left in 1937) Spain was a moral battleground where Democracy fought Fascism. Poling was wounded in battle and captured shortly thereafter. After nine months in a French prison camp, he returned home with a piece of shrapnel in his thigh and "in a dazed frame of mind," his eighty-five-year-old father, Alonzo, told a group of Oklahoma legislators two years later. "He can think and talk of nothing but the [Communist] party." When Alonzo found in his house an orange crate full of "foreign tracts" his son had been getting from the Progressive Book Store, he decided to take action. "My other son and I set 'em beside a tree and set fire to 'em," he said. "They must have been hot stuff. They burned the tree down." Weeks later Alonzo confronted Bob Wood at the bookstore and told him to "quit sending that literature to my house."[31]

Bob continued to court danger by standing on principle. In late May 1938, two of the Scottsboro boys visited Oklahoma City to speak at a rally to raise funds for the defense of others still in jail. The local chapter of the NAACP organized the event. Along with local activist Sis Cunningham and weekly *Black Dispatch* newspaper editor Roscoe Dunjee,[32] Bob met them at the train station. When the travelers stepped off the Jim Crow car onto the "colored" portion of the station platform, Dunjee and Wood approached with Cunningham. A white guard came over and said, "Don't take that white lady through the gate; just go yourselves." "You goin' to stop her?" Bob asked. Dunjee intervened. "You can't interfere with her civil rights." The guard seemed confused. It was obvious to the entire welcoming party the guard's knowledge of local custom was better than his knowledge of the Constitution.[33]

Bob's wife, Ina, was born Sabina Victoria Bush on March 11, 1908, in Lawrence, Massachusetts, one of eight children raised by Lithuanian-born Catholic parents. Her father was a leader in the 1918 Lawrence textile strike, and was once beaten by police in his own home. Ina was an attractive woman of average height with a slightly upturned nose, hazel eyes, and dark brown hair usually brushed straight back. She went to work in the local textile mills at fifteen, contributed part of her earnings to the family, and after graduating from high school (which she attended at night), used the remainder to pay her way through Portia Law School (now the New England School of Law), where she took a particular interest in constitutional law. According to information Bob later provided to the Selective Service Board, he and Ina were married in Elkton, Maryland, in May 1934.[34] In the summer of 1935, Ina traveled to Europe to visit several countries, including the Soviet Union. Throughout the trip she kept a diary; she preferred people to museums, she said, but of Russia she wrote: "I love it all. I love the people. I feel related to everyone of them." A very private person, she always retained a trace of a New England accent that in Oklahoma immediately branded her "outsider." She was much more reserved and introverted than her husband, but was no shrinking violet; she enjoyed dancing with "comrades" at a nearby hall where Bob Wills and the Texas Playboys performed. Ina especially loved the Spanish two-step.[35]

While in Tulsa, she participated in meetings of the Scottsboro Committee. On occasion she coauthored articles, some showing sympathy to the Marxist approach to social problems, others addressing the plight of African Americans. In one, she remarked that African Americans in Oklahoma needed doctors but were not permitted to practice medicine there. Once the Woods moved to Oklahoma City, Ina took a job for two days as "Inez Plunkett" in an Armour & Company packing plant, where she obtained a social security card.

Bob Wood recruited Eli Jaffe to Oklahoma. Eli was born the

second of four children on February 14, 1913, to a middle-class family in Brooklyn. His father, owner of a linen supply company, had emigrated to the United States from Ponevezh, a *stedtl* near Vilna, Lithuania. Eli was raised in relative comfort, joined the Boy Scouts, and became an Eagle Scout. At Brooklyn College (known at the time as the "Little Red Schoolhouse" for its leftist leanings) he served as editor of the school newspaper for a year, starting center fielder on the varsity baseball team, and actor in a theatrical group. He was also winner of a $1,000 first prize in a national one-act playwriting contest, elected president of his senior class and voted its most popular student. He graduated cum laude as an English major in 1937, and was declared an Outstanding Graduate.[36]

After graduation Eli joined the Communist Party, but rather than becoming an organizer he aspired to a career in journalism and writing. Initially, he decided to start a novel about a young man and his pregnant wife in Dust Bowl Oklahoma. For months he researched the subject diligently at the New York Public Library. After drafting the first forty pages he approached Joe Jones, an artist whose paintings of Dust Bowl scenes he admired and who at the time was living in Greenwich Village. Eli asked if he would look at the manuscript. "What you've written is the hysteria of the New York intellectual," Jones said. "If you want to write honestly about the Dust Bowl, why don't you get your ass out there and get to know the people?" Eli thought that good advice; he had just inherited $7,000 from his parents' estate, and unlike many of his peers had no pressing need to find a job.

Because he knew no one in Oklahoma, Eli contacted Oklahoma Communist Party organizer Bob Wood. Bob responded that he was coming to New York for the annual CPUSA conference and bringing with him Bill Ritchison of Claremore. In New York, Ritchison listened to Eli talk about his novel, then drawled, "Why don't y' come to my place n' stay a week, or until y' get weak?" In March 1938, Eli accompanied Bob on a return trip. Because he intended to stay in Claremore with Ritchison and work full-time on his novel, he took plenty of paper and writing supplies. But Bob had other ideas for him. On the trip he encouraged Eli to join the Workers

Alliance, an organization that represented people on relief and was dedicated to obtaining jobs for unemployed farmers and oil-field workers. Its members had already staged several sit-down strikes in courthouses across the state to make unresponsive county officials listen to their complaints. "Unemployment is now the major industry in Oklahoma," he told Eli. "More than half the people are on relief."[37]

Eli joined the Alliance as soon as he arrived in Claremore, where he quickly had an encounter with local officials and their supporters. As fifteen Alliance members gathered for a meeting, a local police chief, an American Legion post commander, and a group of seventy-five Legionnaires "armed with clubs and pickaxe handles" refused to allow the meeting to begin. Rather than force violence, Bob Wood approached the armed men: "Mind if I tell 'em we're callin' it off?" With some relief, the police chief gave him permission. Bob then shouted for all to hear, "Friends, in spite of the Constitutions of the United States and the State of Oklahoma, looks like we're being denied our right to assemble peaceably. All we wanted was to ask for jobs and food for hungry kids." When the armed mob began to shout back, Bob and Eli left quickly. "Bob has no fear," Eli later concluded.[38]

But a subsequent encounter did not end as peacefully. At a public meeting of town and state officials who were discussing how to distribute the few federal dollars available for relief, Eli pointed to a local woman and her malnourished children and shouted: "We demand you give them food!" He immediately recognized he had gone too far. Demands issued to college administrators by idealistic students may have been tolerated in Brooklyn, but demands made by a transplant from New York with obvious ties to the state Communist Party received a much different reaction from Oklahoma bureaucrats. Eli quickly became persona non grata with local officials, who thereafter refused to allow Workers Alliance meetings. Eli recognized he had better leave town. On his way out, however, a local bully confronted him on the street. "You, Bullshevick [sic]!" he shouted, then began punching Eli about the face until he lost consciousness. When his head cleared, Eli found himself in the local jail, charged with street fighting. Initially, Eli refused to pay bond, but relented when Tulsa attorney George Croom bailed him out.[39]

Despite this baptism by fire, Eli's attitude toward politics mirrored Bob Wood's. His Communist Party friends in Oklahoma often referred to him as a "bourgeois humanitarian" much more concerned with the "one-third of the nation" suffering at the hands of the few than with political ideology or spouting the Communist Party line. His actions as an organizer in Oklahoma for all the time he was there showed he was opposed to the use of violence unless personally threatened.[40]

From Claremore Eli traveled to Guymon in the Oklahoma Panhandle, where he stayed for several months with Will and Caroline Henderson, whose *Atlantic Monthly* "Letters from the Dust Bowl" had caught his eye in the New York Public Library. Eli had written Caroline in 1936, and Caroline had invited him to stay on their farm to research his novel should he ever visit the Sooner State. From Guymon Eli wrote stories and articles describing the poverty and social conditions around him. Henderson read several and was impressed with "the flame of your love for humanity" and "the sincerity of your desire to improve the opportunities" for poor people.[41]

Bob Wood was also responsible for Alan Shaw's presence in the Sooner State. Born Alan Lifshutz in 1919 to Russian immigrants (his father was a dentist), he entered Brooklyn College in 1935. Like Eli, he majored in English. He served on the student council for four years and founded the Karl Marx Society. During the summer of his junior year he and a college classmate decided to hitchhike across the country. Upon hearing that his friend's aunt and uncle were driving to Oklahoma — invited by Bob Wood to come out and teach a group of tenant farmers and black sharecroppers — the two college students decided to tag along that far, and hitchhike the rest of the way. But they got no farther than Oklahoma City. Once there they met Bob, who then arranged for them to spend time with the sharecroppers near Bristow. Alan was hooked. Although he deplored the plight of all of Oklahoma's working people, he especially abhorred a set of Jim Crow laws evident in segregated restaurants, transportation facilities, rest rooms, and at water coolers. Bob invited him to return to Oklahoma to work for the state Communist Party after graduation.

Alan graduated with high honors from Brooklyn College in June 1939, and like Eli was voted a leader by his fellow students. But before he moved back to Oklahoma City in August to become Oklahoma City secretary of the CPUSA, he decided to change his name. "When I began to do the type of work that I was doing," he explained later, "I did not want my family to be involved in any of the political discriminations." So he became Alan Shaw, in honor of his favorite playwright, George Bernard Shaw. A cerebral person, he loved to debate ideology.[42]

With Bob and Ina Wood (and later Eli Jaffe and Alan Shaw) actively recruiting, state Party membership jumped from slightly over three hundred in 1937 to five hundred a year later. But organized opposition was not far behind. In 1938, a Tulsa clergyman established the Oklahoma League Against Communism, Nazism, and Fascism.[43] Opposition showed itself in other ways as well. New Deal agencies in Washington were easy (and often justifiable) targets for anti-Communists like HUAC and Hoover. Local offices for these agencies were equally easy (and equally justifiable) targets for Oklahoma officials. Congressman Lyle Boren, for example, worried about the Works Progress Administration. In March 1939, he told an Oklahoma WPA administrator that any WPA supervisor or non-relief employee who was also a member of the Workers Alliance should immediately be removed: "I take a position that a member of the Workers Alliance is as much in sympathy with the Communist Party as a member of the Baptist Young People's union is in sympathy with the Baptist church."[44] But the official waffled. He said the Oklahoma WPA would employ "no known Communists" (he lied), and that it could not discharge relief workers for their political affiliations. "Anyway," he said, in an effort to deflect anti-Communist attention elsewhere, "you hear less about Communists in the WPA than Communists at the University of Oklahoma — and there may be no quarry in the university's 'red hunt.' "[45]

The *Daily Oklahoman* was convinced that Communists permeated the Federal Writers' Project, a New Deal agency that provided jobs for unemployed people of literary bent. "The best place to verify the rumor that the Communists are in the saddle is at the project itself," the *Oklahoman* noted. "The workers who weren't Communists say loudly that the reds are running the works — if you promise not to quote them." The *Oklahoman* was right; several Communists and Communist sympathizers were employed by the Federal Writers' Project. But like Bob and Ina Wood, Eli Jaffe, and Alan Shaw, they were much more concerned with the plight of the poor than with conspiring to overthrow the government. Communist sympathizer William Cunningham (Sis's brother, and author of the novel *Green Corn Rebellion*), for example, directed the Oklahoma Writers Project. Watching over all this was *Oklahoman* editor Luther Harrison, the driving force behind the state's criminal syndicalism law. In the same article on the Federal Writers' Project, Harrison asserted that membership in the state chapter of the Communist Party had doubled to six hundred in the past year.[46]

Despite these relatively low numbers of Party members in the state, Oklahoma officials and their allies ratcheted up the rhetoric. In a speech titled "Communists in Oklahoma," delivered on December 5, 1938, Governor Phillips said: "Our citizens will not stand for Communists in Oklahoma. I have an ambition for such a unity of feeling among our citizenship that I know they'll never do much here." On the other hand, in remarks to a 1938 University of Oklahoma public meeting, Luther Harrison suggested every university student ought to read Marx's *Das Kapital*. "Bring these doctrines out in the open; I have no fear of the results," he said. "The intelligence of the American people has rejected such doctrines every time they have seen and understood them."[47]

On January 6, 1939, the Oklahoma House of Representatives considered a bill to amend the state's criminal syndicalism law in order to outlaw sit-down strikes and peaceful picketing by what they thought were Communist-run organizations. In part, the bill aimed at limiting the Workers Alliance. After two days of hearings, the House passed a watered-down version (the peaceful picketing clause was removed) by a vote of 69–36. When the Senate took it up three weeks later, Paul Stewart, of Antlers, attempted to reinsert the peaceful picketing clause, but to no avail. The entire bill failed to pass either House.[48]

On February 22, 1939, the state Communist Party rented the "Little Theatre" in the Oklahoma City Municipal Auditorium for a rally. Fewer than twenty members showed, where they were out-numbered by 250 Legionnaires there to heckle the speakers and disrupt the meeting, and twenty police officers who had parked their tear-gas truck outside because they feared a riot. At the meet-ing Bob Wood helped reduce tension by joking about the Commu-nist stereotype that some public officials were peddling. "I shave every morning, take a bath once in a while, and do not beat my wife." The audience laughed; a few even cheered. The *Oklahoman* noted that Communist speakers had been so laudatory of President Roosevelt that "the session might have been a Young Democrats meeting, except for one drunk in the back."[49]

After Alan Shaw arrived in Oklahoma City, he immediately be-gan attending city council meetings to speak on behalf of the city's unemployed, its African Americans, and its young people, and in July he asked permission to rent the theatre again for a September 10 meeting. This time, however, the auditorium manager refused, citing the city manager's new policy of barring use by "un-American and abusive organizations." Police could not guarantee security, he argued. "To preserve the public peace and to avoid strife and pos-sibility of riot I find it necessary to reject your formal application," he wrote Alan.[50]

Alan appealed to the city manager, but his request was turned down. He then sought a writ of mandamus to force the manager to rent the theatre to the Party. Again he was denied; the district court ruled in favor of the city. To this decision even the *Daily Oklahoman* objected. Communists "ought to be permitted to meet without mo-lestation and shriek their anger without interference," the *Okla-homan* said in an editorial. "And let us remember that there is only one short step between depriving our neighbor of his rights and being deprived of our own rights." In late August, Alan privately rented another hall for a Communist Party meeting. Again, Legion-naires filled the hall and heckled the speakers. "A young winner of a legion oratorical contest took over the floor for a speech," the *Oklahoma City Times* reported, and, after he finished, "legion members marched out in a body with him." Police were on hand, but no violence occurred.[51]

On August 23, 1939, the Soviet Union and Nazi Germany signed a nonaggression pact, promising not to attack each other. In its immediate wake Hitler invaded Poland, and within weeks France and England joined the war against Hitler, while Russia's Stalin swallowed Latvia, Lithuania, Estonia, and part of Finland. Events in Europe forced Americans of all political persuasions to respond. For conservatives in the United States, Stalin's willingness to ally with Hitler only proved the Soviet Union was as totalitarian as Germany. When the CPUSA parroted the lines sent them by Moscow opposing America's involvement in the war against Germany, conservative forces around the country railed against their hypocrisy. That no word came from Oklahoma Communist Party officials to distance themselves from antiwar positions being articulated by New York leaders only reconfirmed what most of Oklahoma conservative leaders in and out of government perceived as the Party's basic dishonesty.

On the ground in Oklahoma, anti-Communist feelings intensified. At an August 25 meeting that Bob Wood called in order to explain and defend the pact, fifty Legionnaires heckled the speakers. A dozen police were present to prevent violence, but the meeting ended without incident. On September 10, 1939, Oklahoma County Assistant County Attorney John Eberle attended a Communist Party meeting at which several nationally known Communists were scheduled to speak. But because officials in the city manager's office worried about adverse publicity if the increasingly anti-Communist Eberle broke up the meeting and prevented the speeches, they dispatched William Loe, a Special Investigator of Communist Activities for the city manager to confront Eberle and prevent any disturbance. Loe and Eberle quickly got into a heated debate just outside the door, whereupon Loe called the chief of police to send men to restore order. When they arrived Eberle withdrew, knowing he would have other opportunities to press his agenda. The meeting continued, and was only slightly disturbed by hecklers. After it concluded, a *Daily Oklahoman* reporter asked one of the hecklers what he was trying to accomplish. "We're going to bring them to surrender. We will wipe them out of the city."[52]

At a December 17 meeting Bob echoed Moscow's thinly veiled argument that Finland had provoked the Soviet Union to invade for "defensive" purposes. About that time, Eli Jaffe began to notice a shift in opinion. One cold morning he stood with Wilma Lewis handing out Party leaflets outside a Swift and Company packing plant as workers filed in for the morning shift. Most paid no attention to them; some were visibly hostile. Still, Bob and his colleagues refused to curtail their activities.[53]

That same month, another organization held a meeting that added to officials' concerns that Communists were gaining strength in Oklahoma. Between December 28 and 30, 1939, the Oklahoma Youth Legislature (OYL) met for its third conference. In 1936, Oklahoma Communists had helped establish an Oklahoma Youth Legislature affiliated with the American Youth Congress that by this time was dominated by Communists. Its constitution reaffirmed fundamental liberties outlined in the Bill of Rights, and solicited participation by all young people, no matter their race, creed, color, gender, or politics. The OYL, also supported by many University of Oklahoma faculty and by *Black Dispatch* editor Roscoe Dunjee, consisted mostly of college students who debated issues of poverty, militarism, and government support for people's needs. They deliberated on current local, state, national, and international events, and passed mock laws. For most of them, the interracial organization represented an attempt "to get a progressive agenda before the state."[54]

When the OYL met in December 1937, the *Daily Oklahoman* reported it had passed mock laws mandating collective bargaining and a graduated income tax, adopted resolutions calling for a minimum wage and state subsidization of cooperative hospitals, and turned back efforts to segregate white and African American delegates. "Liberalism rampant," the *Oklahoman* noted.[55] The 1938 conference was disrupted by several Oklahoma A&M students who disliked the organization's political perspective and policy of racial integration. They walked out when they thought their concerns had not been fairly heard. In subsequent weeks, the protestors received support from the American Legion, drafted a constitution for a new organization called the Oklahoma Junior Legislature that barred African Americans, and filed incorporation papers. Organizers then called a conference for the same dates and in the same city as the next OYL conference.

Thus, in 1939, on the same days the OYL met at the Shrine Auditorium, the newly incorporated Oklahoma Junior Legislature met at the Capitol, where they "voted" to exterminate prairie dogs, crows, and other Oklahoma farm pests with a special $30,000 appropriation. Then they heartily approved federal government efforts to investigate un-American activities and applauded speeches by the presidents of the state American Legion and its female auxiliary. State senators wandered in and out of the proceedings, glad-handing their young constituents.[56]

In contrast, on the morning of the first day of the OYL conference, registrants were called to order, and, after an invocation, Provisional Chair Nena Beth Stapp used her keynote address to respond to accusations its members were "a bunch of wild and wooly Communists, foreign agents from Moscow, with knives in our teeth and bombs in our beards." Not so, she said. OYL members stood at "the center of progressive youth activities" in the state, and sought only "peace, progress, democracy and liberty." If that was "treason," Stapp argued, "make the most of it." At the end of the session, sixty-one members and sponsors of the Youth Legislature lined up on the steps of the auditorium for a group picture; twenty-one were women (including Nena Beth Stapp and Wilma Lewis); eighteen were African American (including *Black Dispatch* editor Roscoe Dunjee). Eli Jaffe and Alan Shaw stood inconspicuously in the second and last rows.[57] At midcentury, when blacks and whites mixed publicly on the same Sooner State platforms, Oklahoma officials usually saw red.

Beginning in 1940, anti-Communist editorials in the *Oklahoma City Times* and *Daily Oklahoman* became increasingly shrill. After Bob

Wood, Alan Shaw, and Eli Jaffe marched on city council in early January 1940 to demand food and clothing for the unemployed, the *Oklahoman* argued in a January 7 editorial, "Communism is the greatest internal menace for the simple reason that the danger of Communism is almost universally pooh-poohed by a certain type of intellectual 'liberals.' " An April 1 editorial argued that "no matter what offense may be committed by a Communist and no matter what offenses he is charged with, his fellow Communists character- ize him as a 'political prisoner.' " If war should come, the *Oklahoman* argued in its May 17 issue, "groups which preach doctrines contrary to American principles would no longer enjoy freedom of speech and enterprise. The government would not allow any voices to be heard which might stir up sedition, riots, or defeatist attitudes."[58] Thus, another part of Oklahoma's conservative elite made clear its priorities on civil liberties in periods of national crisis.

Oklahoma officials' campaign against Communism also re- ceived support from other nongovernmental organizations besides the American Legion. In early February, the Grand Imperial Wizard of the Ku Klux Klan from Atlanta announced on a visit to Oklahoma City that in order to "educate the people to appreciate the American form of government and to fight un-American activities," his organi- zation was mounting a campaign "to arouse an intensified patriot- ism and point out the advantages of this government over the Nazi, Fascist, and Russian system." The Klan leader praised Martin Dies for doing a "splendid job," and indicated that because Communism was spreading rapidly in Tulsa and Oklahoma City, the Klan was prepared to work for and cooperate with the Dies Committee.[59]

Despite the mounting opposition, Bob Wood and his colleagues continued their activism. In early March they again tried to rent the Municipal Auditorium for an April 28 discussion of "how to keep the United States out of war." Again, the manager rejected their request. Bob and Alan argued that the manager was bowing to pressure from local Legionnaires, who once again threatened to disrupt the meeting if held. In a letter to the mayor and city council members, Bob asked: "What is the reason given for the denial of the auditorium? Simply that a group of hoodlums threatens to break up such a meeting." The *Oklahoman* appeared to agree with this logic. "The opponents of communism will be disserving their own cause whenever they deprive any Communist of any right that is his constitutional own," an editorial stated. "We cannot approve any course of action that abbreviates the constitutional privileges of the most insignificant Communist on earth."[60]

But the newspaper's agreement was only a tease. Three days later the *Oklahoman* announced: "We Have a Remedy." Admittedly, the editorial argued, "the organic law of our country promises every citizen certain clearly specified rights," including free speech and the right to assemble peaceably. Anyone or any group who attempted to interfere with these rights by violence ought to be subject to a "heavy fine" and "extended imprisonment." But the government's obligation to the Communists of Oklahoma ended with a promise to let them assemble and advocate their cause. If, however, they dared to advocate violence against the government, the state of Oklahoma could harness the criminal syndicalism law of 1919 to "inflict the severest kind of punishment upon every mother's son of them." That law, the editorial argued, "is all the protection state and society need." A 1940 ILD survey showed that twenty-five states had criminal syndicalism statutes; thirteen had invoked these statutes in the 1930s.[61] Oklahoma conservatives were obviously not alone in their willingness to use criminal syndicalism laws to combat Communism.

On March 21, one hundred members of the city's two American Legion posts attended a meeting at which they approved resolutions commending the Dies Committee and the Oklahoma City Council for denying the Communist Party use of the auditorium. Just over a month later, several people broke into the homes of the Red Dust Players, threw letters and papers about, took books, and left possessions in a shambles.[62] For several years Oklahoma officials had worried about the Players, a group of part-time Oklahoma musicians who created and sang songs protesting the plight of poor people. In the late 1930s they traveled the state. "Many a night, our 'stage' was the sagging porch of a sharecropper's weather-beaten shack, with the audience seated on the ground in front of us," Sis

Cunningham later recalled. "Lighting was provided by a few ancient lanterns hanging on rusty nails driven into the porch supports." On several occasions, Bob Wood accompanied the Players to address the same audiences. At those performances and speeches, Oklahoma officials and their allies were often lurking in the shadows.[63]

In early May, social worker Elizabeth Green noticed that hundreds of Oklahoma City men and women were being turned away as they lined up every day in the hot sun to participate in a federally funded program that gave unemployed fathers two dollars worth of stamps per month to buy surplus commodities for their families at local grocery stores. County workers in charge of food stamp distribution claimed they could not verify that applicants were unemployed. When negotiations to resolve this problem broke down (Green and Eli Jaffe had compiled a list of WPA workers to help county officials), the Workers Alliance began picketing the office. Green led one end of the picket line. City police intervened on May 16, arrested her (the police chief accused her of attempting "to overthrow the government"), and threw her in jail. The next day a judge pronounced her guilty of vagrancy and fined her nineteen dollars and costs. When she paid her fine, she revealed a bankbook to officials that showed the balance of a legacy left her by her grandfather. Among county officials, she became known as a "fifth columnist," a term originating during the Spanish Civil War to describe those intent on undermining their nation's solidarity.[64]

Oklahoma's campaign against the Communists intensified in the summer of 1940. At the state Democratic convention in early June, Governor Phillips gave the keynote address. "Communism and constitutional government as we know it cannot exist together," he said. He also asserted that the right of free speech was never intended as a license to spread poison. "No person with my knowledge and consent shall work for the state who is not wholly and sincerely in sympathy with our American institutions."[65]

About the same time County Sheriff George Goff organized an Oklahoma County Civil Guard, placing it under the direction of a fellow Legionnaire. To friends, Goff confided that the Civil Guard was organized to help in "getting the Reds." By June Goff claimed to have 2,000 members consisting mostly of auxiliary policemen and auxiliary firemen who were "ready for any emergency on an instant's notice." That summer he sent out a circular to the membership, requesting they "register" their firearms with his office. Similarly, City Manager W. A. Quinn organized the Oklahoma City Emergency Defense Battalion and placed it under a Board of Control, one member of which was overheard to say that "Wood and Shaw should have their throats cut." Although membership in the battalion was voluntary, most who joined (not surprisingly) were city employees. Within weeks the group claimed 2,700 members.[66]

On June 8, Quinn gave the Sunday edition of the *Daily Oklahoman* an extensive interview about the Emergency Defense Battalion. "It will have charge of investigation of all sabotage or attempted sabotage, subversive movements and un-American activities. In general, its job will be to combat the 'fifth column' in the city." Quinn encouraged citizens to report any suspicious activities by telephone or directly to city police. When asked if any fifth columnists had been "located, questioned, suspected or placed under surveillance," Quinn responded, "We have some people we are watching." He indicated that any evidence generated would be turned over to the FBI, with whom "we will work closely." Violations of civil liberties, he said, "will not be tolerated." Quinn concluded by saying the organization "will cooperate closely with oil companies and utilities to prevent sabotage." Although the U.S. attorney general subsequently advised the county sheriff and city manager to disband these organizations because, in his opinion, they were "illegal and unlawful," neither took any action. Both organizations remained viable.[67]

As the Civil Guard and Emergency Defense Battalion organized, folksingers Woody Guthrie and Pete Seeger came through town. At the time Seeger was working at the Library of Congress, primarily collecting folk songs. In early May Guthrie came through Washington and convinced Seeger to join him for a trip to his home state of Oklahoma. When they arrived in Oklahoma City, they initially stayed at a flophouse, but shortly thereafter moved in for a few days with Bob and Ina Wood, who had convinced both musicians to offer their services for a Workers Alliance rally at a hall near the Community Camp.

"There were hardly 50 or 60 people present," Seeger later re-called, "but it included some women and children who evidently couldn't get babysitters. It also included some strange men who walked in and lined up along the back of the hall without sitting down." One of the familiar "strangers" had already come up to Eli Jaffe. "You keep shootin' off your mouth, I'm gonna kick the shit out-a-you," he said. Bob Wood also recognized them immediately, and leaned over to Seeger and Guthrie. "I'm not sure if these guys are going to try to break up this meeting or not. It's an open meeting and we can't kick them out. See if you can get the whole crowd singing." But Guthrie and Seeger were still nervous. "Woody and I got the crowd singing," Seeger later recalled, "and you know, those guys never did break up the meeting. We found out later that they had rather intended to. Perhaps it was the presence of so many women and children that deterred them — perhaps it was the singing."

While staying with Bob and Ina Wood, Guthrie experimented with several songs. One night Ina challenged him: "Woody, all these union songs are about brothers this and brothers that. How about writing songs about union women?" Guthrie sat down at the table. Next morning, Ina and Bob discovered written on a brown paper bag some fresh lyrics:

There once was a union maid who never was afraid
Of goons and ginks and company finks
And the deputy sheriffs who made the raids.
She went to the union hall when a meeting it was called,
And when the company boys came 'round
She always stood her ground.
Oh, you can't scare me, I'm sticking to the Union,
I'm sticking to the union, sticking to the Union.
Oh, you can't scare me, I'm sticking to the union
I'm sticking to the union till the day I die.

Guthrie's "Union Maid" would soon become a crowd favorite.[68]

Ina and Bob Wood "gave me as good a feeling as I ever got from being around anybody in my whole life," Guthrie later noted. "They made me see why I had to keep going around and around with my guitar making up songs and singing. . . . I never had been able to look out over and across the slum section nor a sharecropper farm and connect it up with the owner and the landlord and the guards and the police and the dicks and the bulls and the vigilante men with their black sedans and sawed off shot guns." Like Bob and Ina Wood, Guthrie and Seeger also wanted to change the world for the better, at least as they saw it. To Oklahoma officials, however, Guthrie and Seeger fit a profile already created by the Red Dust Players.[69]

On June 9, 1940, anti-Communism in Oklahoma City got a little meaner. On that day ten young men disrupted a Party meeting at the Progressive Book Store by shouting down speakers. As they left the building they also "scattered books and pamphlets on the floor, threw some into the corridor, and attempted to carry some away in sacks." The landlord intervened, and later complained to police, who promised to investigate. The incident had an immediate effect on Alan Shaw and Eli Jaffe. For months they had been living in a room at the back of the store. After June 9, however, they moved to an apartment house just across the back alley from Bob and Ina. By that time Alan was a married man. During the fall of 1939 and winter of 1940, he and Eli both had fallen in love with Nena Beth Stapp, leader in the Oklahoma Youth Legislature. By spring, however, Nena Beth had chosen Alan over Eli and secretly married him on April 14. Because he worried for his wife's safety, however, Alan continued to board with Eli. Although Eli was disappointed that Nena Beth chose Alan, he harbored no ill feelings toward either. All continued their organizing efforts as close friends.[70]

Three days after the incident at the bookstore, seventy-five men paraded in west Tulsa "waving red and white handkerchiefs over their heads" and distributing copies of a publication called *The People's Voice* that advocated "overthrow by force of the American government." When he read about the incident, Bob Wood rushed to Tulsa, where he insisted to the local U.S. district attorney that the publication was a forgery of the state Communist Party's newspaper of the same name. "The Communist Party never has and does not now advocate the overthrow of government by force," he told the

Tulsa Daily World. "The forgers who circulated the false newspaper are the real enemies of democracy and those seeking to overthrow our democratic form of government." Fortunately for Bob, the district attorney believed him. Bob was "too intelligent a man," he said, "to advocate anything like that in a publication." Others were not so convinced. A local Legionnaire urged state officials to invoke the state's criminal syndicalism law against publishers and distributors of *The People's Voice.* "It is no time to leave unenforced laws which do not forbid the exercise of freedom of worship or speech, but which do forbid advocating the overthrow of government by means of force and violence."[71]

Shortly after Bob returned to Oklahoma City the next day, he hitched a ride with Guthrie and several rural Oklahoma Communists to the Party convention in New York City. "After we got out of the Holler [Holland] Tunnel," Guthrie later wrote, "I says, Well Boys, what do you think of her? One old boy in the back said, I bet I sunburn the roof of my mouth — but it'll be worth it — he looked out the window as we drove down the street and he said, God a mighty, dadburn my hide, is ALL of them people here for the convention?" At the convention, Guthrie was so taken with the sense of community he felt that he gave Bob Wood his new Plymouth for his return to Oklahoma City. Bob used it to travel around the state for the next four years; it became very familiar to Oklahoma officials.

While Bob was in New York, however, the men who raided the bookstore returned. This time, Ina was the only one there. She recognized them as "the identical group" from June 9 and attempted to block their path by holding the railings on either side of the stairway with her hands. Initially they hesitated, then surged to break her grip and knocked her down. They threw books and papers from shelves, ripped scores of books apart, and left the torn pages on the floor. They also stuffed hundreds of books in gunnysacks and carried them away. Ina reported the incident to police, who "renewed their offer of protection" made the week before. No one was ever arrested.[72]

Days later Pentecostal preacher Reverend Edward Frederick Webber announced on "Southwest Church of the Air" — a thrice-weekly morning radio program with an estimated audience of two million he hosted on Oklahoma City's KOMA and ten other stations in surrounding states—that he had just come into possession of certain Communist books. He announced he would sponsor a bonfire to rid the community of these vile materials in the stadium of his Calvary Tabernacle, and invited members of the public to attend. Thousands heard the invitation; somewhere between 500 and 1,000 people showed. While they watched the materials go up in flames, Webber led them in a chorus of "America the Beautiful."

Webber was a celebrity in the Southwest who for years had been railing against "com-you-nists" (that's how Eli Jaffe heard him pronounce the word over the radio). Russians ate their own children, Webber once claimed, not from hunger, but out of sheer bestiality. But the Bible-thumping clergyman hated other groups as well. Jewish groups listed him as an organizer for the local chapter of the Silver Shirt Legion of America, a right-wing organization whose program of "Christian Democracy" advocated that the civil rights of Jews should be abrogated, that Zionist Jews should be prosecuted, and that all Jews ought to be confined to urban ghettos, where they could be watched more carefully.[73] To E. F. Webber, Jews and Communists looked a lot alike.

As word spread of Webber's book-burning activities, ripples of protest began to surface outside the state. Beginning with its July issue, Library Journal carried a quote by U.S. Commissioner of Education John W. Studebaker: "When people are burning books in other parts of the world," Studebaker said, "we ought to be distributing them with greater vigor, for books are among the best allies in the fight to make democracy work." Library Journal continued to run the quote through its November issue, then reprinted it as part of the masthead for its monthly "Editorial Forum" until June 1942.[74]

Other groups besides Communists experienced violations of civil liberties that summer. Jehovah's Witnesses were routinely harassed simply for assembling. The ACLU reported that nationwide in recent months at least forty mobs had attacked Witnesses; they had been beaten, stoned, and jailed, removed from relief rolls for refusing to pledge allegiance to the United States, their literature had been burned, their children barred from schools for refusing to salute the flag. When one Witness who was distributing literature complained to the Oklahoma City Police, Captain Dan Hollingsworth responded that he had been "expecting the members of the sect to run into this kind of trouble sooner or later," and advised him to cease activities.[75]

Also during that summer, as England endured the Battle of Britain and Germany ran over the Low Countries and France, Congress overwhelmingly passed the Smith Act (officially the Alien Registration Act) on June 28. The Act made it illegal "to advocate, abet, advise, or teach the duty, necessity, desirability, or propriety of overthrowing or destroying any government in the United States by force or violence." It criminalized the publishing or circulation of "any written or printed matter" advocating the government's overthrow and penalized the act of belonging to any group that advocated the government's overthrow with knowledge of its purposes.[76]

Elsewhere in the country, officials at the federal, state, and local levels initiated a series of repressive actions to counter what they perceived as fifth-column threats to domestic security. As a result of these actions, Communist Party leader Earl Browder was eventually tried, convicted, and sent to jail for passport fraud. In Pennsylvania, Communists who circulated petitions to put Party members on the ballot were arrested for electoral fraud. In New York, a legislative committee began investigations of Communist teaching in New York City colleges; several faculty members lost their jobs. And in both New York and California, state legislators conducted hearings on perceived Communist subversion.[77]

In Oklahoma, the FBI closely monitored the activities of Sooner State Communists. In a July 1, 1940 report, agent Ralph T. Hood reported that Oklahoma City's chief of police "received information that Wood and other communists in Oklahoma City were plotting an overthrow of the [city] government," and that the City had been prompted to investigate. In response, Assistant County Attorney Eberle began to formulate a strategy to address what he considered the County's most serious threat to the social order.

During the first week of July, the fifth district division of the American Legion held a meeting to "devise ways and means of coping with fifth column activities." And all the while, Oklahoma City's dailies continued their steady drumbeat against fifth columnists, the CPUSA, its members and programs. When one Communist "violates the syndicalism law that penalizes the advocacy of revolution by violence," the *Oklahoman* urged in its July 6 issue, "let him be punished for his positive offense, regardless of the bleating of all the civil liberties bunds in America."[78]

In early August attorney Stanley Belden of Cushing drove to Guthrie to defend a jailed Jehovah's Witness. When two other Witnesses attempted in court to post bond for their friend, the judge also ordered them to jail. Belden rose to object, and the judge asked him: "Are you a Jehovah's Witness?" When Belden said "No," the judge ordered him to kiss the American flag. Belden refused, and was himself escorted to jail. When he was released hours later, jailers led him to a back room, showed him a window, and told him he was free to go. Outside the window Belden saw more than fifty vigilantes armed with pickaxe handles. He insisted on staying in jail until adequate protection arrived.[79]

About the same time, Eli Jaffe noticed at the café where he breakfasted every morning a clean-shaven man in worker's clothes who watched him intently. Bob Wood sensed impending trouble. He took a number of books, put them in watertight containers, and buried them on a tenant farmer's land outside of town. As county officials quietly prepared for the bookstore raids, they circulated photographs of Bob and Ina Wood, Alan Shaw, Eli Jaffe, Elizabeth Green, and Herbert Brausch to arresting officers so they would know who to target; all had been previously arrested for various alleged offenses, fingerprinted, and photographed. On August 15, the *Daily Oklahoman* carried an AP story that identified more than a dozen Hollywood actors named in grand jury testimony as members of or sympathizers with the Communist Party. Included among them were Franchot Tone, Frederic March, James Cagney, and Humphrey Bogart. Mrs. Robert Sharp of Covington, Oklahoma, however, worried for the future of her country for different reasons.

"Something went out of the nation's backbone," she wrote the *Daily Oklahoman* on August 16, 1940, "when the majority of women discarded corsets. Stays held men and women to more rigid morals."[80]

Just before noon on August 17, a number of people were in the Progressive Book Store for a variety of reasons. Because Bob was sick that day, Ina opened the store. Elizabeth Green was there to use the typewriter, Herb Brausch to do some carpentry work. One man and his wife had just stopped in to buy a newspaper. Other customers on site casually surveyed the shelves or chatted with each other. And just approaching 129½ Grand Avenue were Clarence and Hulda Lewis with their two children, Orval and Wilma.[81] At noon, however, as police rushed the bookstore and raided the homes of several Oklahoma City citizens, the lives of those arrested—proprietors, customers, residents, and visitors—changed forever.

CHAPTER THREE

Bob and Alan on Trial, October–December 1940

O f those arrested August 17, Bob and Ina Wood, Alan Shaw, and Eli Jaffe would be the first tried, Bob for owning and selling bookshop materials, the other three for their membership in the Communist Party. At the same time, the trials reflected a larger battle, one which pitted the defendants' civil liberties against Oklahoma officials' concern for domestic security and civil unrest. Issues being debated in the courtroom were not new. Before World War I, many Americans were quite willing to suppress un-American speech, and the nation's judiciary manifested a "pervasive judicial hostility" to nearly all claims of free speech.

But because World War I accelerated repression of free speech, many who before defended repression in the name of patriotism, after the war were far more sensitive to infringements on civil liberties. This new sensitivity did not at first extend to the judiciary, and over and over the U.S. Supreme Court rejected free-speech claims raised by antiwar radicals. But the 1920s witnessed a gradual change in the Court's attitudes. In 1927, the Court for the first time accepted a radical defendant's claim to free speech and reversed the conviction of an IWW member convicted under Kansas's criminal syndicalism act. In 1937, the Court unanimously held that Oregon's syndicalism law did not prohibit a Communist Party meeting and, in another case that same year, reversed the conviction of a Communist Party organizer, holding that mere possession of books and other materials was insufficient for conviction. These subtle shifts suggested that times were changing, but Oklahoma officials did not pick up the cues.[1]

I

The process of jury selection for Bob Wood's trial began in Judge Ben Arnold's district court on Monday, September 30. Arnold had been on the bench since 1934 and in his two campaigns for the position emphasized his membership in the American Legion, the Veterans of Foreign Wars, and the Knights of Pythias, a patriotic fraternal organization that counted President Roosevelt as a member. In this trial, Bob was charged only with distributing books that advocated the violent overthrow of the government.[2]

Sitting at the prosecutor's desk was Assistant County Attorney John Eberle, a slight, handsome lawyer with a fierce but narrow intellect. Seldom did Eberle appear in court dressed in less than a tailored suit with a colorful handkerchief in his breast pocket. Always he slicked his hair back, making sure it sported a very careful part. In court Eberle was given to long speeches he delivered in monotone while parading nervously in front of the bench and jury. (Eli Jaffe thought Eberle's courtroom demeanor made him look like a bantam rooster.) Several who watched the trials noticed Eberle's reluctance to look his opponents directly in the eye. That tendency, however, contrasted sharply with his determination and tenacity.

Appointed to his position in 1932, Eberle was the son of well-to-do German Catholic immigrants (many of whom manifested a superpatriotism during World War I to counter a public perception about their loyalties). He had attended local Catholic schools, Hills Business University, and the University of Oklahoma (OU). He was admitted to the bar in 1930, and was a member of the Catholic

Church, source of a drumbeat of anti-Communistic messages throughout the decade, including Pope Pius XI's March 19, 1937, encyclical "De Communismo Atheo," which denounced "atheistic Communism" as a "Satanic scourge." His parish's copy of the August 1940 issue of *Catholic Digest* carried an article titled "Communism and Religion: A Struggle Unto Death." Eberle was president of a citywide organization of Catholic youth and a member of the Oklahoma Club, Knights of Columbus, Gibbons Dinner Club, and Holy Name Society. As he sat at the prosecutor's table, John Eberle was eager to defend his country—and especially his state—against any enemy from within. That desire manifested itself as fierce anti-Communism. Outside the courtroom throughout the trials, he persistently referred to out-of-state defendants as "those New York Jews."[3]

Also representing the state was Eberle's boss, County Attorney Lewis Morris, a thick-set middle-aged former Marine and a Legionnaire good old boy ambitious for higher political office. Morris received his law degree from OU in 1917, where he headed several debate teams, won several academic prizes, and was president of his law class. Ironically, he practiced law with Moman Pruiett from 1919 to 1923. He was elected county attorney in 1930. In that office during the decade he successfully cracked a local school board scandal and prosecuted several high-profile murder cases. In 1938 he was honored with the state's "Most Useful Citizen" award, which acknowledged how much he did "to restore faith in democratic principles of government."[4] Like Eberle, Morris was intensely anti-Communist. Unlike Eberle, however, he saw in this high-profile trial an opportunity to accelerate his ambitions for the governorship, which would be open two years hence.

Sitting behind the defense table were three attorneys. Lead attorney was David J. Bentall, a veteran labor attorney from Chicago hired by the International Labor Defense, who had only recently arrived in Oklahoma City, and only for the trial. The other two came from the Sooner State. Stanley Belden, courageous defender of civil rights from Oklahoma's eastern oil country, had been a conscientious objector in World War I and most recently had defended several Jehovah's Witnesses in Guthrie. George Croom, thin, balding, quick-witted father of five from Tulsa, had studied law at night before being admitted to the bar. Only occasionally did he raise his voice. Bob and Ina Wood met him when they lived in Tulsa; Croom bailed Eli Jaffe out of jail in Claremore in 1938.[5]

Defense attorneys asked prospective jurors if they believed in constitutional privileges and "the bill of rights, which guarantees the right of free press, free assembly, and free speech." All agreed. Prospective jurors were also asked if they belonged to or had been officers in any organization openly opposed to Communism or the Communist Party, and whether they would be "prejudiced if the defendant happens to be a member of the Communist Party." Most answered "No." Defense attorneys were obviously worried about selecting jurors who might be members of the American Legion, the local sheriff's Civil Guard, or the city manager's Emergency Defense Battalion. Their line of questioning throughout voir dire suggested a defense strategy — "that Wood did not advocate personally nor distribute literature advocating violence in effecting governmental changes," the *Daily Oklahoman* reported, "but merely was a member of a recognized political party in the United States which seeks changes in the social order through peaceful measures."[6]

Although Morris sat at the prosecutor's table, Eberle carried the state's case. "Our evidence will be that Wood advocated violence in gaining revolutionary changes," he said in voir dire. Eberle asked prospective jurors if they believed "the state has a right to protect itself by passing laws on criminal syndicalism. . . . If you find this a proper case to give the maximum penalty, 10 years in the penitentiary and a $5,000 fine, would you do it?" Most responded "Yes." Eberle also asked them if any had received "any letters relating to the cases since you were summoned for jury duty." All said they had not. Once defense and the state had agreed on twelve men (the prosecution struck four, the defense five; almost all of those remaining, the *Daily Worker* noted, were "local businessmen"), Judge Arnold informed them they would not be sequestered, but admonished them not to discuss the case outside the courtroom. Despite their best efforts, defense attorneys suspected that several jurors ultimately selected were members of the Civil Guard or the Emergency Defense Battalion. Throughout voir dire the courtroom was packed with spectators. The *Daily Oklahoman* noticed two observers from the American Legion and "several alleged Communist Party members," including Alan Shaw's wife, Nena Beth Stapp.[7]

The "letters" Eberle mentioned may have been a reference to an organization called the Oklahoma Committee to Defend Political Prisoners that Stapp had formed shortly before the trial began. On September 29, 1940, the *Oklahoma Daily* (the University of Oklahoma student newspaper) reported that Stapp ("who is using her maiden name") had set up an office in Oklahoma City and had already begun sending letters to people across the state to raise money for the defense. Several university professors acknowledged they had received a letter. "It is not merely a group of Communists that are on trial," the appeal stated, "it is DEMOCRACY. . . . Disagree with the defendants, yes — but abandon democracy, never." Outside the courtroom, the city manager's Emergency Defense Battalion "combed the city investigating persons who received letters" from Stapp's committee, which was only "asking aid for the defendants in the case," the *Daily Worker* reported.[8]

The letter also noted that some of the prisoners had been mistreated. "If convictions are obtained in this case and precedent established, fascism in Oklahoma will have scored a great victory," Stapp argued. She urged those who received letters to write the county attorney "condemning these violations of civil rights." She also encouraged them to demand that their state representatives "repeal this fascist Criminal Syndicalism statute." She concluded by asking supporters to "help us provide adequate bail and secure legal defense for the defendants, feed, and clothe their families who now have no means of support. . . . We have nowhere to look for support but to the people." When queried by the *Daily Oklahoman* about the letters, she responded: "We get some help and some protests."[9]

Upon returning to a holding cell after the jury had been selected, Bob Wood wrote a note to his wife, Ina, and her cellmates, Elizabeth Green and Hulda Lewis. "I feel swell about our attorneys. They did a fine job there today." He thought the jury looked like a "good bunch," but worried that "there are no workers among them — the few there were challenged off by the prosecution." He passed on regards from friends in the courtroom, reassured them that "I feel fine," and although he would be staying in the holding cell overnight, he reported that he had brought his clothes and toiletries with him, and "two rip-snorting Westerns." Eberle, on the other hand, told friends, "We are ready — we have our jury picked."[10]

At the beginning of the trial at 9 A.M. the next day, Eberle conceded in an hour-long opening statement that the state would present no evidence to show Bob Wood made threats of violence against the state, or committed any violent acts. Instead the state would introduce as evidence three of the books Officer John Webb had purchased on July 24 — *The Communist Manifesto,* by Karl Marx and Frederick Engels, *State and Revolution,* by Vladimir Ilyich Lenin, and *Foundations of Leninism,* by Joseph Stalin — plus other books and pamphlets in Bob's possession that "taught the use of violence" to effect industrial and political change. "The state's evidence will show that Joseph Stalin has taken a great interest in this country. We'll bring you a picture taken at the University of Oklahoma showing colored and white people standing together," Eberle told jurors. "We merely will read excerpts from these books and that in itself will show violation of the law. We will introduce a pamphlet called *I Didn't Raise My Boy to Be a Soldier for Wall Street.*"

Eberle also indicated that at trial the next day Captain Dan Hollingsworth would take the stand and begin reading excerpts from the books and pamphlets, which would demonstrate "plan, scheme, guilty knowledge and intent." Eberle promised to show that Bob was a member of the Communist Party and that he had "guilty knowledge" of the contents of the books he sold.[11] Already in the room were more than forty boxes of materials. Defense attorneys had not been permitted to see what was in the boxes, nor were they given an inventory of the contents. They also had no idea what percentage of the total number of books and pamphlets seized was contained in the boxes.

"Here is a library, a book shop," defense attorney Bentall responded, "all supposed to teach criminal syndicalism." Bentall asked that the defense be given additional time to analyze the contents of the evidence Eberle intended to introduce, rather than take the time to read it all to the jury. "There may be some we would admit, and some we would object to." When fellow defense attorney George Croom asked, "And suppose we want to read other parts" not excerpted by Eberle, County Attorney Morris responded, "We can stay here as long as you can; read all of them." The defense also argued that because all materials obtained on August 17 and after had been seized in illegal raids, only the books and pamphlets purchased by Officer Webb "could be considered competent evidence."

But Judge Arnold denied defense requests for additional time and held that the state could introduce other evidence to "show scheme, plan, intent, and guilty knowledge." And although he acknowledged that warrants "may have been faulty," he added that the defense's objection was immaterial; in his opinion, the police did not need search warrants. Thus, defense attorneys were put on notice that the judge was not favorably inclined towards their client. "The prosecution was permitted to enter all but a few of the offered exhibits," the *Oklahoma City Times* noted. "They were not permitted to enter a sack containing 15 heavy lead finger rings which Eberle whispered to the judge might be used as 'knucks' in fighting." Later in the trial, when Bentall attempted to make a point, Arnold admonished him, "Whenever you see the judge is with you, don't argue with him. He might change his mind."[12] Arnold's condescension toward this out-of-state lawyer was obvious. Some of Bob's supporters noticed how Eberle, Morris, and Judge Arnold similarly accentuated particular words—criminal sin-die-kalism, sa-butt-ige, con-spir-aicy. They also noticed how often Morris misused "military" for "militant," and how frequently Eberle said "Robert Wood, alias James Stevens,"[13] a name Bob had previously used in his work for the Communist Party.

When Eberle called Dan Hollingsworth to the stand at 10 A.M. and attempted to introduce evidence wholesale from the boxes of books in the courtroom, defense attorneys objected. They argued Eberle had never provided them with an inventory of materials seized, nor were they allowed to see any of it in advance of the trial.

After Arnold sustained their objection, Eberle began one by one to hand over to Hollingsworth 269 pamphlets, documents, photographs, and books (some of which were 300 pages) for identification. Initially, he was permitted to identify them only by format ("a book," "a sheet of paper," "a photograph"), and note where he found it and on what date. After each was introduced, defense attorneys were permitted to review the entire document and decide whether to object. Bob Wood counted "176 times" that Hollingsworth said: "This pamphlet was in the box from 129½ West Grand and taken August 17." Because presentation of this evidence on a hot September day in an Oklahoma courtroom lasted until 4:30 P.M., "everyone, including the jury, were half-asleep & some in the audience completely out," Bob noted. After the jury was dismissed for the day, a frustrated Judge Arnold asked the litigators at the tables before him: "Does anyone know what syndicalism is?" Prosecutors were silent; defense attorney Bentall finally rose to briefly define the origin of the word.[14]

In its summary of the trial that day, the *Daily Oklahoman* reported that the courtroom would probably "become a reading room . . . for an indefinite period." The afternoon *Oklahoma City Times* was less gracious. "Few enough were the interesting points of the trial. Exhibits were mostly humdrum pieces of peace propaganda, pictures of Communist leaders, pep songs and picture books showing conditions in the Soviet Union." In a note to fellow inmates written from the holdover tank that night (where he would spend every night during the trial), Bob reported that because of his attorneys' objections, "Eberle did not wallop thru as he thought he might." He also reported that Orval Lewis had been in court ("He looks fine. I spoke to him a minute or so"), and to allay Ina's fears about how presentable he was in court, he wrote that because he "lay his clothes away carefully at night" they "really need no attention as yet."[15]

If to most in the courtroom the first day of trial went slowly, the second must have seemed interminable. Eberle began by introducing as state's evidence two books confiscated from the Progressive Book Store, *The Red Army and Navy* (which praised the power of

Russian defense forces) and *Red Air Fleet* (which contained pictures of members of the Soviet Army parachuting out of airplanes). Eberle then read several songs, including "Red Air Fleet" (one line of which was, "We are ready for the world's imperialist war"), "Arise Ye Workers" (which advocated Communism and liberty for members of the working classes), the "Internationale" (which urged workers to "advance and conquer the world"), "All Hell Can't Stop Us" (which advocated world revolution), and "They're Talking War" (which argued the rich stayed home and profited from war while workers fought and died). Dan Hollingsworth followed by reading four stories from a Communist second-grade reader published in English in 1935, one of which claimed, "Lenin was the teacher and leader of workers and peasants all over the world," and "taught workers of the world how to free themselves from landlords and capitalists." Defense attorneys objected to each exhibit, arguing that it was immaterial and not admissible. They also objected to Eberle's tactic of reading or quoting only excerpts. "We just don't want the state to distort things by picking out a line here and there and leaving out other lines," George Croom said. Lewis Morris responded sarcastically, "You just ask that all of it be included then."

In an editorial the next morning, the *Daily Oklahoman* proposed a "proper punishment" for those accused. "If the charge is that they have kept the books of Marx and Engels for sale or free distribution, the punishment should be that the offenders be required to read these books and pass a test thereon." The editorial surmised such a punishment might not be constitutional, but concluded: "if all those active reds and pinks and saffrons were forced to master the pages of Karl Marx they would soon become repentant or completely incapacitated." In its report on the trial in the same edition, the paper predicted that because "objections and reading of various books and pamphlets caused the trial to proceed slowly," it was likely to take another week.[16]

Judge Arnold must have felt the same way. When the trial resumed on Thursday, October 3, he declared that at the conclusion of testimony that day he was sending the jury home for the weekend, and that on Friday—and, if necessary, Saturday—the two sides would have to "weed out" state's evidence, settle their differences over its admissibility, and thus relieve the jury of having to listen to the "almost continuous interruptions that thus far have marked the trial." For the rest of Thursday's proceedings, however, the hassling continued. Hollingsworth identified additional evidence that Eberle introduced as state exhibits, and read excerpts from additional documents and pamphlets, including several seized from the apartment of Elizabeth Green. Eberle argued this material would "show scheme, plan and intent" by Bob Wood to carry out the mandate of the Seventh International Congress of the Communist Party to "adopt Trojan horse methods" to foment violent political and industrial revolution. The reference clearly was to Martin Dies's recently published book, *The Trojan Horse in America,* which summarized the findings of his House Un-American Activities Committee. "Communist Trojan horses" — organizations that Dies said denied Communist control — existed across the country in a bid for American youth, the unemployed, blacks, and labor.[17]

Eberle also cited a letter to Elizabeth Green from a high Communist Party official in New York City directing her how to disburse funds. He accused Green of infiltrating the Workers Alliance, "and then seemed to take charge of the organization." In her room police had found an Alliance charter and copies of the organization's constitution and other records. A new practice of the Communist Party, Eberle argued, "is to move into other organizations to spread their doctrine. Evidence shows that the Workers' Alliance headquarters were at 129½ West Grand Avenue, where headquarters of the Communist Party were located." When Croom and Belden objected that the evidence from Green's apartment was not material to Bob's case, Judge Arnold said he would reserve ruling until the next day. "What the state has to prove is that the books and documents Wood offered to the public are syndicalistic," he responded. "It is my theory that if I had one of these books and loaned it to a friend merely so he would read it and find out for himself what the book advocated, it would not be with criminal intent. However," he continued, "if there were many books advocating violence and the man had them in his possession and distributed them to spread the doctrine of violence, that would be another matter and might show criminal intent."

At week's end, the state had introduced fifty books and pamphlets and twenty-five other documents addressing the Russian form of government, treatises on the ruling classes, antiwar propaganda, and Communist Party chapter records. Because all of it, Eberle argued, demonstrated the Communist Party's advocacy of violence to effect political and industrial change, and because most of it was distributed out of Bob Wood's Progressive Book Store, Wood was guilty of criminal syndicalism. Defense attorneys argued that Bob did not advocate violence but encouraged political and industrial change through peaceful means. They also argued that most of the evidence presented by the state had been illegally seized and that much of it could be found in any medium-sized public or academic library. The *Daily Worker* accused Eberle of leading a "campaign to create an atmosphere of Nazi-terror and throughout Oklahoma City to forestall aid to the defendants in this case." The day before, it had announced that the ILD would launch a nationwide campaign to fund "the Oklahoma Defense."[18]

On Friday morning FBI Oklahoma City Agent Harold E. Andersen, who had attended the trial on Thursday, showed up at the courthouse to record names of the defendants and information about the nature of charges against them. When asked by the *Daily Oklahoman* what he would do with the information, he responded: "We are not making an investigation of the case. It is purely a state case and we do not have any men working on it." He did acknowledge, however, that the FBI was compiling a private record for future reference. When asked about Andersen's interest in the case, Eberle and Hollingsworth were "reluctant to discuss" it; Eberle said he did not know "anything about a federal investigation."[19]

State and defense attorneys spent all of Friday arguing over the admissibility of specific materials confiscated on August 17. Eberle told Judge Arnold that he wanted to introduce another ninety books and pamphlets, but Arnold balked. "After so much of this evidence is introduced, after enough has been presented to show the jury the philosophy of the Communist Party and its aims, then I'm going to shut down on you," he told Eberle. "All we're trying to determine in this case is whether the defendant had in his possession and distributed material that advocated violence and thus is guilty of criminal syndicalism."[20] Eberle protested. The state needed to introduce a large number of exhibits "to picture for the jury just what conditions were on the day of the raid." He also argued he should not be held accountable for the trial's slow progress; every time he introduced an exhibit defense attorneys argued the state was trying to "encumber the record by introduction of so many exhibits," and took "30 minutes or so" to examine it.

Arnold was undeterred. He ordered both sides to resolve their differences over evidence by the time the jury returned Monday morning, and "to have a complete list of all evidence to be presented on my desk at that time." By Sunday night, the *Daily Oklahoman* reported, Eberle had decided to introduce fifty additional books and pamphlets at trial on Monday, just over half the total he hoped to submit as state's evidence during the remainder of the week. Arnold had also decided that the jury would be allowed to read excerpts from all documents introduced as evidence.[21]

On Monday, October 7, Hollingsworth completed identification of twenty more state's exhibits, among them the *Communist Manifesto*. When asked its publication date, Hollingsworth responded, "1932." Defense attorneys were quick to correct him; the *Manifesto*, they said, was published in 1848. Although hardly a trick question, they had nonetheless made their point—Hollingsworth was no expert on the literature he was excerpting for the jury, nor on the subject of Communism.

Judge Arnold continued to press both sides to speed up their case. He refused to let Eberle introduce Workers Alliance pamphlets and other literature into evidence. They were "too burdensome" for their "practical value." Defense attorneys spent most of their cross-examination of Hollingsworth contesting the validity of the search warrants used in the August 17 raids. Eberle then called an Oklahoma City police detective and an Oklahoma county deputy sheriff to the stand to discuss their roles in the August 17 raids. Defense attorneys asked that all material seized at the bookstore be brought into the courtroom, in part to force the state to inventory the collection (defense still had not been given a list of the materials) and thus enable them to identify items that would serve the defense's case, in part "to give a clear picture of all books handled at the shop." The court denied their motion.[22]

Just before court adjourned for the day, Eberle said he intended to conclude the state's case on the following day by introducing "a few more" exhibits, including a $2,000 certificate seized from Bob Wood's safety deposit box that Eberle said constituted a loan from the Communist Party in New York to bail Oklahoma Communists out of jail after they were arrested. Judge Arnold sustained defense objections to this evidence. Defense attorneys indicated they would probably subpoena the Oklahoma City librarian to show that "many of the books seized at the bookstore are available on the shelves of the city library." They also said they expected Bob would testify in his own behalf, and that they would need "only about two days" to present their case.[23]

That night Nena Beth Stapp contacted John Romanyshyn, a University of Oklahoma student. She offered him five dollars to check the contents of the OU library for books similar to and exactly like the materials seized in the August 17 raid that the state had submitted in evidence. In a matter of hours Romanyshyn came up with a bibliography of eight books by Karl Marx, six by Lenin, two by Engels, three by Earl Browder, two by Stalin, and 250 "on socialism, communism, and other isms," he later told the *Oklahoma Daily*. Three of those titles matched the books Officer Webb bought at the Progressive Book Store on July 24. "The fact that these books are in the university library, of course," Romanyshyn later told the *Daily*, "is no reflection on the university, for most large libraries have volumes such as these." He had decided to testify for the defense only "as an interesting experiment and for $5. . . . And as for my being a communist, I have never believed in the red doctrines. If I had not taken the job, someone else would have."

Next morning, defense attorneys met with Romanyshyn and reviewed the bibliography he had compiled the previous evening. They also told him they intended to show that other academic libraries in Oklahoma had many of the same books. The defense strategy was obvious. They intended to argue that public and academic libraries also owned materials seized at the Progressive Book Store, and if these libraries could not be held liable for patrons who read the materials for their own edification (the vast majority of whom did not espouse the philosophies contained therein), neither could Bob Wood.[24]

When the prosecution rested its case the next morning, defense attorneys called Romanyshyn as their first witness. Eberle and Morris immediately objected. Romanyshyn's testimony was not competent, they argued, and would not disprove the state's case that Wood possessed and distributed literature advocating violence to effect political and industrial change. Defense Attorney David Bentall jumped to his feet. "The defendant here is not on trial," he shouted in what the *Daily Oklahoman* described as "a fiery argument." Rather, "It is the Constitution and the Bill of Rights and the state of Oklahoma who are on trial," he said. "It is a political trial . . . the only case of its kind where they bring in a whole library. I've seen the same books in the University of Chicago and University of Minnesota libraries."[25]

When Bentall referenced Nazi Germany ("where they burned books and beheaded professors") and implored his listeners: "Let's not do this in the United States because we do not believe what the books say," Judge Arnold intervened. Defense testimony "must be connected up to show the defendant acted in good faith and without guilty knowledge." Romanyshyn's testimony, Arnold argued, "could not show Wood was acting in good faith. The defendant," he continued, "could not commit a crime and then defend himself on grounds someone else had done the same thing."

With that, defense attorneys huddled for a few moments, turned to the judge, and announced they would offer no further defense testimony. The move surprised courtroom spectators, who had expected Bob to take the stand in his own defense. "Defense attorneys," the *Daily Oklahoman* reported, "made it plain that in the event of a conviction, they expect a reversal of the decision by the state criminal court of appeals because of alleged errors during the trial."

Arnold seemed unaffected. He announced he would read instructions to the jury at 9 A.M. the next morning, after which both sides would present final arguments.[26]

Next morning Eberle began the prosecution's closing argument. Wood, he argued, "got the fairest trial in this court that anybody can get under any system of government, and that is the kind of trial we give them under the stars and stripes." He depicted the CPUSA as a Soviet-sponsored organization "seeking to start a revolution in this country from within" by fifth-column tactics. "With the help of God and this good jury," the Communist Party sign he had submitted into evidence "will never again be put up in Oklahoma County." He then launched into the substance of his case against Wood, and for the next nine hours read excerpts from books and pamphlets the state had introduced as evidence, adding commentary on contemporary events wherever he saw relevance. "On this list of books in this inventory, they have got about three books listed that they wrote . . . about poor little Finland. [Stalin], [t]his big bully, jumped on little Finland . . . and it took weeks and weeks to lick that little country," he said, "and the only way they beat them was like France was beaten, to get beaten from the inside. . . . And that is the way they intend to beat the United States," by encouraging Party members to infiltrate and eventually control other organizations.

If left unchecked in this country, Eberle said, "we would have the soldiers shooting their officers in the back" in the event of war. "International conspiracy has been rooted deeper in this state than you know," Eberle told the jury. He then turned to Bob. "This is what you are putting out here at 129½ West Grand Avenue . . . if war breaks out and any officer goes from this town and he is shot in the back, I say that blood will be on your hands, and that it came from reading this literature."[27]

When defense attorneys finally got their chance to address the jury, Croom went first. The criminal syndicalism law had been inspired "by prejudice and war makers," he said, but what was the real reason behind this prosecution? "Could it be because the Communist Party is opposed to war? Could it be interfering with the plans of the munitions makers in this country? I say it is part of a drive for war

and a part of a drive to destroy the American system of government."
Belden then made a few remarks. He cited Biblical passages to show
that Jesus Christ had also been charged with stirring up the people
before his crucifixion. Bentall, however, carried the defense's main
argument. He hammered away at the specific points of the state's
case and Eberle's summary argument. Under the federal constitution, he said, Bob Wood had a legal right to advocate for change by
peaceful means and ought not be penalized by "prejudice stirred up
by the state" against the Communist Party. "This trial is political.
In recent opinions the United States Supreme Court has spoken
strongly on the bill of rights, the right to print books and pamphlets,
documents and leaflets," he said. Eberle, Bentall charged, "criticized the Communists for going underground," yet found the materials seized in the August 17 raids at a bookstore to which all members of the public had access. Supposedly "it was a secret society," yet
"they had a sign right over the door."[28]

Bentall then turned his attention to the three books Officer
Webb purchased at the bookstore July 24 — the only evidence
against his client, he argued, that had been obtained legally. The
Communist Manifesto, he said, had been written in 1848. "Are you
going to convict him on something written 100 years ago?" Lenin's
State and Revolution had been written twenty-five years before,
and addressed only the situation in Russia. Bentall also addressed
Eberle's references to race, which Bentall argued were raised "to
prejudice" the jury. Various groups had called for a solution to "the
Negro question," he noted. "The Communist Party merely made a
suggestion" that one way to answer the "question" was "organization" of African Americans. To listen to Eberle, one could conclude
that "the Communist Party had no right to advocate for betterment
of the Negro." Ultimately, Bentall concluded, "We thought they
would try to prove Wood advocated violence, destruction of property and murder. They did prove he sold books."[29]

After Bentall finished, Lewis Morris rose to present the state's
final argument. If he had shown initial hesitation about Eberle's
raids when he returned from vacation in August, it was obvious by
this time that he had fully embraced the government's case, per-

haps because he perceived it presented him with a political opportunity in his bid for governor two years hence. "It is rather peculiar," he began, "that 22 years ago today I was representing the United States" in the armed forces fighting in France. He then turned to Belden and in an obvious reference to Belden's conscientious objector status during World War I, said, "I set up my Browning machine gun on the Medea Farm in the Champaigne [*sic*] sector, and where were you?" He added, "When I hear people mouthing about the sacred rights of the American citizen, and they are unwilling to act for those rights . . . well, it just kind of makes me sick!" Morris noted that in a recent case he prosecuted in which a husband had murdered and buried his wife, no Communist had talked about her civil rights. "I didn't get a protest from Earl Browder; I didn't get a protest from the Litznies and the Jitznies and Whitznies in New York and Brooklyn. . . . But I put a man in who would tear Old Glory from the Heavens, and keep him a couple of days and boy! Do they start hollering Constitution!"[30]

He then told the story of Red Johnson, whose wife was having an affair. Because of "this constitutional right against unreasonable search and seizure," however, the law did not allow Red to confront his wife's lover in his house, he (incorrectly) asserted. One day, however, Red followed the man out of his house, grabbed him and choked him "until his tongue came out and his eyes rolled and he went limp and went down." But with his hands around his victim's throat, Morris said, Red "kept thinking about that boy and girl of his and he wanted to raise them decent, and he didn't want them marrying Negroes." When the town marshal finally pulled Red off his gasping victim, "old Red stood there with his American blood running through him and with the feel of victory in his pulse." Red turned to the crowd around him and said, "There is one blankety-blank so-and-so that got all of his constitutional rights choked out of him," Morris told the jurors. "What we need in this country is a few Red Johnson juries who will take fellows that will ride with the sacred rights of the Constitution for the purpose of destroying their government, and choke it out of them." Robert Wood — "a Judas Iscariot with 30 pieces of silver from Moscow" — was one of those "fellows," and deserved to be convicted and given the maximum penalty allowed by law.[31] Thus, in wandering remarks Morris had somehow managed to link issues of race, ethnicity, class, gender, creed, state and national loyalty all into an argument against the "outsider," and invited the jury to take a stand with him.

The next morning Judge Arnold issued instructions to the jury and sent them to another room just before lunch. Less than an hour after they finished they returned and handed Arnold the verdict. After he read it silently, he addressed the courtroom. "Now you visitors may have some interest as spectators in what this verdict is, but verdicts of juries are rendered without regard to approval or disapproval of any citizens." In his courtroom, Judge Arnold warned, "there will be no form of demonstration whatever."[32] Arnold had reason to fear an outbreak. On the one hand American Legion members in the audience (always identifiable by their caps) had frequently expressed dismay at defense attorney questions and conclusions. On the other, Bob Wood's supporters showed visible irritation with Eberle and Morris. During the trial writer Gordon Friessen (who would soon marry Red Dust Player Sis Cunningham) was so uneasy at the treatment accorded Bob that he resorted to drawing monsters to keep his hands busy. But he absorbed much of what he heard and began drafting a pamphlet describing the trial as he saw it.[33]

At 1:45 P.M. the foreman delivered the verdict of guilty, and said the jury recommended the maximum penalty of 10 years in the penitentiary and a $5,000 fine. The judge said he would take the recommendation under advisement and pronounce judgment on October 25. He then thanked the jury for their service and dismissed them.

II

Outside the courtroom Eberle told a waiting crowd, "The American people still have the power and the will to protect their democratic institutions from destruction by foreign and un-American philosophies." Defense attorneys told reporters they would appeal the conviction if Judge Arnold turned down their request for a new trial at the time of formal sentencing. Bob's conviction was the first case, they said, where books, pamphlets and other documents discussing the Communist Party were used as evidence absent any effort to prove he had personally advocated violence. Stanley Belden complained that "the charges wouldn't even have been filed except for the generally unsettled conditions." George Croom told a reporter: "The verdict was excessive and in my opinion, unjust. The state convicted the defendant not for what he did but for what he is. It is a blow to democratic principles of government and especially a blow to free speech and freedom of thought and learning." To the *Daily Oklahoman* he said: "The very fact the jury got a verdict in an hour is definite proof the members did not study the evidence of thousands of pages, but acted on prejudice."[34]

That night Bob wrote Ina, Elizabeth Green, and Hulda Lewis. Because the jury was out "approximately 50 minutes," Bob said, "we can surmise the serious consideration given the material." Although he was disappointed that the few "clerks" on the jury helped to bring in the verdict, "I personally (and, of course, for my class) feel proud of the hatred spewed by Lewis Morris, Eberle et al and all they represent." He said his attorneys would perfect the appeal as soon as possible, and that the question of bail would be brought before Judge Arnold soon. In the meantime, he announced he would remain in jail until sentencing day. "I feel fine," he reassured them. "Ate two portions of liver (one of my neighbors is an anti-liverite)." In a note specifically for Ina he said, "We ought to be in conference before long & will see each other. All my love."[35]

By that time word of the verdict had begun circulating the country.[36] "The bulk of the State's evidence was literature seized in a raid on Communist headquarters," the *New York Times* noted on October 12. Edith Walker, student columnist for the *Oklahoma Daily*, was more critical. "If everyone who has read or has possessed allegedly communistic books is guilty of criminal syndicalism, then Oklahoma prisons soon will be filled, row on row, with those convicted of that charge." She predicted the state's efforts would eventually backfire. In fact, "it is fast developing into a laughing-stock."[37] *New Masses* was equally (though not surprisingly) frustrated. "Who stands for force and violence in this country? Get the facts and you will arrive at the proper conclusions."[38]

The ILD quickly announced that Bob's conviction "will be appealed all the way to the United States Supreme Court, if necessary. The only issue in this trial is the Bill of Rights, free speech, freedom of the press and freedom of assembly. No one is safe," the statement read, "if possession of literature which is in any public library is going to be punished. There was no evidence of the slightest action nor the slightest wrong-doing by the defendant." The ILD said a minimum of $10,000 was needed to cover legal costs of the appeals process, and asked for contributions. "A tough fight lies ahead of us in all the Oklahoma cases," the ILD asserted, "but the chances for victory are good, especially if no time is lost in the situation where days count."[39]

The National Federation for Constitutional Liberties, a Washington, D.C.-based political interest group much concerned with the Dies Committee's effect on civil liberties, also joined the chorus. In an October 9 "action letter" subtitled "TERROR IN OKLAHOMA," the chairman reported that the Federation had dispatched to Oklahoma City the executive secretary of the Southern Conference for Human Welfare, who would "assist local groups and individuals in their activities in these cases in defense of civil liberties." He did not say, however, the representative was being dispatched at the request of Norman, Oklahoma, clergyman John Thompson, who with several other like-minded people were contemplating an organization to defend the civil liberties of all Oklahoma citizens. The Federation called on readers to wire Governor Phillips, protest the criminal syndicalism law, and "demand that he extend equal protection" for all citizens of his state. Readers were asked to send the Federation copies of their wires, and make contributions to the Federation to help defray the executive secretary's travel expenses.[40]

In her cell, Ina Wood received a response to a September 26 letter she had written to First Lady Eleanor Roosevelt. The letter had been forwarded to the acting assistant attorney general, and his news was hardly encouraging. "The charge against you involves a purely State matter and, in the absence of a violation of any Federal criminal statute," he said, "the jurisdiction of this Department cannot be invoked, nor can any advice be given you. Your remedy in the event of irregularities in the conduct of your trial or infirmities in the law under which you were charged must be through appeal."[41]

Soon thereafter Ina received another note from her husband. "I want to rise to this challenge by these modern 'witch-hunters,'" he said, "and the wilder and more unrestrained their persecution becomes, the more vigorous I feel." He now saw the issues as "crystal clear—a ten year sentence for reading what one pleases, for bringing to people the issues of the day." He reported a good conference with his attorney and predicted an appeal bond would be successful after formal sentencing. "And should I hit the sidewalk, it will be with all vigor to clear all of us out of these bars and out among the people, where we can work to make clear the fundamental democratic principles involved in these cases." He reported that "thousands are discussing these unprecedented activities" of the county attorney's office, "and we will reach them. I am brimming over with energy—accumulated these weeks of reading Western story magazines, sleeping, eating, and *not* worrying." He concluded, "I love you—for many reasons—and am deeply proud of the poise and calmness you have displayed these many weeks."[42]

The Wood trial was obviously also a subject of conversation on the University of Oklahoma campus. On October 17, an editorial in the *Oklahoma Daily* noted, "Robert Wood's only sin was believing in a way contrary to the American conception of a capitalistic democracy. It seems strange that his prosecutors, failing time after time in attempts to trump up charges against Wood and his clique, finally delving deeply enough to uncover the dust-laden criminal syndicalism law, should be unable to see the Bill of Rights." It was the first editorial in any Sooner State newspaper to take a position against the trials. But not for long. At a conference of 500 high school journalists attending the Oklahoma Interscholastic Press Association conference in Norman several days later, news editor for the *Seminole Producer* criticized state newspapers for failure to defend the civil liberties of Jehovah's Witnesses and Oklahoma City Communists. "It is important" during these times, he said, "for newspapers to wage war against intolerance and to seek to protect minority groups from oppression."[43]

Some time after Bob Wood's trial, Woody Guthrie drafted a new song he titled the "Ballad of Bob Wood."

Bob Wood he studied at Harvard College
To be a lawyer fine
Went out to talk with the hungry and the poor
Said, All your worries are mine.

Bob Wood he was a thinkin' man
When he left the university
He set out to help the workin' man
So they put him in the penitentiary.

Now Bob went down to Oklahoma
Where there's nothin' but oil and sand
Where the land belongs to the yankee bankers
And the people belong to the land

He talked to the farmer and he talked to their wives
Why do you let them treat you so?
They work you like mules every day of your lives
But the banks get all the dough

From Salisaw to Oklahoma City
Muskogee to Tulsa town
Bob Wood went travellin' in a swayback Ford
Said, Don't let 'em push you around

Well, the people listened to what Bob said
And they said, By God he's right
If we want to save our wives and kids
We got to get together and fight.

The American Legion heard him too
And it give them a pain in the head.

Stop talkin' about peace and higher pay!
You are a God damn red!

The deputies busted into Bob Wood's house
Found some radical literature
They took Bob to jail, also Ina his wife
And ten more, just to make sure.

Well the jury they looked at Bob Wood's books
They didn't read 'em but they did agree
Anybody that would read that kind of trash
Ought to be in the penitentiary.

The Judge said, You criminal syndicalist
I'll show you who is boss
I'll send you to prison for ten long years
You agitatin' Trojan Horse!

It took the jury only sixty minutes
To send Bob Wood down the line
The judge give him ten long years in jail
And a five thousand dollar fine.

It's a mighty long road from Harvard College
To the Oklahoma penitentiary.
And while Bob Wood remains in jail
There ain't a workin' man that's free![44]

In an October 21 letter Bob informed Ina that jailers had moved him, Eli Jaffe, Alan Shaw, and several other defendants into the same holding cell, where they now slept on six cots. He was unsure why they were moved, but welcomed the possibility that "maybe we'll get the many" copies of the *Daily Worker* and *New Masses* sent to the jail by friends across the country. He also told Ina they needed a mirror "badly to shave etc. Do youse gals have an extra?" He hoped she could deliver it at the scheduled meeting with their lawyers the next day.[45]

But the meeting did not take place as scheduled, so Bob wrote Ina another letter. Lawyers were busy drafting a motion for a new trial, he said, and he expected the meeting they missed would soon be rescheduled. "We're all swell and feel good in here together," he wrote. "Shaw is back to his punning habit. Jaffe sings all day. Herb [Brausch] gives us apropos Biblical quotations. [Clarence] Lewis jumps thru his hand a la hoop (he's some gymnast)." And because the commissary had visited their cell, he was happily puffing on "a big ceegar." He also reported that their tank had been steamed that day for cockroaches, which had been met "in mortal combat and annihilated." Eli had conducted a class in current events that morning. "We had a good discussion. We hope to make it a daily event." He reported that Alan got a letter from his sister reporting "thousands" raised for their defense. "Yesterday Nena visited Alan and we all spoke to her. Wilma saw her Dad [Clarence Lewis]." Finally, he told Ina he had heard the ILD had issued a "real classy folder" summarizing his case.[46]

But Eli later figured out why the group had been isolated. Because "we did in jail what we did outside: talked to people, listened to what was troubling them, and tried to help," jailers worried the group was "educating the prisoners" to cause trouble. Isolating the group solved the problem. The cell containing them had just enough room for three double bunks, a toilet and a sink. If anyone wanted to use the open space between for exercise, everyone had to pull their legs into their bunks. Alan and Eli often tossed a roll of toilet paper (they had top bunks), while Clarence Lewis took responsibility for insect control by burning invading cockroaches with toilet paper cores. They read the *Daily Oklahoman* for national and international news, and discussed fast-moving events abroad. At night they played poker by spreading an Army blanket on the open space and used matchsticks for chips. Herb Brausch was especially lucky at the game, but Eli noticed he had developed an unusual habit when dealt a good hand. "He would raise up his body and sit on his heels — as so many Oklahoma farmers do — and break wind." Once that happened, everyone would quickly drop out of the pot.

"Herb," Eli howled, "if you had a cork, you'd be the best goddamn poker player in the state of Oklahoma!"[47]

On October 25, the ILD released a letter of thanks it had received from Clarence Lewis, dated October 21. "It made our lot more endurable to get the funds you send us for little necessities that jails don't furnish, especially when we know you are doing all you can for our families as well." And while defendants were honing coping skills inside the jail, on the outside *New Masses* brought readers up to date in an article titled "Oklahoma Okays Hitler." "The state that exiled thousands of families to hungry migrations," it argued, had thrown the Bill of Rights "to the winds — without pretense, without any fine sounding phrases." It urged readers to "write John Eberle a reminder about the Bill of Rights. And so that it will stick," it said, "tell him that next time he entered the County Courthouse he should read the phrase by Thomas Jefferson engraved into the façade."[48]

The same day the *New Masses* article appeared, defense attorneys asked Judge Arnold for a new trial for Bob Wood. They alleged thirty-one points of error in the first trial, and objected specifically to the jury speech of Lewis Morris, which they claimed was inflammatory. The judge quickly denied their request and sentenced Bob to ten years and a $5,000 fine, the sentence to be stayed pending appeal. The *Daily Oklahoman* reported that defense attorneys wanted to postpone Alan Shaw's trial, scheduled for October 28, until after the November 5 general election, and later noted they also wanted to get Bob bailed out of jail before that date, in part because he was a candidate for Congress as an Independent. Although the judge refused a new trial, he did postpone Alan's trial to November 12. He also released social worker Elizabeth Green from the county jail when she posted a $20,000 surety company bond, "one of the largest bonds ever posted in an Oklahoma county criminal case," the *Oklahoman* noted.[49] Green had been in jail more than two months.

The ILD interpreted Arnold's willingness to postpone Alan's trial as evidence of "mass pressure" its efforts had effected. "The indignant protest of hundreds of friends had resulted in certain improvements in the treatment of the Oklahoma Criminal Syndicalism victims," the *Daily Worker* reported, and the ILD "called for an intensified campaign" of protest and financial assistance. "Are you willing to help prevent fascist justice from establishing a stronghold in this country in Oklahoma?" the ILD asked in its monthly newsletter. "Aid to the Oklahoma victims is aid in defense of democracy."[50]

The ILD appeal apparently succeeded. Contributions to bail money for Bob Wood were so oversubscribed ($46,500) that the remainder enabled the Board to fund bail for other defendants. On Monday, November 4, the ILD posted $2,000 bonds for Clarence and Hulda Lewis, who were finally released from jail, two-and-a-half months after their arrest. "We are going to post bonds for the rest of them soon," an ILD representative said, but "we think bonds down here are pretty high." But getting Bob Wood out of jail was taking longer than expected. After putting up the securities and the contract for his bond, the bonding company "rescinded the contract on grounds pressure had been brought on the Oklahoma City branch of the firm," the ILD reported.[51]

Two days after the election on November 5 (Franklin Roosevelt was elected for an unprecedented third term; the CPUSA polled a paltry 46,251 votes; Judge Ben Arnold won a seat on the State Supreme Court; and Bob Wood polled 1,638 votes as an Independent candidate for Congress), Nena Beth Stapp made public a letter she had received from Eleanor Roosevelt along with a twenty-five-dollar check made out to the Oklahoma Committee to Defend Political Prisoners. Stapp told the local press that shortly after forming her organization she had appealed to Mrs. Roosevelt for help, and asked her specifically to write Lewis Morris about the case. "I am glad to make this contribution to the work of your committee," Roosevelt responded. "I cannot write Mr. Morris, as you ask, until I know more about the case."

Stapp was ecstatic about such high-profile support of her group. "With her support and the support of democratic Americans, we are determined to prevent local authorities from riding rough-shod over our bill of rights in their zeal to sentence political opponents to long prison terms because they sold books." After Stapp released the letter, the First Lady explained to the Associated Press she had not given a contribution earmarked specifically to the prisoners, but had instead contributed to the young people working on their behalf. "Everyone has a right to a defense." When the *Daily Oklahoman* asked Lewis Morris about Roosevelt's contribution, he responded, "Well, that's all right with us." John Eberle declined comment. Governor Phillips, on the other hand, spoke freely. The state would not let up on prosecution efforts "[j]ust because a check for $25 came down here from Washington." Elsewhere, some members of the press openly criticized Mrs. Roosevelt for making a contribution to the "Reds' Defense."[52]

On Friday, November 8, Bob Wood finally walked out of jail after the ILD posted bond. With his attorneys he immediately made his way to the Huckins Hotel Coffee Shop, where he had his first meal outside jail in 83 days — a "sizzling steak." There he also answered questions from local reporters. "The jury could not have understood they were sentencing me to 10 years in the penitentiary for selling books," he said. "If this conviction is allowed to stand, the rights of every man and woman in Oklahoma will be jeopardized." For two weeks, he said, he sat in the courtroom waiting for the prosecution to accuse him of some crime. "But the only thing they could say about me was that I read and sold books, most of which are available in large public and college libraries throughout the country." The prosecution attempted to cover up the real issue by slandering the Communist Party, "of which I am proud to be the Oklahoma State Secretary."[53]

The *Daily Oklahoman* could not let Bob's interview go without comment. In an editorial published the same day, the *Oklahoman* noted that in Europe Nazis were burning books, regimenting libraries, and sending university faculty to concentration camps. "Quite naturally loyal American citizens resent the efforts of seditionists to undermine and overthrow their government, and they have little love for the display of revolutionary books on the shelves of public libraries," the editorial argued. "Still, any American is free to read any book he may want to read, our universities are fairly free, and our professors are not dying in concentration camps."[54] Ironically, the

Oklahoman ran the editorial the day before National Book Week started; no one seemed to notice that Bob's trial had been sandwiched between National Newspaper Week and National Book Week.

Bob wasted no time; he immediately began traveling the state in Woody Guthrie's blue Plymouth looking for support for his incarcerated colleagues. He was accompanied by a reporter for the San Francisco–based Communist Party newspaper *People's Weekly*. On the trip "we [saw] in eastern Oklahoma the wreckage and rust and human debris of the shamelessly exploited oil fields," the reporter noted. In western Oklahoma, "the land of the dust bowl, we saw what had happened to the workers of the land." There he also watched "a weather faced grimly sympathetic farmer" tell Bob: "Yes, we know why they are persecuting you 'criminal syndicalist' defendants. We went through the same thing in the last war, those of us who spoke out against it. Exactly the same thing." A boy on a cotton farm looked up from his meal of beans and clabber to tell the reporter, "them that don't have to go, want war. Them that has to go, don't."[55]

The ILD sensed its campaign for the Oklahoma defendants was beginning to strengthen. In a November 12 news release, the organization noted that because "many Oklahomans complained" that "the authorities had gone too far," prospects for getting the remaining inmates discharged were "good." That same day Judge Arnold released Herb Brausch from jail (he had been there 88 days) on $2,500 bond guaranteed by the ILD, and postponed Alan Shaw's trial until November 18 because one of his attorneys was unable to attend.[56]

By this time newspapers and periodicals in other parts of the country also began pursuing the story. *PM*, a combative liberal New York City afternoon daily, sent staff correspondent Duncan Aikman to Oklahoma City for a three-part article. In the first he outlined the series of events starting with raids on the "hole-in-the-wall bookstore" through Bob Wood's conviction. In a second, Aikman noted that the few liberals he talked to in Oklahoma wisecracked that "state politics is becoming a Red-slapping business."

Aikman also reported interviews with Eberle and Morris. Upon meeting Eberle, the assistant county attorney quickly sniped: "How many Communists have you got in New York now?" Aikman took note that Eberle paid no attention to his effort to answer, and instead "stared gloomily at the floor, gloomily out the window, and impatiently at his desk—but never at me—while I interviewed him." When asked if punishment under the criminal syndicalism law was not excessive "for selling a few books," Eberle responded, "We never discuss evidence before a trial or verdicts afterward." Did he consider the Communists—who had polled 132 votes in Oklahoma in the last presidential election—as dangerous to the public order as "the vigilante elements and the Christian Frontiers" in the United States? "I wouldn't know about that," Eberle muttered. "You people on the East Coast ought to know all about it—where you have those things."

Aikman next went to Morris. To the "how dangerous" question, Morris noted that a nephew in Minnesota had recently developed a blister on his foot that later became infected through inattention. Had he taken care of it quickly, Morris said, "he'd have been dancing on that leg tonight. Out here in Oklahoma, we believe in operating on blisters." Without prompting, Morris then connected Oklahoma's Communist booksellers to Oklahoma's African Americans. "Suppose they go sell a lot of that book [he was probably referring to *Reds in Dixie*] to a lot of the down and out no-goods we've got in this state rarin' for trouble. You'd see a race war around here about that time that would make your hair stand on end." Morris also snarled at a civil liberties question. "Who's squawking about these bums in the jail-house? A little gang of Red lawyers, just like the prisoners, a rat who did his stretch in the last war for conscientious objecting and a few hopped-up preachers and college professors." Morris acknowledged that everyone had constitutional rights, but he wondered why he could keep murderers, hijackers and burglars in jail for ten days without charges, and no college professors or conscientious objector of "Civil Liberal Leagues" (probably a reference to ACLU, Aikman surmised) "comes yipping around about constitutional rights."[57]

In his third article, "Jittery Oklahoma Reverts to Old-Time Vig-

ilante Methods," Aikman tried to explain by contrasts the situation
he met in the Sooner State. Oklahoma "is near the old South in
distance and near in time to the old West of the string-em-up-first-
and-argue-it-afterward tradition. It is trying to keep the Negro from
voting," he continued, "and is plagued with falling population, de-
clining oil bonanzas, and scores of thousands of unemployed workers, dispossessed and desperate former tenant farmers, ex-share-
croppers." Many of the latter, he noted, "live in clusters of horrible
hovels like the community camp of evil smells and shivering children on the outskirts of Oklahoma City, but the decreasingly prosperous chamber-of-commerce, American-Legion, worried-farmer,
rancher, oil-speculator Oklahoma is afraid of them." How did Oklahoma officials deal with these problems? By fostering a vigilantism
directed at what it feared — sabotage (which explained why the Civil
Guards and Defense Emergency Battalion were organized), Jehovah's Witnesses (who were given harsh sentences, consistently deprived of their rights, and frequently subjects of beatings from mobs
who forced them to kiss the flag), and now Communists. For the
defendants, Aikman concluded, "the prognosis isn't too good."[58]

The *Oklahoma City Times* quickly countered Aikman's conclusions and went on the offensive. "It is a queer discovery the stranger
makes in our midst," an editorial noted. "All along most of our
people have thought instead of resembling the vigilante system of
the horse thief and cattle rustling days" that the county attorney's
office "has been altogether too slow and too lax with too much delay
and not enough of the pioneer spirit in clearing them up." The
Times fully agreed with these sentiments. "The investigation and
prosecution of these cases seems to be so pussyfootingly uncertain
at times that it is giving rise to the belief that what the city needs . . .
is a revival of an order something like that enforced by the local
Council of National Defense in World War days." A local preacher
agreed. In a special article penned for the *Times* titled "Pastor Asks
Why Christians Defend 'Rights' of Communists," the good reverend wrote that Communists were "the enemies of moral decency,
national freedom, and Christianity."[59]

The *Daily Oklahoman* fumed against Aikman for defaming the

entire state, and lamented that no laws existed to protect Oklahomans against these "unjust charges." "Possibly we have too much of the spirit of the vigilantes in Oklahoma," but among the Sooner State's 2.3 million people, "the reporter finds none who is worthy or commendable; no, not one." The editorial predicted that readers outside Oklahoma would accept Aikman's story as accurate — like they had accepted Steinbeck's *The Grapes of Wrath* — and "die believing that all Oklahomans are vicious and intolerant, and ignorant and depraved. . . . It may take a half century to undo the wrong done to Oklahoma by Steinbeck and the *PM* reporter."[60]

On November 14, George Croom filed a motion to postpone the trials of others until the Criminal Court of Appeals rendered a decision on an appeal defense attorneys were preparing for Bob Wood's conviction. Courtroom tactics engaged in by the state's attorneys consumed so much time, Croom argued, "that it required a case made [appellate record] of over eight hundred pages." As a result, Bob was compelled to pay the court reporter four hundred dollars for a copy of the trial transcript in preparation for his appeal. Oklahoma County had already spent twelve hundred dollars to try the case, Croom said; and because most points of law introduced in Bob's case would also apply to others, an appeals decision, "either affirming this Court or reversing it, will be binding in all of the other cases." Postponing trials for the others would thus save the state and defendants considerable court costs. Eberle would have none of it, however. For him costs to the public treasury were secondary to trying the cases one by one. And the charge against the others differed from that against Bob; they were accused not of distributing literature but of belonging to an organization (the CPUSA was named specifically) that advocated the use of violence for political and industrial change.[61]

While the judge considered Croom's motion, opposition to the cases continued to spread. At the November ILD National Board meeting in New York City, members learned that "the national campaign had given impetus to a splendid local Oklahoma movement in defense of civil rights which culminated in a state conference on November 15 which set up an Oklahoma Committee for Constitutional Rights, which already has the support of the outstanding educators, churchmen, civil leaders, [and] union officials of the state" (to be discussed in more depth in chapter four). The Board also learned that students at Brooklyn College (where both Eli and Alan had graduated) were planning a rally, and hoped to hold a large dinner on December 6, at which New York congressman Marcantonio would speak.[62]

On November 15 Ina Wood became the sixth person released on bail, which Judge Arnold fixed at $6,000. Reporters photographed her as she left the jail carrying a rag doll she had made during the ninety-three days she had been there. Bob met her at the door and promised her "the best dinner in town." She publicly thanked the Oklahoma Committee to Defend Political Prisoners and the International Labor Defense for help they provided in securing her release. That same day Judge Arnold announced that Alan Shaw's trial would commence November 18. It was expected the prosecution would use the same evidence and strategy as they had for Bob Wood's trial.[63]

III

Unlike charges against Bob Wood that solely addressed his ownership and distribution of books, Alan was accused solely of being a Communist Party member, a charge he never denied. The state contended that mere membership constituted a crime even without any overt act by the defendant. Two of Bob Wood's attorneys — Oklahomans Stanley Belden and George Croom — now represented Alan.

Before Alan's trial began, however, Judge Arnold had to decide two issues. First, he had to address a defense motion to postpone other trials until the Criminal Court of Appeals could pass on Bob's appeal. Arnold refused that motion quickly. Second, he had to address a defense request for a change of venue. Croom argued that Alan could not get a fair trial in Oklahoma City because the legal climate there fostered extreme prejudice that was amply demonstrated by high bonds, interference by the Dies Committee (which recently had subpoenaed several local clergymen protesting the treatment of Bob and his colleagues), the activities of the Emergency Defense Battalion and Civil Guard, inflammatory sermons by several local clergy, and the behavior of John Eberle, who had engaged in "building up animosity toward the Communist Party." Morris and Eberle objected, saying they had not been given reasonable notice to prepare a case against Croom's motion.

Most of the morning was spent hearing witnesses address the issue of a venue change. Prosecutors called nine civic leaders (including two chamber of commerce members, an official of the Oklahoma Gas & Electric Company, and two local businessmen who were also members of the Civil Guard), all of whom testified Alan could get a fair trial in Oklahoma City. Testifying for the defense, however, were several ordinary citizens. One witness testified that the trials ought to be held someplace "off in the jungles" where no one knew about the publicity and "hysteria" surrounding them. Because it was the location of Communist Party headquarters, another stated, Oklahoma City was probably the worst place in the state to conduct the trials.

Another witness, William Loe, testified that he had been a special investigator for the city manager and described how he had prevented Eberle from using violence to break up a Communist Party meeting in September 1939. "I never did discover that any acts of violence had been perpetrated or were planned by these youngsters who were in charge of the Communist movement in Oklahoma City." During cross-examination, Loe also said he objected to the way the prosecution had excerpted paragraphs from printed materials and had taken them out of context. "If you could connect a man that way," he argued, "you could take certain paragraphs out of the Bible and convict Jesus Christ about being a Communist."

But the judge was not persuaded; he denied the defense motion for a change of venue. "This thing you call hysteria is all over the state," he told Croom, and in a curious twist of logic that acknowledged and questioned the reality of a hysteria at the same time, concluded: "It is a thing you can't get away from, if it exists."[64] As they left the hearings for lunch, reporters noticed that several Shaw supporters sported buttons reading "Free Alan Shaw" and "Free Alan and Eli."

Asked where they got the buttons, supporters indicated they were being sold for a dollar on the streets of New York by Brooklyn College students to raise funds for Alan's defense. Nena Beth Stapp was quick to note that her committee was not distributing the buttons. The *Oklahoma City Times* reported that county jailors had intercepted one sent to Alan Shaw, and turned it over to Lewis Morris. "A new way of trying lawsuits — by buttons," Morris quipped. "I just got a telegram from one of these New York colleges," he also told the *Times*. "It was signed by 6,000 students. They demanded that these cases be dismissed immediately." Privately Morris told friends about the scores of letters he was receiving as a result of Stapp's efforts, "I'm going to give the FBI every one of these letters. Then, if we get into war, the government will know just who these sympathizers are."[65]

At the opening of trial before an all-white, all-male jury on November 19, Eberle pointed to Alan — to whose name he regularly added "alias Alan Lifshutz" — and characterized him as a "paid professional member of the Communist Party who came to this state to set up the soviet form of government." Both Belden and Croom objected that Eberle's statements were not based on the evidence and were prejudicial. They immediately called for a mistrial. Arnold overruled their motion and invited Eberle to continue. Shaw and his colleagues "intend to put the red flag up in Oklahoma," Eberle said, "and if it is necessary to start a fight between whites and blacks in all the southern states and cause death and destruction of property and all that by violence, they will do it." The state "will prove from their own books that they teach revolutions," he said. The *Communist Manifesto* "divides the people into two classes, the property owners and the proletariat and teaches them to carry on a campaign of hatred between classes." He also quoted from Lenin's *State and Revolution* about the necessity to engage in "Trojan Horse" tactics to influence governments around the world toward Communism, which Eberle defined as a form of dictatorship, "[t]he same kind of dictatorship this defendant wants to set up in the United States, in Oklahoma."

Eberle also introduced as evidence a Communist Party member-ship book bearing Alan's name, and containing stamps indicating he had paid dues. As he closed his remarks, Eberle had six boxes of books, pamphlets, and papers wheeled into the courtroom, and promised to present their contents as state's evidence. Defense ob-jected to Eberle's effort to introduce as evidence the Communist Party sign seized in the August 17 raids. It had not been released from the Wood trial, they said, which they were appealing. Arnold overruled them again and indicated that any evidence introduced in the Wood trial would also be allowed in the Shaw trial. Defense attorneys then presented their opening statement and quickly doc-umented their strategy—they would prove that the state criminal syndicalism law was unconstitutional and that Alan was not guilty of any "overt acts" against the government.[66]

When court reconvened on Friday, November 22, the pattern of Alan Shaw's trial began to mirror Bob Wood's. Over defense objec-tions to each piece, Eberle introduced as state's evidence over forty books, pamphlets, pictures, and documents, including *Struggle for Revolutionary Marxism, 15 Years of the Communist Party, The Ultimate Aim, The War and the Working Class, Stalin, Two Tactics of Social Democ-racy in the Democratic Revolution, People's Road to Power, No Gold Stars for Us—Our Boys Stay Home, Strategy and Tactics, The Dictatorship of the Proletariat, State and Revolution, The Communist Manifesto,* and *The Foundations of Leninism.* All, Eberle said, showed the Communist Party was controlled by Russia and that its aims, program, and meth-ods advocated the use of violence to bring about political and indus-trial change.

Not so, Belden objected. None of the books and pamphlets was binding on Alan, and none stated the CPUSA's official platform at the time. Alan had never endorsed nor sanctioned what these printed materials advocated, he argued. In fact, when a police of-ficer described a protest speech Alan made before the city council, Croom noted that he could only recall that Alan asked for relief and employment for the city's unemployed. "Thus far," the *Daily Worker* later reported, "the prosecution has proved that the Communist Party wants peace, and that Alan Shaw wants work and food for the unemployed." Judge Arnold accepted the exhibits, but withheld ruling on their admissibility until all were submitted. By the afternoon he decided to send the jury home for the weekend and spend it himself reading through the materials the state had presented.[67]

In a November 25 issue of the *Daily Worker,* Bob Wood provided his impression of the trial. "Picture the courtroom: on one side sit the twelve male jurors (women are not yet eligible for jury service in Oklahoma); pacing in front of them is the surly-faced John Eberle," Bob wrote. "Every few minutes he bends over and extracts another pamphlet, a book, a photograph from the dozen or so overflowing cartons on the floor. He marches up to the witness stand. On the stand sits Dan Hollingsworth, ambitious head of the newly created Intelligence Squad of the City Police Department." Hollingsworth would identify where he found the item, Croom and Belden would state their objections, and the judge would accept the exhibits and promise to rule on their admissibility later. "And so goes the whole day."

Major Oklahoma City dailies had their slant on the evidence, Bob noted, but all they reported was "that the Communists were for peace and against the imperialist war." One bright spot emerging out of these events, Bob said, was the creation of an Oklahoma Federation for Constitutional Rights. Especially heartening was support given the Federation by *Black Dispatch* editor Roscoe Dunjee. "If a fair trial is denied Communists, if excessive bail is demanded of Communists, and if free speech is denied Communists," Dunjee editorialized in the piece Bob quoted, "the same rule can be forced upon this writer, his race and all minority groups."[68]

When the trial resumed Monday morning, Hollingsworth again took the stand. After describing in elaborate detail how the police tracked down the materials and arrested the defendants, Croom asked: "But you knew, didn't you, that the Communist Party was listed in the telephone directory?" Under cross-examination, Hollingsworth admitted he had never heard Alan advocate the use of violence or criminal acts to advance the Communist Party program. Why did you order the raids and arrests? Croom asked. "Was it a fact that you had been reading books and papers and you didn't like them?" "No sir," Hollingsworth replied. He also denied that the raids were carried out on a Saturday "so the defendants could not get into court until Monday or Tuesday." When Hollingsworth stepped down, the state called Officer John W. Webb to describe how he had purchased materials from the Progressive Book Store on July 24. On cross-examination, Croom asked, "Why did you let your beard grow?" "I thought I would look like a Communist," Webb replied.[69]

Most of the day, however, was spent arguing evidence admissibility. In response to defense objections that nothing in the Communist Party platform endorsed the Russian system of government, County Attorney Morris read a party constitution preamble that, he said, approved the teachings of Marx, Engels, Lenin, and Stalin. But the state could just as easily have charged the defendants under the syndicalism law for being Nazis, Croom responded. "They found Hitler's *Mein Kampf* at the book store, too." Prosecutors and defense attorneys went back and forth like this all day; ultimately, Judge Arnold dismissed the jury while attorneys debated the legality of the state's exhibits. At the end of a long day, Eberle (whose "truculence," Nena Beth Stapp said, "has changed to surliness under the constant rebukes of the court") told reporters he hoped to complete his case the following morning, after introducing a few more pamphlets and possibly calling another witness.[70]

On the morning of November 26, Eberle introduced a few more books as state's evidence, then called seventeen-year-old Jim Newman to the stand as his last witness. Under questioning, Newman said that while walking one evening in the fall of 1939, he listened to a "street speaker" and then visited the Progressive Book Store and purchased two books. Defense attorney Croom asked him if he was studying government at the university and if he saw anything wrong with reading about other forms of government like Communism and Nazism. Eberle immediately objected that Newman's answer was irrelevant; Judge Arnold sustained him, and Newman was denied the opportunity to answer the question. The prosecution then rested its case.[71]

Defense attorneys had said they were unsure whether to call Alan Shaw to the stand, although Belden clearly thought he had nothing to lose. However, others supporting the defense disagreed, and in the end, Alan sat mute, and the defense rested its case without calling any witnesses. Defense attorneys argued that the state had failed to prove its case.[72]

Just before Alan's trial ended, he was finally released from jail — 100 days after being incarcerated. To cover his $7,500 bail, his mother-in-law offered her property as a $5,000 surety against the sum the ILD could not cover. "The release of Shaw in mid-trial," the *Daily Worker* reported, "is the most dramatic expression of the rising Oklahoma resentment against the prosecutions of the Communists." Only Eli Jaffe and one other defendant remained in jail.[73]

As each of his friends left the jail, Eli's life became more precarious, especially during the day when he was placed in a central cell with the gang that beat him. At night he got his own cell, but had to listen to the screams of recently imprisoned juveniles who were sodomized by some of Eli's assailants. He especially worried about Orval Lewis the second time he was incarcerated. Fortunately, Orval got the cell right next to Eli every night. On one occasion when Eli received cigarettes from friends, the cell gang pressed him to turn them over. Eli picked up a 16-inch dustpan, shook it at the gang leader, and yelled, "Listen, you son-of-a-bitch. You're four inches taller and 40 pounds heavier — but this makes us even. You don't stop pushin' me around, I'm gonna split your fuckin' skull!" Quickly realizing that the gang had surrounded him, he decided discretion was the better part of valor. He dropped the dustpan. The gang leader quickly moved in, wrestled Eli to the ground, took the cigarettes, kicked Eli in the ribs, and walked away.

Eli spent his time writing letters to friends and leftist periodicals and newspapers across the country; his lawyers smuggled them out and mailed them. *The Weekly Review* of New York published one: "I keep remembering Tom Paine's words," he told *Review* readers: "The greater the struggle the more glorious the victory." His lawyers also brought him news of support given by the Oklahoma Committee to Defend Political Prisoners and the ILD. Friends bought him a subscription to the *Daily Oklahoman*, which, after he read it, he used as barter with his cellmates.[74]

But mostly he was lonely and, after hearing about Bob's conviction, very scared. "I had to face the agonizing reality that I, too, might wind up spending ten years" in prison. His girlfriend visited him once, but because of "snide remarks from the jailers, obscenities of the trustees," and the opposition of her parents (with whom she lived), she never came back. The only person courageous enough to visit him regularly was Wilma Lewis, first as part of her routine visits to her parents and brother for the two-and-a-half months they were incarcerated but, after bond was posted for them, just to visit Eli. And at considerable risk. To get to Eli she usually had to "run the gauntlet" of grabbing hands down a central jail hallway, where she also had to endure lewd remarks. On one occasion a prisoner trustee who was leading her turned into a darkened corner, where he exposed himself. Wilma put her head down and kept going. Usually she had to talk to Eli through a glass window; she would bring him news of efforts being made for his release. During these visits Wilma concluded that Eli was "the most exciting thing that had come along." But after a while, the jailors cut off her visits because she was not a member of Eli's immediate family.[75]

On the outside, life was no less dangerous for Wilma, who with her brother, Orval, had been receiving five dollars a week from the ILD on which to live while her parents were in jail. She supplemented this meager sum by working at a diner across the street from her school during lunch hour and study periods. For her services she was paid a burger and a shake. Visits to the jail usually occurred on days after classes at Central High, where her fellow students generally gave her a hard time for political positions she took in her classes. On one occasion she used government documents at the local public library to compile a report critical of the government. Her social studies teacher complimented her on the research and conclusions; her principal criticized her openly. When she distributed literature to her classmates in November about the forthcoming Oklahoma Youth Legislature, the principal stopped her.[76]

In a press release dated November 28, Nena Beth Stapp happily reported Alan's release. She also quoted letters her Committee had received for his defense. "I am sorry to do so little on my part but I have not had any work in four years," one person wrote. "Enclosed is a $1.00 bill to help a little, I hope, and if I get hold of another dollar, I will send it as soon as I get it." Robert Morss Lovett, professor emeritus at the University of Chicago and at the time government secretary of the Virgin Islands, was more forceful. "It is particularly outrageous that this denial of constitutional rights should occur in connection with a national election," he wrote, enclosing a twenty-dollar check. "It is the most dangerous subversion of our form of government to cause arrest without warrant, impose imprisonment by requiring excessive bail, to charge with crime under statutes which have no application and to impose ferocious and unreasonable sentences." A Goucher College professor sent a five-dollar check. "The situation in Oklahoma, as I understand it, is a disgrace to a democratic government."[77]

On November 29, the ILD made public a letter defendant Herb Brausch had sent thanking the organization for posting his bail, and for two boxes of clothing. "The children were thrilled with the clothing and shoes, as they were superior to anything the local charities issue." Because his local union had carried his dues while he was in jail, Brausch said, he was in good standing and back to work. "I take great pride in showing letters from the ILD to my union brothers. Many are interested in the organization," he said. "And my local is the only mixed local (Negro and white) in this jimcrow state." The ILD indicated Brausch's letter would become part of the package of materials soliciting funds for its annual Christmas drive for "labor's prisoners and their families." In a cover letter New York congressman Vito Marcantonio noted that none of the Brausch children had shoes when the ILD representative visited them; he also noted that another defendant's wife could not find work while her husband was in jail. On one occasion she was hired for three hours, but "her pay . . . was 3 pumpkins."[78]

Trial resumed for closing arguments on Monday afternoon, December 2. Judge Arnold ruled that all of the evidence the state had submitted was admissible, and invited both sides to present their final arguments. He imposed no time limits on either. Defense attorneys did, however, ask for a continuance because, they argued, George

Croom was too ill with influenza to come to court. But when Judge Arnold refused to postpone the trial any longer, the ILD quickly flew another attorney from Chicago to assist. Because Croom's influenza flared a second time, ILD ultimately had to fly the Chicago attorney to Oklahoma City twice during closing arguments.[79]

Eberle began his final argument at 2 P.M. Alan Shaw, he said, was "a paid hireling of the Communist Party, a paid revolutionary" who "came from out of the state to teach that doctrine of the party which urges criminal syndicalism." The aim of the Party was to establish Socialism according to the theories of Marx, Engels, Lenin, and Stalin. Party members pledge themselves to fight against "Fascist and imperialist wars, engage in the struggle for equal rights for Negroes, to defend the Soviet Union and to fight for the supremacy of the Soviet Union in this country." And be not deceived by Communist vocabulary, he warned. "When they say worker, they mean Communist. And they work the workers. Examine their hands and they'll be as soft as cream puffs. This defendant never did any work in his life. The Communist down here works the workers, and tries to lead them into economic slavery, like they did in Russia." Several times Eberle told the jurors that Communists "don't believe in God" and "are the enemy of religion." Communists would abolish the family in part because they advocate a "community of women."[80]

On one occasion Eberle waved before the jury a picture of "Comrade" James Ford, and noted that in 1932 the Communist Party had nominated a "Negro" for its vice-presidential candidate. He also showed a picture of delegates to the 1939 Oklahoma Youth Legislature; Communists, he said, had arranged to have "Negroes" and whites together in the picture. He also read from a pamphlet titled *Reds in Dixie,* and after saying, "Let's get down to the meat of this thing," began to quote sections that denounced Jim Crow laws, lynching in the South, and backdoor courtships between white men and black women. "In their Negro liberation plan," Eberle said, Communists "talk about being against white chauvinism. Maybe you don't know what chauvinism is. Well, chauvinism simply means patriotism, and nobody accuses these Communists of being patriots." In his concluding remarks the next day, Eberle told jurors to send the Communists a message. "You let him serve 10 years and his party pay $5,000 and we won't be bothered with very many more Communists around here." In summarizing his remarks, the *Daily Worker* noted that three of the eight hours that Eberle addressed the all-white jury focused on the Communist Party's position on "the Negro question."[81]

Once Eberle finished, Stanley Belden delivered a brief closing argument questioning the legality of warrants that led to the confiscation of materials from the bookstore and Alan's residence, and thus the inadmissibility of these materials as evidence. When he finished, Judge Arnold adjourned the court until the following Monday. He said that he wanted to give Croom a chance to recover from influenza before delivering his final argument. When court opened Monday morning, Croom was there and ready.

"This is the first time in the history of America that books have been brought from the jail each morning," he said, "compelled to stay in the dock all day, testify from the witness stand, and again that evening taken to the county jail and put securely under lock and key." And because the state was likely to get rid of these books if the jurors convicted Alan, "you have the question of deciding . . . whether you are going to give your sanction to the first official book burning in America, or what will happen to these books if you should convict this defendant." Croom said he recollected his fondness for Jack London novels as a youth, but reminded jurors that because London was a Communist, "his books must be burned because they happen to offend some of the more refined natures of a county attorney." He reminded jurors that Oklahoma had thousands of Socialists who voted for Eugene Debs in 1916 and that most of them had a copy of *The Communist Manifesto* in their home. "It was their Bible. Yet nobody seemed to think, gentlemen, that it was such a horrible book!"[82]

Finally, Croom took issue with Eberle's characterization of the Oklahoma Youth Legislature, and especially his reference to a delegate named Billie Croom. "Yes, that is my daughter," Croom said, but he was "glad she was in the Oklahoma Youth Legislature" and proud to be a sponsor. Then he clumsily tried to copy the prosecution's propensity to appeal to probable jury prejudice. But "where is Mr. Eberle's daughter?" he asked rhetorically. "For 10 years he has been on the public pay of this county, and he hasn't had the courage and the manhood to marry and raise a family." Even Eberle did not bother to answer this remark.[83]

In his closing argument prosecutor Lewis Morris noted how he had camouflaged his machine gun in France during World War I, then accused the Communist Party of using the Bill of Rights as a "camouflage" to cover its real purpose. "They camouflage their nefarious teachings of destruction of government and the constitution, and they camouflage it with such things as the constitutional guarantees accorded to men." He then turned to Alan and fumed: "And you camouflage it with freedom of press, with freedom of speech, and you cry about civil liberties." As examples of their efforts to foment revolution, he noted that much Communist literature recommended an alliance between poor whites and blacks to effect economic improvement, including one pamphlet that suggested five million blacks were living in a virtual hell on Dixie plantations. "You go down there appealing to bias and passion and prejudice for the Negro people, and you nominate one of them for vice-president for the United States of America." Defense attorneys objected several times to Morris's courtroom behavior, especially when he waved a picture of an African American worker before jurors' faces while making reference to several Communist pamphlets on the struggles of African American people.[84]

For two hours Morris harangued the jury and at the end connected the issue of race once more to the theme of civil liberties. "When you walk along and you see a fellow talking about burning books and freedom of press and you read this, you know the leaf is dropping a little bit, don't you?" How to resolve this problem? "I say cram all of it down their throats and make them like it," Morris concluded, "and the way to do it is to bring in a verdict in this case of ten years in the penitentiary and a five thousand dollar fine and let that be a warning to these men that you can't do it, that you can't get away with it." Morris later had the telegram from six thousand Brooklyn College students read into Alan Shaw's court record as an example of outside attempts to influence the jury.[85]

When Morris finished, the judge issued the jury instructions and sent them to deliberate at 3 P.M. At 5:30 the jury adjourned for dinner for an hour and a half, then returned to the courtroom to deliver a verdict fifteen minutes later. "Guilty," the foreman said. The jury also recommended the maximum penalty of ten years in the state penitentiary and a $5,000 fine. Alan stood silently beside his wife, Nena Beth, and Bob Wood as the verdict was read.[86]

To reporters outside the courtroom, Alan said, "It is a clear travesty." Nena Beth pledged to broaden the campaign of the Oklahoma Committee to Defend Political Prisoners and appealed to people "who care about the Bill of Rights" to send money to the Committee and protests to Morris and Eberle. Croom was more outspoken. "This is an outrage on justice, a destruction, if allowed to stand, of all rights of minority groups in the United States. . . . The jury could not have read one one-hundredth part of the testimony." Belden declared that "if the verdict was not based on bias and prejudice and passion, why did they give him the maximum that could be given if he had committed some overt act or advocated violence?" Defense attorneys promised to ask for a new trial and, if denied, appeal the conviction.[87]

For his part, Eberle said the state would press on with other cases after January 1. "We'll set the cases and try them one at a time. I do not know who will be tried next." He told the *Cushing Daily Citizen* that the decision would not outlaw all books on Communism in the state of Oklahoma. "We're not going out and search libraries just for copies of communist books." The law applied, he said, "only in cases where revolutionary literature was assembled on a large scale for distribution for propaganda purposes." To a reporter from the *Miami Daily News Record,* he said the verdict "means that any person who is a member of the Communist Party" in Oklahoma "is subject to conviction under the criminal syndicalism law and liable to receive the maximum penalty of 10 years imprisonment and $5,000 fine." He told the *Norman Transcript* that the verdict made party membership "hazardous" and that its activities would now be virtually eliminated. In an editorial the following day the *Transcript* declared: "The Communists should abide by our laws or go to Russia."[88]

Roscoe Dunjee took a different slant in his weekly *Black Dispatch*. He noted that several years previously *Daily Oklahoman* editorial writer Luther Harrison had delivered a lecture at the University of Oklahoma in which he suggested every student in the university be required to read Marx's *Das Kapital*. "Bring these doctrines out in the open. I have no fear of the results," Harrison had said. "The intelligence of the American people has rejected such doctrines every time they have seen and understood them." The *Black Dispatch* "agrees with Editor Harrison," Dunjee concluded, and thus does "not believe that Luther Harrison intended that Oklahoma's Criminal Syndicalism Law should have any such interpretation." In an editorial the following week, Dunjee attacked the racism in Eberle's and Morris's final remarks, and noted that their arguments appealed "to passion and prejudice rather than to reason, justice and right."[89]

Although most other Oklahoma newspapers supported the prosecution, *The Tulsa Tribune* voiced an objection to the way in which the two Communists had been prosecuted. In a December 11 editorial titled "Burning Another Witch," the paper excoriated the "mob of gun-toting vigilantes" who generated the "unreasoning war hysteria" that led to the convictions of Bob Wood and Alan Shaw, "puny little radicals who have no official power and no particular following." The editorial noted that the Communist Party had been tolerated in Oklahoma for more than twenty years and that it "repeatedly conducted public meetings and lectures without serious protest either from the people or from the police." But the editorial then suggested that Congress outlaw the Communist Party first and then, "if the Party continues to be active, its members may be prosecuted with some degree of justice." By going after the members before the Party was outlawed, "the democratic ideal has taken a licking from the well-meaning but befuddled patriots of Oklahoma City."[90]

Outside the Sooner State reaction differed considerably. The *Daily Worker* called it a "shocking and dangerous trial . . . a danger signal to the entire labor movement." The *Miners' Voice,* a labor union journal in Butte, Montana, called the trials dangerous violations of "every important provision of the Bill of Rights." The *Nation* criticized the "vindictive" sentences, and argued, "It would be difficult to find a more flagrant example of judicial outrage of the Bill of Rights." The *New York Times* carried a short story on the front page of its December 10 issue, decrying Alan's conviction. And under the heading, "We Have Our Own Hitlers Who Would Destroy Civil Liberties," the *Capital Times* of Madison, Wisconsin, reported, "Here we have an astonishing situation in which a man is given a prison term because of his beliefs." Under such logic as applied by Oklahoma courts, Detroit autoworkers could not distribute handbills, Pennsylvania mineworkers could not freely assemble, University of Wisconsin students could not express themselves on the war. The *American Guardian,* a Socialist newspaper edited in Oklahoma City, reprinted the *Capital Times* editorial in its entirety.[91] On December 6, several people in Brooklyn hosted a dinner at a local hotel to raise money for the Oklahoma defendants. Not only was it "financially successful," it also "won several hundred persons for active assistance to the defense and established a base for greater activity in the Oklahoma campaign in New York," the ILD reported.[92]

But Oklahoma officials had their own allies, who fought back in their own way. When Brooklyn College students continued to irritate, the *Daily Oklahoman* countered by running a story on December 5 under the title "Prexy Says Reds Use Colleges in New York for Their Activities." The story quoted the Brooklyn College president, who told a New York legislative investigating committee that, although the "overwhelming majority of students and faculty was anti-Communist, a very small minority" sought to "exploit the future of the college for their own ulterior motives." Two days later the newspaper reported a speech by Oklahoma's Fifth District U.S. Representative Mike Monroney before a postmaster's convention in Oklahoma City. Monroney told his audience to be on the alert for fifth-column activities. "You people are the main, and oftentimes

only, contact with the federal government that most people have."
And in the library at John Eberle's home parish in Oklahoma City
was the December 7 issue of the Catholic periodical *America*, which
carried an article titled "Must the Constitution Protect Those Who
Would Destroy It?" "America's safety in this world crisis demands a
thorough cleaning out of the destructive forces in our midst," the
author argued. "If we persist in winking the legal eye at something
we know in our hearts to be destructive and un-American, we shall
later pay the penalty, perhaps much to our sorrow."[93]

On December 14, Martin Dies drove up from Dallas to Oklahoma City to address members of the Oklahoma chapter of the
National Patriotic Council in the Municipal Auditorium (the same
room denied Bob and Alan earlier that year). When he arrived he
told the *Daily Oklahoman* that the House Un-American Activities
Committee would expand its investigations to the Sooner State and
that there was a possibility hearings would be held in Oklahoma
City. He refused to comment on the specifics of the Wood and Shaw
trials, but said he thought Oklahoma's problems with Communist
infiltration were relatively minor. "I don't think the Oklahoma situation is anything comparable to that which exists in the eastern
cities," he said. "There is very little un-American activity here, com-
paratively speaking."

In his speech that evening, he addressed issues raised in Bob's
and Alan's trials point by point without specifically mentioning the
defendants. Communists in America were not members of a political party, "but a foreign conspiracy masked as a political party. It is a
front for spies, saboteurs and enemy agents." The ILD "is nothing
more nor less than an organization to defend Communists in court
trials." The American Youth Congress, "while willing to denounce
Nazism, refused to denounce Communism because those in control
were members of the Young Communists League." He hoped, he
said, to never see happen in America what happened in France,
where people fled from Paris before Hitler's marching troops.
"That was the result of Trojan Horse operations," he said, "of Fifth
Column work." The *Daily Oklahoman* featured the Dies lecture on
page one.

On December 17, the American Legion National Commander addressed members of the Oklahoma City Junior Chamber of Commerce. "Whether democracy survives, and in what form," he said, "depends upon America." He praised agencies that awakened the country to fifth columnists, and specifically commended Lewis Morris, the county attorney in the audience who had successfully brought convictions against two Communists. The crowd applauded.[94]

The day before, Eli Jaffe was finally released on $5,000 bond, 121 days after his arrest. The last few weeks had been depressing for Eli, who lacked visitors and nearly lost hope. He might have heard about Lewis Morris's comments to the press that defendants were slow to exercise their right to have bail reduced because they wanted to stir up sympathy for their cause. "Worried 'bout your friends forgettin' ya?" jailers had teased him. "My gut suggested I was being kept in jail by the International Labor Defense to keep the 'Oklahoma Book Trials' alive. Sympathizers, I knew, had a greater incentive to contribute money when one of the victims of a frame-up was still in jail." But several days earlier he had received a letter from Bob Wood that his bail would soon be posted. When Eli left the jail, Wilma Lewis was there to take a picture. "It showed a pinchfaced, perplexed-looking individual with a wry look-at-the-camera smile," he later recalled. "It didn't show a mouthful of cavities, impaired vision and a deep-in-the-fabric trauma."[95]

On December 19, Alan Shaw returned to the courtroom, where he was formally sentenced to ten years in the penitentiary and fined $5,000. On many of the days during trial he showed up in the same faded-blue cotton slacks and polo shirt he was wearing when arrested; this day he wore a suit. "You didn't testify in this case," Judge Arnold said after delivering the sentence. "Would you like to say anything at this time?" Alan was ready. "Over the entrance to this courthouse there is an inscription with a quotation from Thomas Jefferson, 'Equal justice to all men, regardless of state or persuasion, religious or political,'" he began. "That inscription and those words have been disregarded in my case. It has been a mockery from the very beginning."

He then looked toward Eberle and Morris, sitting at the bench immediately to his right. "I was tried and convicted through the bias, prejudice, hatred, venom, and sectionalism of these two men." He noted that both were rumored to be ambitious for higher office — Morris for governor, Eberle for the county attorney's office Morris would vacate should he win; Alan argued that both wanted to use his trial "as a stepping stone" for their personal ambition. "Throughout my entire trial . . . no act of violence was shown, no act of violence was hinted at, not one witness testified from the stand that I have ever advocated any criminal act," he concluded. "The entire prosecution was one based on race hatred built up in the mind of the jury by the prosecuting attorneys, of prejudice on one question or another."[96] As he left the courtroom Alan declared to reporters: "[T]he two most peculiar manifestations of the roots of fascism are anti-Semitism and discrimination against the Negro people." Morris and Eberle made heavy use of both, he said.[97]

Over the next several months the focus of the Oklahoma City trials shifted from the courtroom and expanded into the nation's public sphere, where each side struggled to maintain its position, and where each took on new allies.

CHAPTER FOUR

Both Sides Mobilize, August 1940–April 1941

O ne cannot fully understand the bitterness of the conflict surrounding the bookstore defendants unless viewed in the context of a wider battle over radicalism, race, and civil liberties in
Oklahoma and the nation. The trials garnered state and national
attention in large part because of tensions created by that wider
battle. As a result, the trials also became a symbolic battleground for
a variety of forces on both the left and right.

Just one week before the bookstore raids, for example, Professor Streeter Stuart of Southeastern State College in Durant, Oklahoma, wrote his congressman, "I call upon you as my representative to . . . vote against any form of conscription of individuals," he
said. "War is insanity." The congressman forwarded Stuart's letter
to Southeastern's president, who fired Stuart effective August 31.[1]
On October 17, just one week after Bob Wood's trial ended, Presbyterian ministers meeting in Norman for the annual state synod conference passed a resolution asking Governor Phillips and the State
Board of Education to investigate the Stuart firing. Two days later
the University of Oklahoma chapter of the American Association of

University Professors sent a letter to university president William Bizzell voicing its concern as well.[2]

On the morning of October 19, Nena Beth Stapp sent a telegram to the ILD's Chicago office. "Dies Committee attempting to smear civil rights movement in Oklahoma," she said. She reported that Nick Comfort of the Oklahoma School of Religion in Norman, the Rev. John B. Thompson of Norman's First Presbyterian Church, and the Rev. Paul Wright of the First Presbyterian Church in Oklahoma City, had been summoned to appear before Wick Fowler and E. T. Seale, staff members of the Dies Committee who had come to Oklahoma City to survey un-American activities there. "Civil rights movement here fighting dismissal of Professor Streeter [*sic*] who opposed conscription, fighting persecution of Jehovah's Witnesses, fighting criminal syndicalism frame-ups," she continued. "Vigilante terror and tight censorship make necessary immediate funds from whole Midwest."[3]

Fowler and Seale had subpoenaed Comfort, Thompson, and Wright to appear at the courthouse on October 21, and to bring with them "all financial and membership records of the Communist Party of Oklahoma and letters, books, papers, and other written matter concerning the Communist Party and members thereof." After consulting with Attorney Stanley Belden, who "informed them . . . that they need not testify since this was only an investigator and not a member of the committee," the three decided to appear anyway. In the room the three ministers asked: Why us? Fowler refused to reveal the source of his list. Was Eberle involved? they asked. Fowler would not confirm or deny. Fowler told Wright that because he had been observed working with Alan Shaw on an unemployment welfare committee, "you became identified with the Communist Party. You know, preachers sometimes become so interested in humanity that they likely are to become gullible." Wright responded, "I just like to be a little more wide awake than the fellow next to me and be aware when liberties are being threatened."

Comfort was more aggressive. "I am not and never have been a member of the party or associated with it," he told Fowler and Seale.

"I have fought for civil liberties and will continue to fight for them."
Do you know the Red Dust Players (which the *Daily Oklahoman* identified as "a labor dramatic group")? Comfort answered "No," but
wondered later why Fowler "seemed particularly interested in that."
When Fowler then began lecturing Comfort on being a liberal and
"in these days sticking his neck out," Comfort responded, "Young
man, it's a shame to see such a nice fellow as you working for such a
rotten boss like Martin Dies."

Thompson was asked if he knew of any Communists or Communistic organizations on the University of Oklahoma campus. "No,"
Thompson responded. When asked to list organizations to which
they belonged, Comfort reported the AAUP, the American Federation of Teachers, the Oklahoma Education Association, the Southern Conference for Human Welfare, and the Norman Forum.
Thompson listed Phi Beta Kappa, the American Peace Mobilization
Committee, the ACLU, and the Southern Conference for Human
Welfare. Wright noted the Oklahoma City Chamber of Commerce,
the American Legion, the Community Fund Budget Committee,
the Council for Social Welfare, the Men's Dinner Club, and "oh yes,
the Oklahoma City Rose Society."[4]

After the session, Fowler and Seale were eager to tell the *Daily
Oklahoman* that the inquiry did not imply those subpoenaed were
Communists or associated with Communists. But Comfort, Thompson, and Wright were not kind in their response. They voiced their
suspicion that "back of this is an effort on the part of local reaction-
aries to intimidate or discredit those who are trying to uphold
American constitutional rights and democratic processes in a time
of world and national crisis." Nor were they reluctant to name the
individual most responsible. After noting that a federal subpoena
had been delivered to them by an Oklahoma county deputy sheriff
and an Oklahoma City detective, they concluded: "All our attempts
to discover who is responsible for this attempt to discredit us lead to
John Eberle's office." To a *Norman Transcript* reporter Comfort
noted: "There are forces in Oklahoma City who are trying to knock
down the ears of every liberal in the state."[5]

The following Monday Fowler concluded his investigation and

told the *Daily Oklahoman* he would report his findings to Chairman Dies, who would then decide whether to conduct an investigation of Communist and Nazi activities in the Sooner State, and perhaps hold hearings in Oklahoma City. Fowler denied Eberle had anything to do with his preliminary investigation and counseled the clergymen before him on Saturday not to be alarmed. "The fact that a person is summoned to appear before a Dies Committee investigation does not imply he is connected in any way with un-American activities. Information in the possession of respected persons frequently sheds light on others who should be the subject of investigation." The *Daily Oklahoman* was much harsher on the Dies Committee staffers. "In the case of Robert Woods [*sic*] such a subpena [*sic*] would have been perfectly proper," it editorialized on October 23. But in the case of the three ministers "the use of the subpena [*sic*] duces tecum was an asinine performance." Thus, even the *Daily Oklahoman* recognized a problem with "overdoing witch hunts. . . . The most formidable handicap confronting those who are doing genuine and effective work against communism," the *Oklahoman* argued in an October 25 editorial, "is the fact that some red-hunters overdo the job and attempt to put the red mark on innocent victims."[6]

Past activities may not have been the only reason the Dies Committee and the county attorney's office were interested in the three men. By that time, planning for a civil rights watchdog organization had been going on for months, and organizers had been in touch with civil rights organizations across the country for advice. On October 22 they launched it. The Rev. Paul Wright and a University of Oklahoma philosophy professor (who had been state chairman of the ACLU for three years) issued a circular (also sent to every Oklahoma newspaper) headlined "Oklahoma Committee on Constitutional Rights." It invited them to attend a state conference in Oklahoma City. "A small group of Oklahoma citizens have recently had a number of discussions of the urgent problem of preserving constitutional rights in this state," the letter said. "We have worked out a statement which we think may well serve as a working basis for cooperation and for beginning this task."[7] Accompanying the circular was a separate call that stated that "those inalienable rights, free speech, press, worship, and peaceable assembly which our fore-fathers specified in the Constitution are in danger" in the Sooner State. It specifically cited persecution of Jehovah's Witnesses, the dismissal of Streeter Stuart, and the criminal syndicalism trials.[8]

Oklahoma officials did not hesitate to lash back. On October 28 the Oklahoma city manager warned fellow Oklahomans "not to stick your neck out" by joining a movement to organize a statewide civil liberties committee. "People can still say what they think, but they've got to be responsible for their statements," he said.[9] At a November 12 press conference, Governor Phillips warned OU faculty members against attending the "State Conference on Constitutional Rights." "They're hired to teach school down there in Norman," Phillips said, "not to go around the state working on something which does not concern them." He wondered out loud whether "they don't have enough to do." Should anyone from OU attend the meeting, how-ever, Phillips said they would be identified. He later added that he would turn over to the FBI any letter he received from anywhere in the country that protested the criminal syndicalism trials.[10]

ACLU director Roger Baldwin worried about something else. Because the Communist Party so readily shifted its position in lock-step with Moscow and said nothing about Stalin's purges, many ACLU members questioned just how committed American Com-munists were to civil liberties, and some recommended that the ACLU put some distance between itself and Communist Party ac-tivities. Baldwin was particularly sensitive to public perception that connected the two organizations. Indeed, earlier that year the ACLU barred from its governing committees and staff any person who supported totalitarian dictatorship in any country. On Novem-ber 14 he wrote ACLU Chairman E. A. Ross that he was not able to determine how much the organization of the Oklahoma civil liber-ties group was "being promoted by our friends or by the Commu-nists, who do most of their work nowadays through the National Federation for Constitutional Liberties." He suspected the Federa-tion was not involved in Oklahoma, but told Ross: "We rather de-pend on you for advice on that, if you can get the facts."[11]

Although the major Oklahoma City dailies only lightly reported on the core documents the committee sent out to generate interest for the conference, they spared little ink in reporting on the conference itself. And it had plenty of fireworks to attract attention. Two hundred people attended (only the *Black Dispatch* noted they were "black and white"). The day began at 10:00 A.M. with a brief address by ACLU Chairman E. A. Ross, then quickly moved to a series of meetings. "While majority and minority members kept the air hot with their thrusts and jibes," the *Daily Oklahoman* reported, an Oklahoma Federation for Constitutional Rights nonetheless was formed.[12] A motion on the syndicalism trials "brought a storm of protest," the *Oklahoman* reported. "We're not making any criticism of any particular public official, but we think somebody has been making martyrs out of this bunch of punks," declared one attendee. Another objected, "It's time to put our feet on the neck of every Communist in the United States and send them back to Russia." Adding to the cacophony on the floor were similar protests shouted from the balcony.[13]

Later that day, the assembly adopted a resolution: "We hold that the foundations of democracy are in danger when any law can be made the tool of special persecution of any group, that the freedom of the press is threatened when citizens may be punished for possessing or distributing books; that the 8th amendment to the Constitution is abrogated by the imposing of excessive bail; and that justice itself is made a travesty when convictions are secured on insufficient or irrelevant evidence." The resolution concluded: "Fully conscious of the implications of such actions for all of us . . . we condemn the extra-legal and illegal treatment of any minority group and demand further safeguards of the rights granted in the 4th and 8th amendments of our Constitution."[14]

After the conference passed a resolution affirming the Constitution and Bill of Rights and condemning "the use of a national emergency on the part of any interests to destroy the legal equitable rights of labor," the group elected an executive committee and state council. At the concluding session that evening, the Rev. Wright read to an audience of four hundred ("attended by both whites and Negroes," the *Black Dispatch* again noticed) nearly fifty telegrams from civil liberties groups and notable educators across the nation (including philosopher John Dewey), all encouraging the new organization to press on in Oklahoma. In a keynote that followed, Ross commented, "We don't want to change the form of government, we don't want to change the constitution — that's what we're trying to preserve, the rights of the people under the constitution no matter what form they advocate. What we want," he concluded, "is to protect Oklahoma against the rise of night riders."[15] With that line, Ross received a standing ovation from most members in the audience. The Oklahoma Federation for Constitutional Rights had made its position clear.

Across the state reaction to the new organization was mixed. County Attorney Lewis Morris connected the formation of the Federation to the criminal syndicalism trials and accused the group of "trying to prejudice the jury ahead of time." OU President Bizzell regretted "the embarrassing situation due to the feeling on the part of some of our so-called 'liberals' that they must protect the civil rights of people who may or may not be entitled to have their rights protected," he wrote one of the Regents.[16] About the meeting the *Daily Oklahoman* noted: "Some fine, sincere folks are getting excited over civil liberties. The peril to such domestic bugaboos pales into insignificance compared with the danger of the triumph of nazism, communism and fascism, all of which have ruthlessly throttled civil liberties as soon as they have achieved power."[17] The International Labor Defense rather precipitously called the new organization "a powerful bulwark in defense of democracy through the United States." The *Wilson* (Oklahoma) *Post Democrat* was also supportive. "A bunch of professors, ministers and others are getting themselves in a tub of hot water by having the audacity to organize a civil liberties league and plug for the rights of individuals as guaranteed by our national and state constitution," it said.[18]

Roscoe Dunjee pulled no punches. He harbored no sympathy for Communist dogma, he said, but as an African American in a Jim Crow state he did recognize violations of civil liberties when he saw them.[19] Perhaps the most balanced editorial came from Edith Walker, campus columnist for the University's *Oklahoma Daily*. She noted that the Federation had received encouraging support from liberals across the country "to stem the outrages which have been perpetrated against the rights of citizens," and she wished it well. "Between a communist and an American who seeks to preserve the rights of a communist, there is a vast difference."[20]

To kick off its membership drive, the Federation printed a ten-page pamphlet listing its officers, explaining its goals, and soliciting membership. The pamphlet specifically addressed the criminal syndicalism cases, which it judged "a constant source of infringement of the Bill of Rights." It then quoted a November 7 letter from Attorney General Robert H. Jackson to Eleanor Roosevelt. "You are assured that the office of the Attorney-General has issued no statement suggesting the use of State criminal syndicalism laws," Jackson wrote the First Lady. "In fact, at the recent Federal-State conference of Federal and State law enforcement agencies, the Oklahoma statute was specifically pointed out as an example of the sort of legislation that is unnecessary and undesirable."[21]

Like the book trials, the existence of the Federation functioned as a catalyst for opposition. To protest the creation of the Federation, "Radio Pastor" E. F. Webber arranged to bring *Red Network* author and noted red-baiter Elizabeth Dilling to Oklahoma City for a speech at the Shrine Auditorium. What Americans needed was a good dose of common sense, Dilling argued. People with common sense "won't give civil liberties to cancers. Getting some Communist out of jail," she concluded, "they call that civil liberties?"[22] Governor Phillips invited Martin Dies to speak in Oklahoma City on December 12. Dies told an audience of five hundred in Municipal Auditorium that state and local governments were justified in taking steps against un-American activities in the absence of federal action. Both Eberle and Morris were in the audience.[23]

The next battle between Oklahoma's conservative forces and civil liberties activists over the book trial defendants was the annual meeting of the Oklahoma Youth Legislature in Oklahoma City in late December 1940, several weeks after Alan Shaw's conviction. When the *Oklahoma City Times* reported the OYL meeting on December 28, it led with a picture of Eli Jaffe and Wilma Lewis (both representing the Young Communist League), smiling at the cameras. The caption beneath their picture noted their connections to the criminal syndicalism trials, which was also emphasized in the article that followed. After "a dramatic session" highlighted by a speech by Jaffe, the *Times* began, "Communist and anti-Communist members" of the OYL Commission on Democratic Liberties — "the most important" of the Youth Legislature — "joined . . . in unanimously criticizing Oklahoma's criminal syndicalism law."[24]

What drew most of the *Times*' attention, however, was a stormy session that pitted Eli against a handful of representatives from the Oklahoma City Young Businessmen's Club, the VFW, and OU. One of them charged, "We have a red death creeping across the State of Oklahoma acting behind our backs." Another shouted, "The reds drew up the constitution of the group." Eli responded, "I represent the Young Communist League and I'm proud of it. Not the Communist Party but your place in American democracy is really on trial in the criminal syndicalism trials here." But his opponents blasted the Communist Party for "advocating the use of violence." When they had spoken their piece, they bolted the conference and were joined by several fellow OU YMCA delegates and the representative of the University's Christian Youth Fellowship. When the OYL later adopted a resolution placing it on record against the principles of the Communist Party, Eli and Wilma asked to be placed on record as "abstaining."[25]

Half a continent away supporters of the Oklahoma defendants hosted several fund-raising events. Already on October 18, the *Brooklyn College Vanguard* advised students that they could best aid BC alums Alan "Lifshutz" and Eli Jaffe by contributing to defense funds set up by the ACLU, the ILD, and the National Federation for Constitutional Liberties. They could also send protest letters to prosecutor Eberle. A month later they were selling buttons on the streets of New York reading "Free Alan Shaw" and "Free Alan and Eli."[26]

On December 6, the Committee for Civil Rights in Kings County, New York, sponsored a dinner at a Brooklyn hotel to raise money for Eli's bail. Featured speakers included well-known artist Rockwell Kent, Congressman (and ILD President) Vito Marcantonio, and writer Irwin Shaw, whose fiction regularly appeared in the *New Yorker.* Two weeks later a Committee to Defend Alan Shaw and Eli Jaffe sponsored a fund-raising party at the Muriel Draper Studios in New York City. The "pipelines of democracy flow from Brooklyn College to Oklahoma City," read the announcement, which also indicated African American singer Hudie "Leadbelly" Ledbetter would provide entertainment. Admission fee was 25 cents for students, 39 cents for all others.[27]

Shortly after the conclusion of Alan Shaw's trial on December 9, Alan and Nena Beth, Ina Wood, and Elizabeth Green traveled to New York City. After they arrived they issued a statement through the International Labor Defense thanking the ILD for all its help. "We know that the support the ILD has given us in the legal defense, in bringing the facts of our case before the American people, in raising bail in assisting us while in jail with prisoners relief, was made possible by the support of the people." They also made several public appearances on the ILD's behalf. On January 10, the *Brooklyn College Vanguard* published an interview in which Alan claimed jailers had separated all defendants into different cells, then "passed whiskey and dope among the other prisoners as a bribe to beat us up." Shortly thereafter flyers went out across campus announcing a "MASS DEFENSE RALLY" sponsored by the Student Council. "Hear a Victim's Account of Fascism in the U.S.A.," it read. At the rally, Alan told three hundred students that the Oklahoma cases showed how war hysteria had been created to justify a "widespread attack on the basic tenets of Democracy in America."[28]

Alan also spoke at an intermission of a January 12 performance of an off-Broadway play. Part of the performance's proceeds went to the ILD for the Oklahoma City defendants. To drum up additional support, the *Daily Worker* carried an announcement of the event and ran a picture of Alan Shaw and Nena Beth Stapp; *New Masses* told its readers "a flesh-and-blood political prisoner" would speak at the event. On January 13, Alan appeared at the Lenin Memorial meeting in Madison Square Garden to speak about violations of civil liberties he had experienced in recent months.[29]

On January 22, 1941, the ILD held a "mass defense rally" for the

Oklahoma defendants at the Manhattan Center. Nearly one thousand attended. Alan spoke briefly, and was joined by an impressive cadre of speakers representing groups that made manifest the increased attention the book trials were getting across the nation. Included among the speakers were Vito Marcantonio and mystery writer Dashiell Hammett. Also on the dais were the executive secretary of the American Peace Mobilization, the chairman of the American Labor Party, the secretary of the National Negro Congress, and representatives of the Church League for Industrial Democracy, the National Federation for Constitutional Liberties, and Brooklyn College. Defense attorney Samuel Neuberger also spoke.

After Alan Shaw described his experiences in Oklahoma City, others responded. The National Negro Congress secretary said, "I think I know why Alan Shaw and Robert Wood and the other defendants have been given the kind of treatment you have heard. They had the audacity to believe the Negro people were entitled to democracy. We of the Negro Congress will join with you in the fight to free these defendants." Vito Marcantonio spoke last. "We recognize full well that the two-bit district attorneys in Oklahoma are only seeking to emulate that which is being carried on by the FBI, the Dies Committee, and gentlemen who occupy seats of the mighty in the Department of Justice. Their kind of 'sovereign government' does not derive from the sovereignty of the people. It derives from the teachings and practice of Adolph Hitler — none other." By the end of the meeting the ILD had raised $462.35 for the Oklahoma defense.[30]

That same month the ACLU wrote an open letter to the president and Congress of the United States about the "attitude of our government towards the Communist Party." Among allegations they noted that in Oklahoma "two young men have been sentenced to ten years in prison and to $5,000 fines under a state law which forbids advocacy of the violent overthrow of the government, one without proof of anything except membership in the Communist Party, the other without proof of anything except possession of Communist literature." They then addressed a law pending in Congress that would deprive Communists of the right to work in defense industries. The writers argued that all of these laws "take away from Communists those constitutional guarantees which must be kept open for all if in the future they are to be available to any."[31]

Oklahoma's Governor Phillips had a different agenda. In early January 1941, he gave his blessing to a special "Americanism" committee of the legislature, from which several bills had recently been introduced that were designed to keep the Communist Party off the ballot. On January 15, the Oklahoma House of Representatives unanimously passed without floor debate a bill denying the Communist Party a place on any state ballot and forbidding anyone holding a position in the Communist Party or "indirectly affiliated" with an international organization from running for office in the Sooner State. The Senate passed a similar bill a day later.[32]

The Oklahoma Federation for Constitutional Rights reacted quickly. At a closed meeting of the council and executive committee on January 18, the Federation passed a resolution asking for a public hearing on the House bill. To many Oklahoma legislators, it looked very much like a gauntlet had been thrown before them. Several were eager to pick it up.[33] But before they could act, on January 23 several OU professors appeared uninvited at a meeting of the Senate Committee on Privileges and Elections to press for hearings on the bills.[34] Committee member Senator Paul Stewart, of Antlers, angrily told reporters, "That's enough for me. There is nothing in this bill but the outlawing of parties disloyal to the American form of government." He then announced he was also considering scheduling hearings to investigate Communist influence on state college campuses. The Federation, which later labeled Stewart "one of the most vicious labor-baiters in the state," had taken on one of Oklahoma's most powerful politicians.[35]

Into this mix entered the Ku Klux Klan, which for several weeks had been watching the situation develop from the periphery. Among other things, the Klan worried about the CPUSA's position on racial segregation, and especially its advocacy of African American civil rights. From its own offices in Oklahoma City, the Klan issued a flyer shortly after the Federation was formed. The flyer put all on notice that despite attacks against it, the Klan would continue to "insist that Communism, Fascism, Nazism and all other foreign isms be banished" from the United States. "When we tolerate the intolerance of those who would destroy our Government, then tolerance ceases to be a virtue and becomes treason. . . . Intimidation and threats of violence by subversive alien rats have not and will not stop the Ku Klux Klan in its American program."[36]

In late January 1941, the Klan published a pamphlet warning Oklahoma citizens against the Federation and reviewing the Federation's history by connecting a series of "facts." At the Federation's organizational meeting "KNOWN Communists" were in attendance; the "American dupes" who organized the Federation "were very abusive in their denunciation of Congressman Dies" when he visited Oklahoma City in December; one Federation organizer was chairman of the American Peace Mobilization Committee, and the Federation intended to cooperate with the American Civil Liberties Union — both known "Communist-front organizations"; and "Roscoe Dungee [sic] (Negro), editor of the Black Dispatch, is listed as a member of the 'Executive Committee.'" The Klan announced it would give its "hearty support" to the Senate Committee on Privileges and Elections in its efforts "to rid the state of ALL subversive individuals and organizations" and "weed out all subversive groups and individuals" from state institutions.[37]

Such events drew the attention of others around the country. "Civil rights must be jealously guarded in this period," declared a "Statement of [five] Principles" endorsed by prominent social workers and printed in the January 1941 issue of Social Work Today.[38] The St. Louis Post-Dispatch was even more proactive. Shortly after the first of the year it sent staff correspondent F. A. Behymer to do a story on the Federation. In its January 26 Sunday edition, the paper ran his story under the heading "Hunting Witch-Hunters the Aim of New Civil Rights Organization Fighting War Hysteria in Oklahoma." Behymer wrote: "[T]o check the rising tide of hysteria" that began in May when Hitler marched through Belgium and France, Oklahoma officials organized their home guards, Pentecostal preacher E. F. Webber held a public book burning, and County Assistant Attorney Eberle supervised the August 17 raid on the Progressive Book Store.

And "just now," Behymer concluded, "the Federation is locking horns with the witch-hunters" in the legislature.[39]

Oklahoma officials and their allies retaliated. Governor Phillips did not mince words. "This organization about constitutional rights is the height of folly," he said. "No one is denied constitutional rights in Oklahoma." At dedication ceremonies for new church facilities at Trinity Baptist Church on January 26, the chief minister enumerated his concerns about the Federation, which were automatically amplified to the rest of the city through his radio audience. "When churches are infested with Communists and fifth columnists, as we have some evidence of their being here in our own city, it's time to do something about it," he said. The *Daily Oklahoman* gave his remarks front-page coverage the day before the Senate committee scheduled hearings, at which Federation members were expected to testify. That same day, one rural county legislator introduced a resolution calling for an investigation of "red" activity at OU and Oklahoma A&M.[40] With all the hype, the hearings on the bills promised anyone involved a high-profile platform and generous press coverage.

Senator Joe B. Thompson of Ardmore called a hearing of the Senate Committee on Privileges and Elections to order on Tuesday morning, January 28, and although any senator could attend and ask questions, Thompson specifically named Paul Stewart, of Antlers, to sit with him. Stewart had made no secret of his desire to run for a seat in the U.S. Congress; his opponents suspected he would use the hearings to increase his popularity. Among those in the audience were Bob Wood, Eli Jaffe, several state legislators, an Elks Club representative, members of the American Legion, including its state commander, the Ku Klux Klan Grand Dragon, and numerous reporters. Eli Jaffe later wrote the *Daily Worker* that the room was filled with "suspected Silver Shirts" and "KKK."[41]

Senator Thompson began by reading the Senate bill and asserting that "[i]t is the intent of the legislature to pass good laws, necessary laws." But before opening the hearings to testimony, he also read a letter from a local labor union suggesting sarcastically that legislative members should recess a week and read the U.S. Constitution before deliberating. Thompson did not take kindly to the advice. He then polled everyone in the room, asked them to state their names and affiliations, and identify on which side they wished to be heard. Bob Wood said simply that he wished to oppose the bill.[42]

The American Legion representatives said their organization "feels the Communist Party is not entitled to any place on the ballot in any state. Neither do we feel that any member of the Communist Party, the bund, or any foreign subversive group should have the right to hold public office, either appointive or elective." The Elks Club representative also spoke in favor of the bill. One legislator said the bill did not go far enough; it should bar all Communists — whom he referred to as "rattlesnakes . . . from the soil of Oklahoma." As he pontificated at length, calls of "Amen" and "Pour it on" came from the rear of the room. "After three hours of spirited argument, and the threat of at least one fist fight," the *Norman Transcript* later reported, the committee quickly voted unanimously to recommend to the full Senate approval of the measures.[43]

Bob Wood and Eli Jaffe immediately stood and demanded to be heard. Bob said both wanted an opportunity to speak against the bills, but Stewart said he did not care to hear either of them, and the committee refused them the floor. Bob continued to press for an opportunity to speak because the "Communist Party was what was being carved," but the senators ignored him. As he exited the hearing room, however, Bob issued a statement to the press. "The outrageous undemocratic manner in which the senate committee conducted its 'hearing' this morning is final proof that the suppressive legislation they seek to foist on the citizens of our state is inimical and subversive," he said. "Every professional enemy of the organized workers and farmers was present," and the committee "gave these spokesmen of reaction all the time they needed for their un-American mouthings." Representatives of the "common people," however, "were not allowed to speak." The attacks were "a warning what these storm trooper mentalities have in store for the population in general."

When committee members heard about Bob's "grave charges," Thompson instructed the senate sergeant-at-arms to order Bob and

Eli to appear before the committee the next morning. After an executive committee meeting of the state Communist Party that night, however, Bob told the *Daily Oklahoman* he would defy the order. "If a regular hearing is called, we will be glad to go. But we won't attend an unfriendly hearing if we are isolated as the only group. . . . It wouldn't be an open hearing and the questioning wouldn't be impartial."[44]

The next day under the tag line "No Can Find Reds," the *Oklahoma Daily* ran a picture of the committee sitting behind a long table while the sergeant-at-arms reported he could not find Bob and Eli. Thompson later said Bob had sent him a telegram saying he or another member of the Communist Party would appear if a date were set for "an open hearing." Despite their absence, however, the committee pressed forward. More than a hundred people were present in the hearing room, including photographers, radio announcers, and numerous members of the American Legion. At the end of the session the committee decided to "educate the public about what is going on in the state" by expanding hearings to investigate radicals and radical sympathizers at Oklahoma's colleges and universities. In seeking subpoena power and an allocation of $100,000 for its investigations, Senator Stewart said, "I want this committee to have full authority to subpoena Robert Wood, Eli Jaffe and a lot of college professors I'd like to talk with. I think we can learn a lot." In a January 30 editorial, the *Oklahoma Daily* quoted an unnamed Oklahoma City church paper referring to a "thousand Communists at the University of Oklahoma."[45]

The local press quickly dubbed the expanded investigation a "little Dies Committee," and a number of senators seized the opportunity to make public statements. One senator wanted to "put those monkeys" behind prison walls. Another wanted to "hold them in concentration camps until a boat load is herded together and then ship them across the ocean to the countries they like." A third wanted "to put them all in a boat, and ship them half way across the ocean, letting them swim the other half." By the end of the day the committee had prepared a list of witnesses to subpoena — thirty-three college professors and all officers of the Oklahoma Federa-

tion for Constitutional Rights. It was obvious the Federation was a
target. Others subpoenaed included Nena Beth Stapp and bookstore defendants Bob and Ina Wood, Eli Jaffe, Alan Shaw, and Elizabeth Green.[46]

In an article published in the February 2 issue of the *Daily
Worker,* Eli Jaffe summarized what he saw. "The people" were fighting against three enemies, he said — the "lunatic fringe at the State
House" (who did not "know the difference between communism
and rheumatism" but were ready to launch "a tirade of red-baiting,
red-hunting and red-faced Senatorial elocution" with "the obvious
intent of blackjacking progressive voices"); Governor Phillips, a
"stooge for the oil and utility interests and the reactionary leadership of the American Legion;" and Paul Stewart, a "250 pound
Southern bourbon." "Plain folks" he listed included the Oklahoma
Federation for Constitutional Rights; the Oklahoma City Trades
Council of the AFL (whose secretary stated: "We have definite reasons to believe that the State Administration is determined to destroy the gains we have made through the struggles of many years");
the 22,000-member Farmers Union, which was pushing for a graduated land tax and cooperative hospital bill; and Sooner State African Americans, led in large part by Roscoe Dunjee, who decried the
"Buzzards of Every Age" ready to violate the constitutional rights
and civil liberties of all people.[47]

On February 4 the Little Dies committee commenced hearings.
Governor Phillips was the first to testify before a crowd so large the
hearings had to be moved to the Senate lounge. He lumbered into
the room and settled his 300-pound frame onto a strong chair.
"This is a very proper activity for the Senate," he began. "I pledge
my personal support and the support of my office to your investigation." He told the committee that for the past two years he had been
turning over to the FBI all the information on Communist activity
in Oklahoma that had come across his desk, including correspondence on behalf of the criminal syndicalism defendants.[48]

But hearings the next day drew most attention. Bob Wood was
scheduled to appear; his wife, Ina, accompanied him into what the
Daily Oklahoman called a "sparkling matinee in the senate cham-

ber." Once again the room was packed. After the sergeant-at-arms informed Chairman Thompson he could not find Eli Jaffe, Alan Shaw, Nena Beth Stapp, or Elizabeth Green to serve them subpoenas, Thompson called Bob to the stand. He told Bob he could not extend immunity and required him to take an oath to tell the truth. Bob agreed. Thompson then asked him where his friends were. Green and the Shaws were attending a meeting in Chicago, Bob said, but he was unsure about Eli, who might have been off on a speaking engagement. "More Oklahomans, you see, know about us since August 17, 1940, than we could possibly reach with all our literature." "I agree," replied Thompson, as he reached across the table to light Bob's cigarette. Bob promised to find Eli and bring him to the hearings the next day to help persuade senators that "hysterical voices are rising in our midst."[49]

"Given a chance and an audience," the *Oklahoman* reported, Wood then "unburdened himself with metaphors and allegory on the fraternal uplift of the Communist movement, its martyrdom in the fight against 'that rascal Hitler,' and some of its inner workings." In the process, he also "exchanged bantering repartee" with Thompson and Stewart. "As far as I know," he said, no Oklahoma professors were members of the Communist Party. He acknowledged that the Party had hosted an annual convention in Oklahoma City attended by Party members from thirty cities. "Thirty?" Thompson repeated, asking him to name the cities. Bob could only come up with twenty and admitted: "Maybe I exaggerated." He refused to divulge the names of members, however; knowledge of the membership rolls "is limited on purpose. We're not disloyal, and we're not stupid." He said that Communists are "against war, passionately," and although they recognized there were just wars, they did not believe in revolutions to put the Party in power. "Then it's just a matter of what side you're on?" Thompson asked, "No!" Bob replied sharply. "We're not on either side in this war. We're never on the side of imperialistic wars and we hope we never get into it."[50]

The *Daily Oklahoman* loved the drama. "Gesticulating, laughing, swiveling his chair occasionally as if he wished to address the audience, Wood warmed to his subject and spoke more rapidly when permitted to expand, so that the senate recorder had to ask him to repeat," the paper reported on page one. "The touch of pink at his cheekbones spread and he laughed, 'I guess I'm off on a fast track.'" Accompanying the story were three pictures of Bob under the tag line "Communist Secretary Lectures Senate." One clearly showed the scar on his head from Birmingham five years earlier. When asked why he did not bring local Communist Party records and books as the subpoena directed, he said they were currently in the hands of city and county officials who seized them on August 17. "Wood was an adroit and impassioned witness," the *Times* reported, "as he parried committee questions and sandwiched subtle justification of his party ideals and methods between careful revelations of party organization work."[51]

While Bob was "gesticulating," Mr. and Mrs. Alonzo Poling walked into the room; it was obvious Thompson was waiting for this couple, because he dismissed Bob immediately and called Alonzo — an eighty-five-year-old veteran of the Spanish American war — to the stand. At Thompson's invitation, Poling related the story of his son, who had returned wounded from the Spanish Civil War imbued with Communist ideology after fighting for the Loyalists. "He can think and talk of nothing but the party," Poling told the senators. The elder Poling also recounted how he burned the Communist literature he had discovered in his house while his son was recuperating there, and how he had traveled to the Progressive Book Store to tell Bob Wood to "quit sending that literature to my house."

As the *Daily Oklahoman* described the scene, Bob was seated opposite Poling and "looked as if he wanted to resume his impassioned speech on the brotherhood of man which the entrance of Mr. and Mrs. Poling had interrupted." The *Oklahoman* ran a picture of the Polings. She sat with a small purse and a hat adorned with prairie chicken feathers, he in a handmade suit coat that looked two sizes too big. After Poling finished his testimony, the committee recessed until the next day, but Bob was asked to return to the stand and bring Eli with him. That evening Bob told the *Oklahoma City Times* that Eli had phoned him to say he had just heard about the subpoena and would be in Oklahoma City the next day. "Of course, we both knew from the papers that subpenas [*sic*] had been issued for us, but we didn't know they would be returnable so soon."[52]

The hearings resumed at 9:30 A.M. on February 6, and Bob Wood again took the stand. More than two hundred people crowded into the Senate lounge. For two hours "Wood and Committee members exchanged barbed comments and observations to keep the audience laughing throughout the session," the *Norman Transcript* reported. All parties agreed that Hitler had to be stopped and the American form of government had to be preserved from a Fascist dictatorship, but differed on whether the United States ought to be socialized. Would he accept a position in private industry for fifty dollars a week? Stewart asked him. "In fact," Bob responded, "I'd be glad to run your newspaper for $20 if you would let me write the editorials." Bob also said he was registered for the draft and was prepared to "fight and die to prevent Hitler . . . from extending Fascism to this country. We believe that the working people of Germany and England should rise up and stop this war before others are slaughtered. Then the working people could establish a society to eliminate . . . men who live off the work of others." By the close of the hearing Stewart and his colleagues were calling him "Bob" and asking his opinion on how to stop Hitler.[53] The easy nature of the Little Dies Committee hearings suggests that the politicians considered Bob Wood and his fellow Oklahoma Communists much less dangerous than their public rhetoric indicated.

Thompson dismissed Bob and shortly thereafter surprised spectators by calling for an executive session. The *Daily Oklahoman* later discovered why. The paper reported that senators were "concerned about whether the committee . . . or the reds are getting the better of it in the red hearing." Some committee members thought Bob certainly bested the committee on publicity. And the *Oklahoman* reported, "Those thinking the senators would trip him up and make him admit he took his orders from Moscow were fooled, the senators agreed." Nonetheless, the committee scheduled another hearing for the following Tuesday, February 11.[54]

The circus atmosphere that characterized the hearings during the first week continued in the second. About a hundred people attended; many sported Legion buttons, but most seemed sympathetic to the OU faculty members who were being interrogated. All were asked about Communist connections or sympathies and membership in the Oklahoma Federation for Constitutional Rights. Senator Thompson, who admitted to no more than a third-grade education, asked one professor for copies of his publications to analyze them for potentially subversive ideas. Several involved integral calculus, but the legislator looked confused as he passed some to colleagues. "This stuff may be mathematics," Thompson said, "but it doesn't look like anything I ever studied." Eli Jaffe thought he overheard one legislator mutter that the publications might be "Communist code."[55]

Although *Black Dispatch* editor Roscoe Dunjee had not been subpoenaed, the committee questioned him anyway. Dunjee was asked about his membership in the Federation. "Can you tell this Committee anything about the Bill of Rights?" Dunjee could not resist. "I don't know whether I can tell you all that's in the Bill of Rights. I know, however, that as a Negro, I'm not getting my civil rights."[56] A number of spectators erupted in a volley of cheers, and Stewart halted the proceedings immediately and scanned the room. "What's your name?" he asked one of those who cheered. "I haven't been subpoenaed," said Duane Spradling, an OU student from Pauls Valley. "You just think you haven't," Stewart responded. "Sergeant-at-arms, subpoena this man as John Doe. Now tell me your name." Spradling was then marshaled out of the room with twenty-nine other people who had laughed (including two OU students and two OU alumni), and marched into an antechamber, where they were sworn in as witnesses and issued subpoenas to appear the next day.[57]

When religion professor Nick Comfort took the witness stand, he was asked for examples of civil rights violations. So "plain-spoken" was Comfort, one observer noted, "that the hearing became a comedy." Comfort easily listed several: the beating of an African American charged with murder in Hugo; the raid and arrest of a leftist speaker in Oklahoma City; the firing of Streeter Stuart; the excessive bail for criminal syndicalism defendants.[58] "Do you sympathize with Communist ideas?" interrupted Stewart. "No," Comfort responded,

Defense attorney Herman Rosenfeld greets C. A. and Hulda Lewis in the Court of Criminal Appeals, August 1942, in part of the effort to overturn the convictions of the Oklahoma Communist Party members. Nena Beth Stapp and Alan Shaw sit apprehensively in front of them. Shaw had been convicted on criminal syndicalism; Lewis was awaiting trial on similar charges, which were not pursued when the appeal was successful. Copyright 1942, The Oklahoma Publishing Company.

Bob Wood in jail in Oklahoma City, September 11, 1940. The state secretary of the Communist Party had been charged with criminal syndicalism and faced a maximum sentence of ten years and a $5,000 fine. Copyright 1940, The Oklahoma Publishing Company.

Nena Beth Stapp and Alan Shaw, as the latter is released from jail, November 1940. Photograph courtesy of Ms. Judith Wheeldon.

Bob Wood (center), released from jail in November 1940, is met by two of his three defense attorneys, Stanley Belden (left) and George Croom. Belden was approached to
defend Wood by the ACLU because he was fearless when acting on principle: Belden
had been a defiant conscientious objector in World War I and had worked for the
NAACP with attorney Thurgood Marshall on an Oklahoma civil rights case in which a
murder confession had been beaten out of an African American tenant farmer.
Belden had also represented Jehovah's Witnesses in the state. Croom had been
retained for Wood's defense team by the International Labor Defense (ILD), a New
York–based legal services agency controlled by the Communist Party. Photograph
courtesy of Mr. Timothy Wood.

Ina Wood shortly after her conviction and sentencing in June 1941. This "glamour shot" photo was printed in hundreds of newspapers across the nation. Photograph courtesy of Mr. Timothy Wood.

A still-defiant Eli Jaffe, December 1940, upon his release from jail. Courtesy of the Western History Collections, University of Oklahoma Libraries, Norman, Oklahoma.

The cover of a pamphlet, *Oklahoma Witch Hunt,* describing events of the arrest and trials of the defendants, that became one of many that circulated the country as part of the effort to raise funds for the defendants. As secretary of the Oklahoma Committee to Defend Political Prisoners, writer Gordon Friessen had attended the trials of the four defendants. Largely to keep his hands busy—and his mouth shut—he drafted the pamphlet and its illustrations during court proceedings. Courtesy of the Cunningham/Friessen estate.

"probably not half as much as you do, senator." What about the display of red flags? "It depends on what the flags mean," Comfort said. "I was out in western Oklahoma the other day and saw hundreds of red flags waving in the fields and I was about to call Governor Phillips' attention to it when I discovered they were surveyors' flags." The crowd laughed, but Stewart demanded a straight answer "without the comedy." Comfort said he had no objection to the display of red flags. How about foreign influence on the United States? Stewart asked. "I don't want any foreign influence in this country. . . . Let's make up our own minds," Comfort responded.

The Rev. Wright also testified. Asked to define a Communist, Wright offered a definition he once gave to a high-school student. "He is one who believes in dialectical materialism." "Dia-what?" the court stenographer interrupted. "You mean that's the definition you gave that high school girl?" Stewart asked. "Yes, and what's more, she was intelligent enough to understand it." The "crowd roared" as Thompson rapped for order, the *Daily Oklahoman* later reported.[59]

That afternoon, Eli Jaffe took the stand (the *Tulsa World* described him as a "willing witness"). Was he editor of a recently commenced publication titled *New Appeal to Reason?* Yes. Did he have a copy of the mailing list used by the Oklahoma chapter of the Communist Party? No. To distribute his paper, Eli replied, he used the mailing list of the Oklahoma Committee to Defend Political Prisoners, which, he claimed (rather disingenuously) had no connection to the Communist Party. "Do you think the Communist system could be established under our constitution without doing away with it entirely?" "Yes sir," Eli replied. "We Communists are striving for the common welfare."[60]

Stewart questioned him about activities in the Oklahoma Youth Legislature, and Eli reported he had also been a Boy Scout. "I still carry an eagle badge with me now." As he reached into his coat pocket, however, Stewart cut him off. He noted that Eli was a Jew, but were his parents "Russian or German Jews?" No, he responded, "I believe my parents were Lithuanians." "Lithu-what?" Stewart asked as he leaned over. "What's that?" After briefly hesitating, Eli responded: "Lithuanians, from Lithuania — that's one of the countries in Europe." Stewart then laughed as Eli continued. "It's one of the countries that voted to join the Soviet Union." At this another senator erupted in laughter. "Voted to join! I suppose Finland voted to join, too?" "Some parts of it did," Eli responded, revealing a loyalty to the Communist Party line that defied historical reality. He ended his testimony by responding to questions that showed he did no manual labor, supported himself by writing short stories and plays, and survived on a small inheritance from his father. Eli was then excused.[61]

Clyde and Irene Richardson, expelled in 1939 as members of the Oklahoma chapter of the Communist Party, were then called to the stand. Clyde went first. In a "thin and tired voice" that often caused Thompson and Stewart to tell him to "speak up," he was hardly a forceful witness. Was a program of force and violence ever taught by Bob and Eli at Party meetings? Stewart asked. "No," Clyde replied. "You don't hear it from them." "Didn't the Communists finally move in and take over" the Workers Alliance? Stewart asked. "Well, I couldn't say," Clyde responded. "When it became known the Communists were active in the organization, a lot of people scatted out." Why were you ejected from the Party? Stewart asked. "Inactivity and failure to carry out duties," Clyde responded. Irene was more forceful. She was ejected from the Party at a "persecution trial," she said, because Communists "tried to tell us how to do things" in the Alliance "and we wouldn't take dictation." She refused to sell pamphlets or attend meetings regularly. They did talk about overthrowing the government when the "day" came, she recalled, but "they never did discuss anything that was downright unlawful." Were Wood and Jaffe dangerous? "Yes," Irene said, "because I'm afraid they might do bodily harm to me or my children."

Although Stewart and Thompson kept pressing for names, the Richardsons were unable to supply any not already known. With the conclusion of their testimony, hearings ended for the day. If committee members expected testimony from the Richardsons to reveal how Communists huddled in cellars while plotting revolution, the *Daily Oklahoman* reported, they were gravely disappointed. Instead, "their testimony on inner party workings indicated that the local chapter is beset by the same troubles as many women's clubs, the big shots heckling lax members for not selling enough pamphlets or rounding up customers for their meetings."[62] Committee members seemed desperate to come up with something damaging to someone.

When the hearings resumed the next morning, KKK Grand Dragon J. R. Reed sat in the audience, took notes, and passed out a recent Klan pamphlet. "Excited members of the 'Little Dies Committee,'" observer Roscoe Dunjee later reported in the *Black Dispatch* (in which he also reprinted the entire pamphlet), "afraid that such close relationship with the night shirt brigade might hurt them," issued an order to building employees: "Scoop 'em up and spade 'em in." Senators wanted to make sure, Dunjee said, that copies of the pamphlet "were hard to find." Reed told reporters that the Klan had forty-four chapters in Oklahoma and a state membership of 40,000, some of whom were on the OU faculty. "They make reports on other faculty members who have radical tendencies," he said. "We have the dope." He applauded the efforts of the Senate Committee on Privileges and Elections to undermine the Oklahoma Federation for Constitutional Rights and also indicated that all information his members were generating on subversive activities in Oklahoma was being turned over to the FBI.[63]

While the Little Dies committee hearings were drawing most press attention, prosecutors and defense lawyers in the criminal syndicalism trials were engaging in battles that most newspapers overlooked. Prosecutor Eberle had wanted to begin the remaining trials January 13, but defense lawyers managed to get them postponed to February 17. The ILD learned that the cases were generating so much interest that "a special class for 25 lawyers" was "meeting weekly" in New York, "in which experts in their respective fields in labor law are studying criminal syndicalism and related cases together."[64] In a February 1 press release, the ILD appealed for more funds and circulated a message crafted by defendants Alan Shaw, Elizabeth Green, and Ina Wood "expressing our deep appreciation to the hundreds of New Yorkers who gave us such splendid cooperation and support during our stay in this city. We are now going back to face new trials." While in New York, the three defendants attended many small meetings and "raised a considerable sum of money for the Oklahoma Committee to Defend Political Prisoners." In early February, defense lawyers managed to get the trials postponed to April 22, and although Ina and Elizabeth returned to Oklahoma, Alan Shaw remained in New York to secure additional support by visiting local trade unions. At its February 14 meeting, the ILD National Board laughed at the comic nature of the Oklahoma "Baby Dies" committee hearings, which had by this time concluded inconclusively, but had nonetheless helped to draw considerable attention to other attempts to outlaw the Communist Party across the nation.[65]

On March 7 the ILD National Board planned a refined strategy for a national campaign. With Bob Wood and Alan Shaw present, members decided to organize West Coast and Midwest tours for them and two other defendants, Ina Wood and Eli Jaffe, to raise interest and money. Members also decided to encourage interested parties to write the county attorney directly, demanding that he postpone further trials until the appellate court had an opportunity to rule on Bob Wood's appeal. They decided to make the content of the appeal "a central point" in the forthcoming national conference so all representatives might learn about the potential for criminal syndicalism legislation in other states. But they also had some concerns about the Criminal Court of Appeals, and one judge in particular. In March, one of the defendants' attorneys worried about Judge Thomas Doyle, "a very ardent Catholic" like his "protégé," John Eberle. The defense even gave some consideration to taking the unusual step of attempting to get Doyle disqualified.[66]

Between their appearances before the Little Dies Committee and the beginning of Eli's trial in April, most of the defendants returned to New York. On March 28, Eli was interviewed by the *Brooklyn College Vanguard*. Seated in the *Vanguard* office "with his legs folded under him, Buddha-fashion" and with an "amiable, boyish grin" that faded when "his eyes grow sober," Eli recounted his imprisonment. "It isn't the kind of pleasant experience one likes to talk about," he said. "Excluding flogging, the authorities made the jailhouse a concentration camp—withholding letters, heckling visitors, making it difficult for legal counsel to consult with us, and provoking physical violence against us by getting the other prisoners drunk."[67]

That same month the National Federation for Constitutional Liberties issued a pamphlet titled "Investigating Committees and Civil Rights." Because so many legislative bodies "operate under vague grants of power, exceed the scope of any proper investigation, and disregard the established principles which protect the rights of individuals and organizations called before them," the pamphlet said (it specifically mentioned the federal Dies Committee and similar legislative investigating committees in California, New York, and Oklahoma), "they warrant public condemnation and determined resistance against their invasion of individual and private rights." The pamphlet then enumerated a number of problems characterizing these committees that mirrored what happened in Oklahoma in previous weeks. "Such committees are easily identified by their lack of discrimination and care in proceedings; by their public use of rumor and hearsay; by their appeals to prejudice; by their indiscriminate use of newspapers and other publicity to carry on 'smear' campaigns." They also "abuse witnesses," show little concern for "disclosing *actual existing facts*," "scatter unsupported charges to the winds, using press and radio to broadcast unsupported sensational accusations," have "little regard" for Constitutional rights, and offer witnesses little or no opportunity for defense. They act, the pamphlet concluded, "as extraordinary courts where hearsay, rumor, and prejudice run riot; where accused persons have no rights, and from which there is no appeal."[68]

On April 20, 1941, Edwin S. Smith, the head of the National Labor Relations Board, addressed a mass meeting of the National Action Conference for Civil Rights in the District of Columbia cosponsored by the National Federation for Constitutional Liberties and the Washington Committee for Democratic Action. Speaking on "Civil Liberties in the Present Crisis," he decried what he called "mounting violations" across the nation in recent months, which he traced to a war hysteria. "The public can be, and is, easily misled by appeals to popular prejudice which seek to rally laudable and patriotic feelings behind a drive against civil liberties on the ground that the proponents of such attacks are themselves defending democracy and civil liberties." He called for renewed efforts to resist these violations wherever they occurred.[69]

Many chose not to act, however, including lawyers in Oklahoma and around the country. As early as November 1940 the ACLU had asked defense attorney Stanley Belden if "any other lawyer of standing" in Oklahoma might be willing to sign an amicus brief for Bob Wood and Alan Shaw. None would. In December the ACLU contacted the American Bar Association (ABA) and asked whether its Committee on the Bill of Rights might file an amicus brief. Although the ABA declined ("it is not the policy of this Committee generally to appear in a case until the case reaches the United States Supreme Court"), it contacted the Oklahoma State Bar Association to suggest it "look into" the situation. A few months later Belden reported he had spoken with the state bar Civil Liberties Committee chair, whose "personal opinion" was "that a communist could not get a fair trial in Oklahoma." The chair agreed to call a meeting if Belden wanted him to, but at the same time expressed an opinion that "we should be willing to give up some of our Constitutional rights in time of stress." In early April, Belden requested a meeting with members of the Committee to present the facts of the case and seek their support. In June the committee chair advised him that although a meeting had been called, the quorum necessary to hear him ("five members scattered over the State") was "not able to attend." For the entire three years the cases were pending, no Oklahoma attorney could be found willing to sign an amicus brief.[70]

By April, Bob and Ina Wood were winding their way back from New York to Oklahoma City for Ina's and Eli Jaffe's trials. On April 24 they stopped in Kansas City, where Bob was scheduled to give a speech. He had sandwiched this engagement between a lecture in Omaha on the 23rd and St. Louis on the 26th. As usual, he was carrying with him boxes of shoes and clothing donated by friends in New York for poor people in Oklahoma. Because they had very little themselves, the defendants often picked through the boxes to find clothes and shoes they could wear for their court and other public appearances. The sponsor for the Kansas City speech was a local group called the Human Rights Club, which had arranged for five dollars to rent a clubroom at the Athenaeum, site of a prominent but conservative Kansas City women's club. When Human Rights Club officials submitted their deposit the previous week, they did not inform members of the Athenaeum that Bob was a Communist.

On the night of April 18, someone raided Club headquarters. Because only membership lists and records (but no funds) were taken, club officials suspected Chief of Police L. B. Reed. Then, the morning Bob was scheduled to speak, the *Kansas City Times* carried a story that Athenaeum officials had only recently learned he was a Communist. It came "like thunder out of a clear sky," said one Athenaeum member. She wanted the people of Kansas City to know "we are not sponsoring this meeting," but there was little the Athenaeum could do to stop it. Hours after the *Times* edition appeared, Chief Reed and several policemen approached Bob and Ina Wood while they were eating lunch in their hotel coffee shop. "I have cancelled your engagement tonight," Reed told them. "I am going to accept full responsibility for doing it. I am going to relieve the good women of the Athenaeum from having to deal with you." He then took them into custody, searched their hotel room without a warrant, confiscated a "private file and Communist Party literature" (he did not confiscate the shoes and clothing they were transporting), and questioned them for five hours, advising them that he hated Communism "worse than . . . rattlesnakes."

During the interrogation Bob Wood admitted to being a Communist and indicated he was giving this round of speeches to raise money for the defense of criminal syndicalism defendants in Oklahoma. When asked if she was a Communist, Ina refused to answer. "I prefer to be tried only once," she responded, "and in Oklahoma." To that Reed responded: "We're going to photograph you, fingerprint you, and then run you out of town." He then placed Bob and Ina in a patrol car, had his detectives take them to the train station, forced them to buy one-way tickets to Oklahoma City with their own money, and made sure they got on the train. He ordered two of his officers to get on the train as well, "but not to sit with Wood, not to touch him, and that when Wood and his wife got on the train they were not to be in police custody." He simply wanted to be sure they "rode out of Kansas City and did not get off the train within the city limits." He also telephoned Oklahoma City police to meet the train at 12:30 A.M., "and keep them down there. We have no room for them in Kansas City." At Oklahoma City, local newspapers had photographers ready to take their picture as Bob and Ina stepped off the train. That same day, officers arrested four members of the Kansas City Human Rights Club on charges of vagrancy. The charges were dismissed the next day for lack of evidence.[71]

In the immediate wake of these events, the Oklahoma Committee to Defend Political Prisoners (which by this time had become the intermediary through which the ILD was funneling funds for the defendants' living expenses) protested to the U.S. attorney general that the actions of Kansas City Chief of Police Reed were illegal and constituted an act of kidnapping people and transporting them across state line. "The refusal to end the dangerous anti-democratic trend in Oklahoma was a direct invitation to Chief Reed," the committee said. "If undisturbed, this tragic reversion to force and violence in dealing with our citizens . . . cannot but lead to even more rapid and progressive deterioration of all cherished American ideals."[72]

Although the *Kansas City Star* acknowledged the need "to guard against subversive elements," a next-day editorial suggested that Chief Reed overreacted. "The constitutional right of free assembly and free speech still exists," the *Star* said. "Even under stress we should keep our heads. This is still America." The *Kansas City Journal* was even more critical. In an editorial titled "Stalin and Chief Reed," the *Journal* excoriated Reed for handing Wood an opportunity to make headlines across the nation, "precisely what the Communist leaders want the police to do." Two days later the *Journal* continued to worry about Reed's "low esteem for the Bill of Rights."[73]

On April 29 Oklahoma Criminal Court of Appeals Judge Bert Barefoot gave Bob Wood permission to leave the state for medical attention, but forbade him "to make speeches outside this state with reference to the trial of his case." Because defense counsel did not want to alienate Barefoot while he had Bob's appeal under consideration, his order effectively squelched plans the ILD had to enlist him in fund-raising tours across the nation.[74] By that time, however, all parties connected to the litigation were bracing for the next set of trials.

In March 1941, *National Geographic* published an article titled "So Oklahoma Grew Up." In it the *Geographic* painted a positive picture showing Oklahoma as a state that had made much progress since pioneer days. Many photos accompanied it, including pictures of oil derricks around the capitol, local festivals (some Native American), government buildings, attractive women in Western regalia, rodeo competitions, and cattle ranching. The periodical ran no pictures of — and did not discuss — the Sooner State's Hoovervilles (two of which were a short distance from the capitol building), its segregated public facilities, its underfed people represented by tens of thousands of unemployed, or the blighted land in the western part of the state. Instead *National Geographic* saw only sunshine and health.[75] Because Oklahoma did not often get favorable treatment from "eastern writers," the *Norman Transcript* noted in a February 25 editorial, "We can be thankful" the *National Geographic* "on this occasion also reported many favorable things about the state."[76]

The *National Geographic*'s article contrasted starkly with a statement about the trials issued in mid-April by Theodore Dreiser, author of the critically acclaimed best seller, *An American Tragedy* (1925). "The whole of this crusade is not only to put down the rights of the American people to express their protest to established national policy," he said, "but to shut them up as well and not allow them to have anything to say in the affairs of their government or their own physical welfare. Of course these specific cases should be taken to the Supreme Court, where they will promptly be reversed. At least there are a few Americans yet on the Supreme Bench."[77]

CHAPTER FIVE

Eli and Ina on Trial,
April–August 1941

I n early April 1941 the International Labor Defense issued a single-page trifold. Titled "Defending Democracy in Oklahoma — 240 Years in Prison, for What?" the flyer explained the ILD's active involvement in the Oklahoma City bookstore cases. Criminal syndicalism laws, it noted, hung "as a constant threat over the heads of labor and all progressives in many states, particularly over trade unionists who have been the majority of the victims." Because in Oklahoma the AFL was already being threatened with criminal syndicalism prosecutions, the ILD said, "Oklahoma is where it must be halted." The trifold suggested a series of actions: send money; pass "this story of Oklahoma on to your friends"; get "your organization to take necessary protest action," and contact Oklahoma County Attorney Lewis Morris.[1]

I

On April 23, Eli Jaffe's trial began in the district court of Judge Lucius Babcock. Eli was represented by local attorneys George Croom and Stanley Belden, and ILD attorney Samuel Neuberger,

149

whom Eli thought "self-confident and articulate with a flair for the dramatic." But not everyone liked Neuberger. During one recess a man approached him in a public restroom and said: "You Jew bastard—you oughta get your goddamn head stomped in!" When he returned to the courtroom, Neuberger told the judge he "had just been threatened with physical violence." The judge made no comment, and took no action.[2]

During two days of voir dire Croom asked each prospective juror if he had anti-Communist prejudices or if he belonged to the local Civil Guard or Emergency Defense Battalion. "Great difficulty was experienced in obtaining a jury," the *Oklahoma City Times* explained, "man after man being excused because he was prejudiced against Communists." The *Daily Oklahoman* saw the same situation. "Examination of the jurors constituted a virtual parade of anti-Communist prejudice. One prospective juror said he was so bitterly opposed to Communists he would convict Jaffe even if the evidence showed he was not guilty." When the twelve-member jury was finally selected, five admitted to being members of the Oklahoma County Civil Guard. Little wonder Eli wrote in his notebook that day: "The wheels of capitalist justice start to grind. The impartial jury of my peers is picked. The county attorney reads his incomprehensible charge with all its legal mumbo-jumbo—and equal justice is under way." Court recessed at 5:30 P.M. on April 24, but the judge agreed to a defense request to keep the jurors together in a hotel during nontrial hours.[3]

In his opening statement the next day, Prosecutor Eberle signaled his intention to use the same strategy against Eli he had used against Alan. Communists "get the people fighting over peace or war, and try to create a civil war," he began. The Oklahoma State Communist Party "is part of the national party and that's part of the Comintern, and these people take their orders from Joe Stalin in Moscow." Croom objected; what went on in other countries should not have an impact on Eli's case. The judge overruled him. Eberle then said he was prepared to introduce quantities of printed materials to prove his case. Just like Christianity was taught from the Bible, Eberle argued, "these books are the Communist bible."

Again the defense objected. No evidence existed to prove materials seized at the Progressive Book Store had been approved by the Communist Party as representing its program. For the moment, Judge Babcock appeared to agree. "The question is whether you are properly proving they are the Communists' bible," he told Eberle. Shortly thereafter, however, he ruled the materials admissible.[4]

Eberle quickly seized the opportunity and began to carbon copy the case he ran against Alan Shaw. With Eli, however, he had a trump card. Eli had admitted to being a Communist during his initial interrogation in August. Because defense attorneys were convinced that their best chance at success rested with the Wood and Shaw appeals, because they decided they could not win a case with the jury before them, and because prolonging the proceedings would only end up costing more money, they decided not to press their case. Despite Eli's wishes, they chose not to put him on the stand. "I was angry and frustrated because I did not have the opportunity to take the stand and call Eberle the kind of liar I knew he was." As in previous cases, defense lawyers decided that "inasmuch as the prosecution had not proved that I had ever committed or advocated any overt act of violence, taking the stand in my own defense would not be advantageous."[5]

On Monday morning, April 29, after both sides rested, Eberle began his closing remarks. For the next six hours he read excerpts from scores of books and pamphlets to show how the materials advocated the use of force to overthrow governments and effect political and industrial change. At one point he looked up from his reading to address the jurors: "You notice that they always refer to themselves as 'the workers.' . . . But there ain't none of them workers," he said, pointing to Eli. "This boy got out of Brooklyn College and went to work organizing the workers. They've got automobiles and they eat three times a day." He also flashed Eli's driver's license before the jury and pointed out it carried only a first and a last name. "The funny thing about these fellows is that they don't have a middle name. That's funny! You are supposed to give everybody a middle name. I don't know why they don't have one. That may mean something and it may not."[6]

Next Eberle read from a pamphlet titled "The Communist Position on the Negro Question," which, he said, outlined a program for establishing a "Black Belt Republic" across the South independent of the U.S. government. "All the land would be confiscated for the use of Negroes and, among other things, the intermarriage of Negroes and whites would be permitted." While talking, he flashed the picture of Eli at the 1939 youth conference showing white and African American delegates posing on the steps of the Shrine Auditorium. "There is a nigger in the bushes there, something underneath." As for religion in this new "republic," Eberle said, "the party does not subscribe to belief in any god." Some American Communists even talked about defending themselves "with force of arms as our fathers did" during the American Revolution. "I don't know where these Communists' fathers were in 1776," Eberle commented, but then he pointed to Detective John Wade Webb, who was seated in the courtroom in a regular army uniform with medals bedecked across his chest. There was a perfect example of an American who emulated the ideals of the nation's forefathers, Eberle said.[7] The gesture was obviously staged. In his final statement the next day, he charged that Eli was a "criminal," a dangerous "man without a middle name" who represented "a plot against our flag and country. I congratulate the twelve men who have tried this case impartially and fairly and am proud we live in a country where justice can prevail."

After Eberle ended in early afternoon, defense attorney Sam Neuberger asked the jury to decide the case based solely on the facts and not on prejudice or emotion. "Considering the sentiment of the times," he said, "it will take courage to come out with a verdict of not guilty. . . . You cannot convict a man for what he thinks. . . . There is not one scrap of evidence to show that Eli Jaffe advocated violence, sabotage and revolution." County Attorney Lewis Morris then offered a "vigorous closing argument," calling for the maximum sentence. "Serve notice on the world with a verdict," he told the jury, "that says you can't come down here and use the constitution and the guarantee of free speech and press as a camouflage to cover up a nefarious revolutionary party to destroy the constitution and bring about violence and suffering."[8]

At 6:30 P.M., April 29, jurors entered the jury room to begin deliberations. Box loads of books and pamphlets went in with them. When the jury requested permission to retire for the evening without reaching a verdict five hours later, some courtroom observers surmised they probably did not have time to read much of the evidentiary material. Others speculated it was deadlocked. The Wood jury had taken only ninety minutes to convict, the *Daily Oklahoman* noticed, the Shaw jury two hours.[9]

The next morning, after deliberating an additional fifteen minutes, the jury pronounced Eli guilty and recommended the maximum sentence of ten years and a $5,000 fine. The *Daily Oklahoman* reported that some jurors said "there was not disagreement on guilt but several ballots on the degree of the sentence, some feeling at first the maximum was too much for Jaffe." Outside the courtroom Eberle announced that Ina Wood would go on trial June 2. Eli told reporters, "This verdict is a danger signal. Let all who believe in the right of the people to think as they wish take warning from it."[10]

By now, increasing numbers of people across the nation were watching the trials. The *New York Times,* the *Christian Science Monitor,* and the *New York City Post* ran short stories on Eli's conviction. Many people wrote letters to the Oklahoma Committee to Defend Political Prisoners that were reprinted in its newsletter. "Frankly," one Oklahoman attending Harvard Law School wrote, "I am personally resentful of the fact that people whom I meet here label me as being from 'the state where those funny trials are going on.' " The ACLU cabled: "The Oklahoma cases are rapidly becoming a national issue." A farmer from Hitchcock, Oklahoma, said: "I hope you folks will succeed. Enclosed $5.00." A VFW member from Coalgate, Oklahoma, wrote: "Very sorry I can't give anything to the cause. I am unemployed, have a family of 4 to support and not a chance. If there is anything else I can do for the cause of freedom let me know."[11]

Prosecutors responded. "By attempting to influence the decision of the criminal court of appeals you can see how much confidence these revolutionists have in the American system," Lewis Morris told a reporter from the *Oklahoma City Times*. "I have received a few letters from Brooklyn, but for every letter trying to stop these prosecutions I am getting ten letters from red-blooded Americans who applaud getting rid of these fifth columnists." Eberle took a different tack. "I have already looked up some law on this question," he said. "It is entirely possible that we will ask the court to issue contempt citations" against parties who write letters to appellate court officials.[12]

Between the end of Eli's trial and the beginning of Ina's, the spotlight shifted back to the University of Oklahoma. On May 7 the Little Dies Committee issued a report that the Communist Party had 1,000 members in Oklahoma, was well financed, and functioned as "a propaganda agency for the Soviet Union of Russia."[13] It recommended passage of pending legislation to abolish the Communist Party in the state, and in the event of a national emergency, to put known and suspected Communists in a detention camp "as they are truly part of the fifth column within this nation." In garbled terms it also made clear its patriotic and Christian fervor: "The time may come in the near future when this nation may be offered only 'blood, sweat and tears,' " the report read. "Therefore, let us all help to hoist high the stars and stripes and to it once again, renew our pledge of loyalty. . . . For the consecration of mankind to the cause of Christianity Jesus Christ the Savior allowed his blood to bathe the cross . . . when the young men of America unselfishly and patriotically, stand ready to bathe a million crosses in their blood, to say the least our citizenship can relieve them from the pain and burden of carrying the cross to Calvary." The report also acknowledged the American Legion for "unwavering patriotism." The State Senate adopted the report with a unanimous vote the next day.[14]

Adoption of the Senate report came on the heels of efforts to pass laws in the Oklahoma Legislature to deny recognition to any political party whose purposes included the violent overthrow of the government and to forbid members of the Communist Party from holding any elective or appointed public office. Bills creating such laws passed the legislature by huge majorities on May 8; both were forwarded to the governor.[15]

The Senate Report, along with Eli's conviction, further energized those who sought to bring public pressure to bear on Oklahoma officials and signaled a turning point in the trials. Hereafter reaction from across the nation appeared to put Oklahoma officials on the defensive, and its threats seemed less intimidating as the story of the book trials circulated the country. In fact, befriending the Oklahoma defendants came to symbolize a principled stand for basic freedoms and the Bill of Rights. For example, when Ina Wood was invited to address gatherings in St. Louis after Judge Barefoot prevented Bob from doing so, the *St. Louis Star Times* wanted its readers to know in advance of her arrival that "this country is a democracy, and in this city the constitutional guarantees of free speech, free press and free assembly are respected . . . and cherished." And although the *St. Louis Post-Dispatch* said Kansas City "identified itself as a place where the fundamental civil rights of free speech and free assembly are blacked out," the *Kansas City Star* ran a story titled "Oklahoma Hears Some Back Talk," and the *Kansas City Journal* editorialized: "This thing called Americanism is in a perilous state when its defense is in the hands of men like Chief Reed." The Oklahoma Committee to Defend Political Prisoners, which reprinted these editorials in its May 20 *Newsletter,* referred them all "to the attention of the County Attorney's office." But Eberle's response was predictable; he tried intimidation. In early May, he charged that the letters and wires he received constituted "contempt of court."[16] Insulated in the cocoonlike culture of Oklahoma officialdom, he and his colleagues could not see that sentiment was shifting against them. They were too committed to a particular course of action, too sure of their cause.

ILD attorney Sam Neuberger also sensed a shift. In his report to the National Board on May 9, he stated that "the local atmosphere was much more sympathetic to the defendants" than during the previous trials and urged a continuing public campaign. He announced that the ACLU, the National Federation for Constitutional

Liberties, and the National Lawyers Guild were preparing amicus briefs and that scores of other organizations would be discussing resolutions in future weeks to protest the trials. Although the ILD had hoped to send the defendants out on speaking tours in order to raise awareness of the cases and defense funds, those plans suffered a setback when Oklahoma authorities threatened to revoke bail for any convicted defendants who left the state to make speeches. The Board temporarily cancelled the tours.[17] Students at the University of Chicago protested when they learned that Bob Wood could not come to address a May 8 gathering. "Criminal syndicalism laws . . . constitute a major threat to civil liberties," one student told the University newspaper, which noted in an editorial that the Oklahoma courts were "[e]vidently fearful that Wood's speaking engagements were not good advertising for their state."[18]

On May 22, Eli Jaffe was back in court for formal sentencing. Before he pronounced sentence, however, Judge Babcock asked: "Have you any reasons why that should not be done now?" Like Alan Shaw, Eli had an answer at the ready. "Yes, sir," he began. "This sentence that you are about to pass is not a sentence against the individual, Eli Jaffe. Rather, it is a sentence against American democracy itself." He argued that he was tried under a war hysteria manipulated by "a fanatically-minded assistant county attorney and the politically-ambitious county attorney." Over the years he had tried to help the unemployed in Oklahoma by getting them food, shelter, and clothing, to champion the rights of working people to join unions and organize themselves, to help "dead end" young adults get out of poverty, and to resist a movement toward a war supported by the rich and powerful that would be fought by the poor and powerless. For each of these efforts, he asked: "Is that a crime?" "I challenge John Eberle to tell me exactly when and where I actually advocated or committed acts of force and violence. . . . Both history and the American people," Eli concluded, "will render a far different judgment than was rendered by a jury inflamed by the prejudice and irrational words of the assistant county attorney." After Eli finished, Babcock pronounced sentence: ten years in the penitentiary and a fine of $5,000. Babcock also increased Eli's appeal bond from $5,000 to $10,000, and sent him back to jail. He released Eli the following day, but gave him only ten days to raise the remaining $5,000 or he would be sent to prison June 5.[19]

On a sunny afternoon several days later, Eli was driving Wilma Lewis home in his old Plymouth. When it suddenly hit him that he might be in prison in five days if the ILD could not raise the additional $5,000, he broke into a cold sweat. He turned to the high-school junior seated next to him, the person who had been among his few visitors in the county jail between August and December, and who for the past year had frequently placed herself in danger by publicly working with and outspokenly defending him, and asked: "Wilma, if I have to go to the penitentiary for ten years, will you wait for me?" Wilma started to cry, but still managed to blurt out "Yes." Fortunately for both, the ILD posted Eli's bond the next day. Eberle quickly reminded the *Oklahoma City Times* that the ILD was "an organization directly responsible to Communist authorities in Moscow."[20]

By that time defense lawyers were preparing for Ina's trial, scheduled to begin June 2. On May 30, however, events took another curious twist. Early that morning defense attorney George Croom was driving from Tulsa to Oklahoma City in the blue four-door Plymouth Woody Guthrie gave Bob Wood that was so well known to Oklahoma officials and the FBI ("Oklahoma license 71-141," Bureau records noted). When he stopped at the home of an African American client just outside Bristow, an Oklahoma State Police trooper pulled up and asked him what he was doing "talking to a Negro." Croom sensed this was not a spontaneous encounter. He "had business" with the man, he replied, then permitted the trooper to search the Plymouth. There the trooper found "several types of literature belonging to Wood" and Croom's criminal syndicalism case files for Ina Wood's upcoming trial.

Because Croom could not show he owned the car, the trooper said he would have to take him to the Bristow jail. On the way into town, however, Croom overhead him radio ahead: "I have the prisoner." Croom remained in the Bristow jail for half a day, then was transported to the Oklahoma County jail seventy miles away. To arresting officers Croom repeatedly identified himself as a defense lawyer in the Oklahoma criminal syndicalism trials, and repeatedly asked why he was being arrested. And repeatedly he was told, so the FBI could examine him. He spent the night in jail and for the twenty hours he was in custody was allowed no visitors. The next afternoon state officials and representatives of the FBI told him that they had confiscated and searched the materials seized in his car, but they refused to identify any charges on which he was being held. Croom was released shortly after the FBI interview.[21]

By that time the local press was on the story. "Croom in Jail under Mysterious Circumstances," the *Oklahoma City Times* reported. "Officials Are Mum," said the *Daily Oklahoman*. Reporters interviewed the FBI agent, who said that he had concluded the Bureau had no jurisdiction in the case. The papers also summarized a statement by Croom that Ina Wood released through the Oklahoma Committee to Defend Political Prisoners, in which Croom accused Eberle of orchestrating the arrest and detention to "mess through my personal files."[22] Word of this treatment drew editorial condemnation on the East Coast and in the Midwest. "Left unchallenged, and the officials of the state and the FBI men unpunished, it would not take long for an American Gestapo to develop," the Duluth, Minnesota, *Herald* said. The Calumet, Michigan, *News Journal* agreed. "The old 'third degree' was bad enough, but this sort of thing would leave few people safe from spite or plain viciousness." *The New Republic* reported that the ACLU had asked Governor Phillips and the U.S. attorney general to investigate the situation.[23]

On June 11, the ACLU contacted the American Bar Association's Bill of Rights Committee regarding Croom's arrest. Again the ABA referred the matter to the Oklahoma Bill of Rights Committee. The Committee's secretary later reported that he had spoken with Croom, who told him he was stopped because of defective lights, that the trooper was simply overzealous, and that the matter had been "settled." The committee secretary concluded that "the prosecution of the criminal syndicalism cases had nothing whatever to do with" Croom's arrest.[24] Consequently, neither the ABA nor the Oklahoma State Bar Association took action.

At a pretrial meeting for Ina Wood on May 31, Croom asked that the trial be postponed because of his arrest, arguing that Ina could not possibly get a fair trial given the events of the past two days. The judge granted the motion, but only until June 9. At the same time he overruled defense motions to suppress evidence seized in the August 17 raids and for a change of venue. It looked like Ina's trial would replicate Alan's and Eli's, and to some extent Bob's.[25] Several related stories appeared between Croom's arrest and the beginning of Ina's trial. In a press release dated June 5, the ILD appealed to women across the country. "Prosecutors John Eberle and Lewis Morris . . . must hear from the women of America who refuse to permit them to railroad Mrs. Wood . . . to the penitentiary. . . . Letters from women in every part of the land should reach these gentlemen at once."[26]

On June 6, the *Oklahoma City Times* carried the headline "Lewis Morris Admits His Eye Is on Governor's Race in 1942." When questioned, Morris said, "Yes, I may run. Don't you think I'd make as good a governor as some we've had?"[27] That same day the *Tulsa Tribune* ran an editorial: "We never dreamed we'd get euchered [*sic*] into saying a good word for Communists in Oklahoma or anywhere else, but the hysterical anti-Communist trials in Oklahoma City are no longer humorous." The editorial focused on the legislative investigation, "which reached new highs in camp meeting oratory and patriotic breast-beating," the three high-profile trials already concluded, Ina Wood's impending trial, and recent actions against her defense attorney, who was "clapped into jail and held incommunicado." Oklahoma Communists "unknown a few months ago . . . are now national figures. The severity of their sentences has drawn to them thousands of sympathizers. . . . Moreover," the editorial lamented, "the cruel beast of mob hatred is now abroad in the state to threaten any minority group which the mob fears or does not understand." Just "what kind of insanity is this?" the *Tribune* wondered.[28]

Two days later the League of American Writers, "a voluntary association of writers dedicated to the preservation and extension of a truly democratic culture," met in New York City for its biennial conference. Press releases announcing the conference forecast considerable discussion of censorship and specifically mentioned the "bookburners of Oklahoma" and "the imprisonment of booksellers." At the conference, delegates chose Dashiell Hammett as president and Theodore Dreiser as honorary president. Delegates then passed resolutions denouncing persecutions and violations of civil liberties. Included among them was specific mention of the Oklahoma syndicalism trials. The League also sent a petition to Governor Phillips signed by four hundred writers "protesting the Hitler-like persecution of Oklahoma citizens for possessing and selling literature legal everywhere else in the country." Among the signees were award-winning and best-selling authors such as Erskine Caldwell (*Tobacco Road, God's Little Acre*) and Richard Wright (*Native Son*), and well-known playwrights such as Clifford Odets (*Paradise Lost* and *Golden Boy*) and Lillian Hellman (*The Children's Hour* and *The Little Foxes*).[29]

II

Ina Wood's trial began the morning of June 9. More eyes across the nation watched these proceedings than any of the previous trials. Coverage by *Tulsa Tribune* capital correspondent Joseph E. Howell clearly demonstrated that gender offered a different lens on the book trials. "You would think she was another spectator as she sits at the lawyers' table in her green outfit — cocky green hat, matching green jacket, and green and white print dress. She seems so unconcerned." Howell was unaware these were used clothes.[30] "Her lip doesn't even tremble" as John Eberle asks jurors if they could give her the maximum punishment. "Occasionally she smiles a little," sometimes making notes during some legal argument on a sheet of yellow paper. She is a "smallish woman with dark features" who sits alone, except for her attorneys. Her husband, she explained in an interview with reporters after the first day of jury selection, was resting at a friend's farm. "I'll join him when this is over." Reporters covering the trials "think she is the smartest of the group," a "good egg."

Although she gave her age as thirty-three, she looked more like twenty-eight, Howell said. "She wears no jewelry except a gold trinket giraffe on her jacket and a plain silver wedding ring on her middle finger." She lost weight after getting married, she said "with a grin and a wrinkle to her slightly uppity nose." The Woods had no children, Howell reported. "Asked if she is responsible for much of her husband's fervor for his job, she replies, 'It is pretty much of a complementary situation. I feel I need him. I hope he gets a little good from me, too,' and there is a twinkle in her hazel eyes." To an accusation by one Oklahoma City reporter that she enjoyed being the center of attention, she protested: "I don't see how any one can say I am happy. I would rather this had never happened." Then why wasn't she crying, the reporter pressed. "The trial isn't a reflection of me," she responded. "I understand the place I occupy in American history, the processes that made it possible."[31]

Jury selection mirrored previous trials. Despite defense attorneys' efforts to show that county jury commissioners illegally eliminated from the jury pool anyone not owning property, Judge Albert Hunt, a former Oklahoma Supreme Court Justice who had returned to the bench after eight years of private practice, refused to expand the pool from which they had to select. "Probably aware that they would be the victims of public censure if they returned a verdict of not guilty," one observer noted, "many members of the jury pool said they had opinions about the Communist Party and that they couldn't serve on the jury." One prospective juror said: "I have no respect for a woman who feels a Negro is her equal." Another admitted he was opposed to minority parties "because they might pull the majority over to their side." After three days, however, the defense and prosecution finally settled on twelve white men.[32] On the final day of jury selection, the *Daily Oklahoman* noticed that Ina had changed from "the green and white combination starring a huge-brimmed hat that kept the courtroom's audience from seeing her bronzed face" to a "white blouse and dark skirt wearing a blue-black sombrero type straw hat with sweeping lines and an impertinent false feather." The *Oklahoman* was unaware these were also used clothes. The paper noticed that ILD attorney Sam Neuberger's nervous doodlings had "switched from ovals to Saturns with encircling rings, a complicated form of doodling, presumably imported from New York."[33] For the *Oklahoman,* Neuberger's every move said "outsider." Every day the courtroom was packed, and "all the principals in the cast sense that they are playing a part in an unusual drama," *Tulsa Tribune* reporter Joseph Howell observed. Morris and Eberle "have found public sentiment approved what they are doing. It may be the road to the governorship for Morris, and the road to the county attorneyship for Eberle."[34]

Trial began June 13. Again, defense attorneys asked for time to analyze the boxes' contents. They had never been allowed to review the materials, they complained, and had never been given an inventory. Again, Eberle objected, and then the two sides got into extended arguments that sometimes wandered off point. "Typical of arguments was that between Eberle and the defense attorneys about whether two exhibits should be held together with a paper clip," the *Daily Oklahoman* reported. "Neuberger contended they should be kept apart, and Eberle said they should be kept together by the clip. The court upheld Eberle."[35]

Eberle trotted out his army of now familiar witnesses; all told by-now-very-familiar stories. During Croom's cross-examination of one witness an incident occurred that demonstrated a connection between Eberle and Judge Hunt. Before Croom "could ask a certain question, Eberle objected and was sustained by Judge Hunt," an observer noted. "Neuberger arose and went over to the court reporter and insisted that the record show that the judge had ruled on a question before it had been asked. Finally, Croom was allowed to ask the question which had already been over-ruled." At one point Eberle jumped to his feet: "We object to counsel using such big words and so many words, and object to it as incompetent, irrelevant and immaterial."[36]

By this time, Eberle and Hunt had developed a courtroom call-and-response cadence. "Several times when Croom or Neuberger objected, Judge Hunt sat in his chair without saying anything" an observer noted. "After a brief pause, Eberle would resist the objection. Judge Hunt would then overrule the defense on exactly the grounds stated by Eberle." The only variation from patterns set in previous trials centered around the testimony of an employment officer at Armour & Co. stockyards, who testified Ina had applied for a job the previous summer under the name of Inez Plunkett, and had worked for two or three days before quitting. When Eberle sought to introduce an application blank he said Ina had filled out with this misinformation, Croom and Neuberger objected. Hunt overruled. Why were his objections being overruled, Croom pressed. "To show the actions of the defendant as a member of the Communist Party," Hunt replied. "There is nothing illegal about a Communist or anyone else seeking employment," Neuberger huffed.[37]

When making objections, Neuberger regularly cited cases relevant to legal points he wished to raise. Eberle regularly objected, saying that "in Oklahoma we simply object, saying incompetent, irrelevant, and immaterial." Judge Hunt ruled that Neuberger could make objections, but that he could not cite cases. Neuberger ignored Hunt's admonitions, however, and cited cases anyway, no doubt to create a record he could use on appeal. Outside the courtroom Neuberger continued to be treated with hostility. A number of people were overheard talking about that "damned Jew" defending Ina. "That Jew's going to have to behave if I sit in here," commented one man in the gallery. "It's all right for you to be their lawyer," another told him to his face in the halls, "but if you think the way they do, we'll lynch you."[38]

At the end of the day, Eberle had more than forty boxes of materials seized in the August 17 raids wheeled into the courtroom. He asked that the court admit the material as evidence, but Hunt refused. No matter; Eberle had made his point. He wanted to impress the jury with volume but did not want to have to read more excerpts. After Judge Hunt refused his motion, the prosecution suddenly rested its case. In its report of the day's proceedings, the *Daily Oklahoman* expressed surprise that from the mass of evidence available to Eberle, he had not read from the diary Ina Wood had "kept during a tour of Europe, including Russia, several years ago."[39]

Not unexpectedly, the defense rested its case the following Monday morning, June 16, without calling a witness. Like Bob, Alan, and Eli, Ina did not testify. Judge Hunt then issued instructions to the jury, to each of which the defense objected. Hunt ignored every objection. At 10:00 A.M., Eberle rose to give his final argument. Everyone braced for a lengthy monologue; Eberle did not disappoint. In a closing argument the *Oklahoma City Times* described as "a ripping, biting, scathing attack on Communists and Communism," Eberle pointed out that some wars were indeed "necessary. . . . Underneath the sweet and honey phrases they use to combat war, we find dastardly and sinister reasons for their stand against war, or what they call 'imperialist' wars."[40] George Croom objected to Eberle's use of the term "imperialist." " 'Go get on a soapbox,' " snapped Eberle. " 'I'll be glad to meet you at a soap box or any place else, Mister Eberle,' " Croom shot back, "his face red." Eberle then turned his back on Croom and resumed his argument. "This blue-printed treason they put out — ". Up jumped Sam Neuberger to object to Eberle's choice of words, but to no avail. Hunt overruled him.

"Ina Wood sold books," Eberle continued, "and the books that she sold scream revolution — bloody revolution — from every page." One observer noticed how Eberle would pace the floor, "hissing" the phrase "bloody revolution"; he also noticed that when Eberle stopped reading from the books and pamphlets, he "was often incoherent." To demonstrate, the observer wrote down several examples. "This is an international conspiracy aimed at setting up a slave state." "They work women like men, and they're glad to do it because they get something to eat." "These people don't even have a God to swear to. They can't even take an oath." At 5 P.M. when he was still in the midst of his final argument, court recessed until the next morning. In summarizing Eberle's remarks, the *Daily Oklahoman* again expressed surprise he had not mentioned Ina's diary.[41]

In his remarks the next day (and perhaps in response to the *Daily Oklahoman*'s prompting), Eberle finally pulled out Ina's diary. He quoted from it extensively, though much of it reflected the simple musings of a young woman on her first trip abroad. He particularly focused on her positive view of Russia and its people: "I love it all. I love the people. I feel related to everyone of them," she had written. Next Eberle turned to the issue of race and devoted the next few hours associating Ina Wood with equal rights for African Americans. First he quoted from a pamphlet titled "Questions and

Answers" that Ina had coauthored; it revealed, Eberle said, Communist plans for revolution in the Black Belt where African Americans formed a majority population. "Under the evidence in this case they engage in the breaking of laws. . . . They advocate the breaking of our laws such as the breaking of the Jim Crow laws and such as the laws of marriage between the races; they advocate the breaking of those laws."[42] Finally, Eberle turned to Ina and pointed his finger. "This woman wants equality," he said: "In Russia they say that men are equal to women in everything, and in this country they are equal before the law. . . . I'm asking the court to give her equality. I'm asking the court to give her ten years, just like they've given the men." He finally sat down, ten hours after he started.[43]

Defense offered its final argument the next day. "Books, books, books," George Croom began. "When did it become a crime for an American citizen to own a book? John Eberle sets himself up as censor to tell 250,000 people of Oklahoma County what they can read and what they cannot read. That is his real intention; that is what he stands for." Croom had even harsher words for Lewis Morris. He was "fascist-minded, "consumed by violent political ambition," and willing to "walk to the State Capital over the innocent bodies of women." Why did "he not bring up the real issues of Oklahoma — unemployment, dispossessed farmers, deplorable health, low wages, poverty, women slaving for $5.00 a week?" Croom then reminded jurors that "only a stone's throw from this building live 3,000 people in the most deplorable, vermin-ridden conditions human beings can possibly endure. Why not discuss them? Because Mr. Morris prefers to ride into the governor's mansion across the bodies of innocent women."[44]

"What did Ina Wood do?" Sam Neuberger asked again and again throughout his final remarks. Although she "worked and tried to get better hospital conditions for Negroes," that "is not a crime," he said, "but isn't that part of the foundation of John Eberle's accusations?" The prosecution argued repeatedly, Neuberger pointed out, that Communists were attempting to hide behind the Constitution, "but I tell you jurors, John Eberle is trying to hide the constitution!" Neuberger also mocked Eberle by parroting the words "bloody revolution" in hissing tones. "Never in the history of the United States has there been any prosecution for possession of books."[45]

Tipping its hand that the defense did not really expect to win, Neuberger charged that Judge Hunt had overruled so many defense motions that it appeared he had entered into "a conspiracy with Prosecutor Eberle to railroad the defendant." How else to interpret Hunt's ruling in favor of the prosecution when it dumped into "evidence" in less than an hour 10,491 pages of reading material from 99 books that Hunt himself admitted he had not read? "If you permit these books as evidence, you will condone this book-burning without flame, this destruction of free press by the whims of an assistant county attorney." And how can one possibly blame "the ills of the world on a young woman who stands trial for her liberty in Oklahoma City?" he concluded. "Smear, smear, smear. Drag a red herring across the trial. Somebody must suffer, the county attorney declaims. He hasn't got Stalin. He hasn't got Marx. He hasn't got Moscow. So let's give it to Ina Wood."[46]

As always, Lewis Morris gave the final statement, in which he did little more than sling words connecting prejudices. One ACLU observer thought he "used everything in the books. . . . He dramatically approached the jury and asked them questions which he never expected to be answered." And as at the previous trials, Morris addressed the issue of race. "The Communist Party distributed 4,000 pamphlets of propaganda among Negroes influencing them to hate," he remarked. The Party also believed in anti-lynching laws. "Is this the form of government you want?" Specifically for Ina Wood's trial, however, he also included gender. "The defendant should be convicted and sentenced to the penitentiary," he argued. "The mere fact that she is a woman doesn't make any difference. They think by sending women out they can depend on the chivalry of American juries to turn them loose. I feel sorry for people who are misguided, but she's not misguided. She's one of the inner-ins." Defense counsel immediately moved for acquittal because of Morris's "highly inflammatory, impassioned and unwarranted" speech, but Hunt denied their motion.

In his argument, the *Daily Oklahoman* observed, Morris used his "usual tactics of addressing remarks directly to the defendant and the defense attorneys." George Croom sat "tightlipped," Neuberger "smiled back at the shouting prosecutor, apparently unruffled." Ina Wood "preserved her composure" and "showed no emotion" but for the "tightly clenched fists" in her lap. The ACLU observer noticed other things. "Unable to catch the meaning of many of Morris's statements," he preserved a series of quotations. Among them, "It's a propaganda shop [the Progressive Book Store], and that's an overt act." "The U.S. Government has a right to tell a clique to exercise their constitutional rights decently." His obvious favorite, however, occurred when Morris wanted to read the judge's instructions to the jury, but mislaid his reading glasses. Instead, he picked up Judge Hunt's spectacles and said, "I want to read the instructions with the judge's glasses. We see eye to eye."[47]

The jury received the case late Wednesday afternoon, June 18, just before recessing for dinner. Less than an hour after returning from dinner, they came back with a verdict. In the room to hear it were Eli Jaffe and Alan Shaw. Like Ina and her attorneys, they knew what was coming. Ina Wood was guilty, the jury foreman said, and for that crime the jury recommended she be sentenced to ten years in the penitentiary and fined $5,000. When the verdict was read, Ina showed no emotion. Judge Hunt immediately doubled her bail, then announced that formal sentencing would take place June 23. If Ina could not meet bail, she would immediately be transported to the state penitentiary.

Outside the courtroom reporters crowded around all parties. John Eberle announced that he was pleased. He noted that the jury took less time to agree on this trial than the previous three; his clear implication was the evidence was even stronger in the Ina Wood trial. Croom commented, "We now have a prototype of what happened in Germany here in Oklahoma County." "I haven't done anything. I haven't committed any crime," Ina told reporters. "My conscience is clear. . . . I don't expect to go to prison. I can't believe that the higher courts could sustain a farce on justice such as this has been."[48]

The ILD issued an immediate appeal for additional funds necessary to meet Ina's new bail: "Mrs. Wood cannot be permitted to become the first American woman victim of the war hysteria of World War II." From New York Bob Wood telegraphed in clipped prose a message that was part political—"Morning's paper carries story barbarous verdict. Am certain great majority fellow Oklahomans as people over entire country will be outraged by malicious brutal sentence;" and part personal—"I know cool objective eyes you focus on this travesty justice. Am proud my magnificent wife. Hope see you soon. All my love."[49]

III

If attitudes toward the defendants had subtly shifted just before Ina went to trial, they crystallized into a noticeable momentum in the wake of the jury's verdict. The Associated Press circulated an attractive photo of Ina under the title, "Gets 10 Years on Red Charges." The *Daily Worker* titled its editorial: "Mrs. Wood's Conviction Insults the Instincts of All Decent People." Such a conviction, the paper argued, could only be obtained by a "hand-picked jury."[50] That the *Daily Worker* condemned the conviction was hardly surprising, but now major newspapers across the nation also weighed in.

A June 20 *St. Louis Post-Dispatch* editorial, titled "A Woman of No Importance," led the way. "For what was Mrs. Wood convicted?" the *Post-Dispatch* asked. "What she did was think thoughts, read books and express ideas which the Ku Kluxers of Oklahoma did not like. For that she is to spend 10 years in prison, more years than many of our foulest criminals have served." What evidence did John Eberle present to demonstrate her crime? "Copious extracts" from books and pamphlets seized from the Progressive Book Store, including many works to be found in all libraries. "If the FBI should raid the St. Louis Public Library, it could establish the same kind of case against [the] Librarian and his staff." The Ku Klux "spirit runs amok" in Oklahoma, and has gained an ascendancy evident in the civil liberties violations state and local officials perpetrated against Communists, Jehovah's Witnesses, African Americans, and Jews.

Contrast the Oklahoma decision with a recent decision by the

Iowa Supreme Court, the paper said, in which a St. Louis labor leader was absolved of violating an Iowa criminal syndicalism law.[51] The fact that he was Communist, the court ruled, was irrelevant. "We had better pause in this moment of our history to decide whether or not we are going to throw away our liberties, scrap the Bill of Rights, throw our cherished judicial decisions into the discard pile and engage in a hysterical nation-wide witch hunt, or whether we are going to preserve the principles on which this country was founded." The *Post-Dispatch* then quoted a recent speech by Franklin Roosevelt at Oxford University. "We rejoice . . . in the great cause of preserving the free learning and the civil liberties which have grown stone upon stone in our lands through the centuries."

Powerful words, the editorial argued, but "they can be clothed with meaning only if the case of Mrs. Wood, the woman of no importance, is merely a savage exception to the principle of free thought rather than a forerunner of a nation-wide witch hunt." Next to the editorial the newspaper carried a political cartoon showing the Statue of Liberty, but covering her torch was a cone labeled "Oklahoma Criminal Syndicalism Prosecutions." On June 28, the *Christian Science Monitor* reprinted the editorial in its entirety. Other newspapers reported similar sentiments. The *News-Sun* of Springfield, Ohio, said the Oklahoma syndicalism defendants "are being prosecuted for the contents of their minds, the thing our history, our tradition, abhors and which our Constitution forbids." Small-town newspapers in Indiana, Iowa, Pennsylvania, Wisconsin, Minnesota, and Florida printed an AP column titled "Keep the Silly Season in Its Place" that condemned convictions for selling books "found in any civilized library." A *Los Angeles Times* columnist sneered: "Oklahoma has interpreted 'criminal syndicalism' to mean the selling of 'Grapes of Wrath.' "[52]

Two days later Hitler invaded the Soviet Union. For two years before that date many Americans saw Hitler and Stalin as two evils who had combined their ambitions to dominate the world. After that date, however, Americans underwent a seismic shift in their thinking. Suddenly the Russians were fighting the same evil as Great Britain and its allies and, indeed, it was highly probable that the

United States would enter the war in the very near future and fight side by side with the Soviet Union to defeat the dreaded Hitler and Nazi Germany. The Roosevelt administration quickly began sending aid to the Soviet Union to help the fight against Hitler. Along with the policy shift came a shift in language coming out of official Washington describing the Russian people. But the shift in thinking occasioned by this watershed event was perhaps most transparent in the American CPUSA leadership. Before June 22, it was against the "imperialist" war; after that date it pushed for U.S. entry into the conflict. In the next few weeks Communist Party leaders admonished loyalists to follow the party line.[53] Among the loyalists were members of the Communist Party in Oklahoma.

Before the Party leadership circulated its new orders, however, Ina Wood appeared before Judge Hunt for formal sentencing on June 25, two days later than originally scheduled, by which time the ILD had raised enough money ("in record time," it said) to keep her out of prison while her case was being appealed. Not surprisingly, Judge Hunt gave her the maximum sentence — ten years in prison and a $5,000 fine. He then asked if she had anything to say. Her words were obviously crafted for a national audience. "All the techniques of Nazi fascism have been used in this trial," she said. "People who are responsible for the abuse of political rights in this case would not lift a finger to correct the evils of Community Camp. They are the ones who lose entirely the little Christian principle they have when it appears that their profit will be diminished in the least." All of the syndicalism trials, she concluded, "are part of a diabolical, unprincipled attack upon our democracy. They shall be a blot upon Oklahoma history." Judge Hunt responded: "This court gets no pleasure out of sentencing anyone, particularly women, but a jury of 12 men has found you guilty of a violation of a state statute and set your punishment."[54]

Ina's trial had not interrupted a growing cacophony. On June 22, more than two hundred members of the League of American Writers signed a letter to Governor Phillips and County Attorney Morris condemning the persecutions suffered by the defendants as "a most serious miscarriage of justice." Among the books held in a jail cell and carted out for each of the four trials in more than forty boxes, the letter noted, were John Steinbeck's *The Grapes of Wrath,* Richard Wright's *Uncle Tom's Children,* Andre Malraux's *Days of Wrath,* Leo Tolstoy's *War and Peace,* Leane Zugsmith's *Home Is Where You Hang Your Childhood,* and *The Collected Works of Jack London.* "If this conviction is upheld," the authors argued, "the books now occupying a room in the county jail will be burned. For, no longer needed as evidence, the county officials will destroy them. This will be the occasion for the first official book-burning in our country."[55] Several weeks later novelist and Book-of-the-Month Club selection committee member Dorothy Canfield Fisher, social reformer and turn-of-the-century settlement house organizer Vida Scudder, and writer/poet/screenwriter Dorothy Parker joined other well-known women writers to protest to Governor Phillips "the crime committed against the Bill of Rights and an innocent young woman" in his state.[56]

Between June 23 and 27, the American Newspaper Guild hosted its annual conference in Detroit and unanimously passed a resolution condemning the lengthy prison terms and hefty fines meted out to the Oklahoma defendants for "the mere possession of books and literature which are obtainable in virtually every public library." The Guild noted that "two members of this group . . . were allegedly kidnapped in violation of the Lindbergh kidnapping law" (referring to Bob and Ina's expulsion from Kansas City) and decrying that this act "has not been punished, which indicates the extent to which irresponsible and vicious public officials will go in an atmosphere of hysteria." On June 25, Ina was interviewed by the *St. Louis Star-Times* on her way back to New York. "Practically the whole case against me was based on books seized at the book shop," she said. "You will find the same books in any well equipped library."[57]

By this time the ILD and the Oklahoma Committee to Defend Political Prisoners were circulating 8,000 copies of the *Post-Dispatch* editorial (the *Post-Dispatch* had donated the first 6,000) around the state and nation. Most Oklahoma newspapers did not like the editorial. On June 29, the *Daily Oklahoman* addressed it directly. "The Ku Klux theory is absurd," the *Oklahoman* said. "There was no public hysteria and not a great amount of interest. . . . There was no preliminary propaganda in the press or elsewhere." The Oklahoma syndicalism law clearly separated the political from the criminal, and the four convicted Communists were criminally guilty of syndicalism. "Mrs. Wood and her colleagues were given a fair trial by jury and there was nothing savoring of unfairness or miscarriage of justice," the *Oklahoman* concluded. On July 12, the *Christian Science Monitor* reprinted the *Oklahoman*'s editorial in its entirety.[58]

Other Oklahoma newspapers joined in the criticism of the *Post-Dispatch* editorial. The Duncan *Banner* denied Klan influence, and the *Chelsea Reporter* wrote: If Oklahoma was indeed a "Ku Klux hotbed," then the Sooner State would be "an ideal place for communists to keep away from. And while we are on the subject," it added, "we have no recollection of the people of this state asking for a new form of government." The *Post-Dispatch* "overlooks the facts," said the Payne County *News* of Stillwater. Oklahomans would not let fundamental freedoms be threatened by Communists. They wanted what was best for all, not what pleases a minority dedicated to overthrowing the government. The *Okmulgee Times* observed that the "vast majority of people of the United States will have far more respect for Oklahoma's efforts to send communists to the penitentiary where they belong," and the *Okmulgee Daily Record* added that Ina and Bob Wood got "just what they deserved; it'll never be our policy to print one word in their favor." The *Tulsa World* and its sister publication, the *Tulsa Times,* on the other hand, agreed with the *Post-Dispatch.*[59]

On July 5 *Publishers Weekly* told its readers why the Oklahoma trials were "Important to Books and Booksellers," and why the cases had several "alarming aspects." If the verdicts were not reversed, "a precedent in Oklahoma and perhaps elsewhere will be established for the seizure not only of controversial literature but of other material on the same shelves, the arrest of bookshop customers present in the same shop with the material. And of booksellers offering it for sale." That was scary, *Publishers Weekly* concluded. "The point at issue is not whether the books circulated exert a good or bad influence, but whether they, rather than overt acts of illegality, constitute evidence for conviction."[60]

Other publications joined the growing chorus. Many editors had obviously read the *Post-Dispatch* editorial. In her weekly column in *Midwest Labor* of Duluth, Minnesota, Irene Paul wrote on June 27: "Trade unionists and workers especially must fight now for civil liberties for all, or we shall end up with civil liberties for none." In a July 2 editorial, *Christian Century* argued that the Oklahoma situation "does not involve mob action, but subverts the legal mechanism of the state itself by making it an instrument for the punishment of unpopular opinion."[61]

"And what shall the church say about the violations of civil liberties for those who are politically or religiously in a minority?" asked *The Christian Evangelist*. "The Supreme Court will rectify this injustice, doubtless, if the defendants have money enough to carry their cases up on appeal." The very conservative *New York Herald Tribune* reminded readers it "had no truck with Communist ideology," but "Oklahoma has been making a monkey of herself" in the criminal syndicalism trials. "No people in fighting a menace of the sort can afford to sacrifice in the process the fundamentals it is defending." That fact, the *Herald Tribune* warned, "should be appreciated in Oklahoma too, lest in these emotional times a match applied there spread to the tinder of hysteria elsewhere."[62]

United States Week quoted Oliver Wendell Holmes. "If there is any principle of the Constitution that more imperatively calls for attachment than any other it is the principle of free thought—not free thought for those that agree with us but freedom for the thought of that we hate." The *Dayton Herald* soundly condemned "Alienism in Oklahoma." The four convictions showed "anyone who happens to believe anything which is objectionable to the powers that be in Oklahoma could be imprisoned. . . . Unhappily and unwisely, the state of Oklahoma has undertaken to save America from foreign isms by substituting alien practices for American ways."[63]

The *Beacon Journal* of Akron, Ohio, marveled at the breadth of Oklahoma's syndicalism law. "Under such a section a man could be sent to prison for owning a copy of the speeches and papers of Abraham Lincoln. . . . The zealots who put the criminal syndicalism law on the statute books injured their state's reputation." In its August 18 issue, *The New Republic* contrasted the *Post-Dispatch* editorial about subversive books lurking on the shelves of the St. Louis Public Library with a quotation from Governor Phillips: "Why should we give free run to those left-wingers, pinks, reds, Communists and those of the lunatic fringe who advocate overthrow of our government?" It saw in the raids the beginning of a campaign to violate civil rights with an unparalleled cynicism and terrorism directed at anyone who disagreed with public officials.[64]

All these editorials became grist for the ILD's publicity campaign. It reprinted the *Post-Dispatch* cartoon on the cover of the spring issue of *Equal Justice* and quoted liberally from the closing arguments made by defense lawyers and Oklahoma County prosecutors and from Ina Wood's remarks at her formal sentencing.[65] The ILD also published separate pamphlets in which it quoted editorial comments from across the country to bolster the fund-raising campaign and raise the profile of the cases. The newspapers it quoted expressed condemnation of the convictions from the political right and left, demonstrated that the ILD's defense of civil liberties in the Sooner State was generating widespread support, and tended to isolate Oklahoma officials from the rest of the country.[66]

In its July 29 issue, *PM* ran a full page on the trials that particularly focused on Ina Wood and Elizabeth Green. "New York Gets a Look at Two Oklahoma 'Criminals,'" it was titled. The article outlined the history of the case, but also noted detail. "Ina Wood is a handsome, intelligent woman of 32, who worries about her weight." Elizabeth Green "was wearing a girlish red-print dress and a white straw hat she kept balanced in the wind with difficulty." Neither looked "dangerous," the article noted; neither wanted "to talk much while the trials were still going on. Oklahoma justice is swift. But both seemed very chipper considering what they had been through." "I've had lots of sympathetic letters from women, farmers and working people out there," Ina said. Elizabeth commented, "I thought the whole thing was funny at first, and couldn't take it seriously." Now, the article noted, "she isn't amused at all. Even a little scared." The ILD had thousands of copies of the page printed up for wide distribution, on the back of which it also reprinted the *St. Louis Post-Dispatch* editorial, and sent many of those copies to Oklahoma City.[67]

They arrived around the same time a new controversy hit the Oklahoma City area. On the morning of July 16, many Norman residents woke up to find two pieces of literature on their doorsteps. One was a CPUSA "manifesto" titled "A People's Program of Struggle for the Defeat of Hitler." It reminded readers that Great Britain had just entered into an alliance with Russia, and called those individuals leading the antiwar fight "spokesmen of the most reactionary circles of the bourgeoisie." The other was a mimeographed sheet urging Oklahomans to drop prosecution of the criminal syndicalism trials as one way to help the Soviet armies. In an editorial the next day, the *Norman Transcript* warned: "We should be wary . . . of the new propaganda Communists are spreading in this country, trying to gain sympathy for their cause. . . . Be not deceived by the Communists."[68]

Six days later, in four automobiles, Grand Dragon J. R. Reed led members of the Ku Klux Klan "wearing white robes and hoods, but not masked" to the OU campus and Norman's downtown area about 9:30 P.M. There they passed out copies of the same pamphlet that circulated the state capitol building during the Little Dies Committee hearings. Contacted the next day by local newspapers, Reed said the Klansmen would return to campus soon with the "whole crowd. It's about time to do something down here." When asked about plans, he would only say "it will be legal" and "will take place soon." In an interview with a *St. Louis Post-Dispatch* reporter, Reed said he was motivated to undertake the trip by the *Post-Dispatch* editorial.[69]

The *Oklahoma City Times* found the event comic. "After years of going around in its civilian negligee, the Oklahoma Ku Klux Klan Tuesday night shook the mothballs out of its bed sheets, put on its dunce caps, and played spook on the campus of the University of Oklahoma . . . hoping to spook the daylights out of any Communists thereabouts." Governor Phillips hoped Oklahomans would not succumb to "this Ku Klux hysteria," and warned KKK members not to take the law into their own hands; otherwise they would find themselves in a prison cell "next to the Communists." A week later the Oklahoma Federation for Constitutional Rights issued its own pamphlet attacking the Klan leaflet point by point, and reaffirming its determination to defend the Bill of Rights in Oklahoma and the defendants in the criminal syndicalism cases.[70]

The *Tulsa Tribune* did not mince words, however. In an editorial titled "The Klan Is Back," the *Tribune* concluded: "We are in the middle of a growing season of screwballism." It was obvious that "the inhabitants of the region around Oklahoma City are currently undergoing a distressing epidemic of brain fever." Evidence? "They have recently sentenced an inoffensive young woman to ten years in the penitentiary for no other crime than being a member of the yet-legal Communist Party. And, worst of all, they performed this sorry outrage with all the enthusiasm of a medieval mob at a mass burning of the Huguenots."[71]

Eli Jaffe was less polemic in his description of events published in the *Daily Worker* and the San Francisco–based *People's World*. "Progressive" Oklahomans believed the Klan was attempting to resurrect itself in the Sooner State, he reported, because of growing sympathy for the Soviet Union in its fight against Hitler. He also speculated that the Klan wanted "to become the center of vigilante and hooligan elements to replace the now defunct Oklahoma City defense battalion and the Oklahoma County civil guards [the U.S. attorney general had ruled in June that such organizations were unconstitutional and illegal] to stem the rising progressive tide in Oklahoma." Less than three weeks later, the *Daily Worker* noted that the forces behind the prosecutors "are all on the defensive" and that the Oklahoma defendants "have become the symbols of the fight against native American fascism."[72]

Supporters of the defendants continued their efforts elsewhere. On July 29, Chicago Attorney Pearl M. Hart sent out a plea to friends and acquaintances stating that Ina Wood was convicted for "dangerous thoughts" and that Elizabeth Green was scheduled for trial on September 13. "After her comes the hard-working father of 8 children; then an aged farmer. Then his wife . . . and after these . . . it is anybody's turn . . . unless a stop is put to this 'blitz' against civil liberties." She had already donated $944.16 of "borrowed money" for Ina Wood's appeal . . . but said she could afford no more. "Will you help me?" She included a pledge card with the note: "All money sent to me to help pay for the Ina Wood appeal will be applied directly on specific bills." She also enclosed a sheet that contained the *St. Louis Post-Dispatch* editorial on one side, and the *PM* article on Ina Wood and Elizabeth Green on the other.[73]

At its August 17 meeting, the ILD National Board plotted strategy to expand the campaign. Defense attorneys were nearly finished with appeals, which were scheduled to be heard September 9 and 10. Because the Oklahoma chief justice was out of town until August 22, however, attorneys had been unable to secure a postponement for other pending trials. As a result, the defense would have to be ready for Elizabeth Green's trial September 13. For the appellate arguments, the ILD hoped to mobilize "as large as possible a group of observers from different parts of the country to attend." The board also approved several motions — one to postpone as long as possible the oral argument so that New York congressman Vito Marcantonio could join defense attorney Stanley Belden and ILD attorney Sam Neuberger in presenting that argument, another to schedule defendants to speak at fund-raising events in the fall, and yet another to forward all publicity material to the Oklahoma State attorney general "urging him to drop the prosecutions." Several weeks later the ILD began contacting numerous organizations, asking them to pass resolutions supporting the Oklahoma defendants. "Please send copies of all resolutions adopted to us, and to Governor Leon C. Phillips."[74]

On August 17, the Oklahoma Committee to Defend Political Prisoners held a one-year anniversary "celebration" of the 1940 raids by issuing a statement to the press. "Times have changed much in the last year," the statement began. Most right-thinking people around the world, including "Oklahoma City men and women," had come to realize that "[w]e cannot go on living until

Hitler is defeated." That meant rearranging the priorities of the nation, the state, Oklahoma County and Oklahoma City, shoring up defenses everywhere, and dropping distracting issues of much less importance. Among the latter were the syndicalism trials. Devoting any more attention in the courts to these cases was a futile effort and waste of important resources, the committee said.

The *Daily Oklahoman* quoted the statement in full and noted it was authored by Nena Beth Stapp, wife of Alan Shaw, and that it accused local police of unprofessional conduct. "The Gestapo could hardly have had more power" was one quote the paper pulled from the statement. In a next-day editorial, the *Oklahoman* particularly questioned the link the committee made between defeating Hitler and dropping the syndicalism cases. "Our none too perfect statutes are going to look like a corroded sieve if one of them is nullified every time a calamity erupts anywhere abroad."[75]

As a leader with the committee, Nena Beth Stapp was often the target of criticism from the Oklahoma press. In a heated exchange of letters with the *Stigler* (Oklahoma) *News-Sentinel,* she stood her ground. The paper fired the first volley. On July 24, it attacked the *St. Louis Post Dispatch,* calling it a "decadent diurnal of the once-great Pulitzer Publishing company. . . . It is an ironic thing when a resident of the corrupt municipality of St. Louis, birthplace of American gangsterism, cess-pool of crime and fountain-head of corruption, should offer criticism of a sovereign state that is attempting to keep America safe for democracy by ridding it of the undesirable vermin" like Ina Wood. The rest of the editorial attacked the "grimy, smoke-filled atmosphere" of St. Louis, "whose waterfront is the breeding place for two kinds of rats." Stapp answered on August 7, calling the *News-Sentinel's* editorial "childish" and accusing the paper of "intense bias and prejudice approaching the point of hatred and absolute intolerance." In response, the paper invited Stapp to respond. On August 21 she did: "I think you have proved the futility of name-calling and vitriolic attack, so I shall stick to the facts." She then outlined the case made by defense attorneys. The *News-Sentinel* published her letter, but in a bold-print paragraph also stated: "Miss Stapp is an artful propagandist and evidently is glad to get free space in a paper to spread her communistic views — however she's harmless if watched carefully."[76]

Efforts to mobilize support for the defendants picked up momentum when Frederick G. Melcher, well-respected editor of *Publishers Weekly*, penned a scathing editorial in his August 23 issue. "The book-burning episode in the Oklahoma Stadium last year and the trial of those who had any connection with the Progressive Book Store in Oklahoma City constitute the most disheartening assaults on the freedom of speech guarantees of the Bill of Rights since this war began." He ended by quoting from Harvard law professor Zechariah Chafee's widely cited *Freedom of Speech*, a text, Melcher said, that "might be made required reading for the prosecutor" in the Oklahoma cases. "The effect of suppression," Melcher quoted from Chafee, "extends far beyond the agitators actually put in jail."[77]

Into this political crossfire stepped Charles Lindbergh, *Spirit of Saint Louis* national hero in 1927. By 1941 he had become the foremost spokesperson for keeping the United States out of war. On August 29, he was scheduled to deliver an address in the Municipal Auditorium sponsored by the Oklahoma City chapter of the America First Committee. On August 26, however, 250 people showed up at a city council meeting to protest use of a city building for Lindbergh's speech. Most vocal among the groups were the American Legion and the Knights of Pythias. City council members listened carefully, then voted unanimously to deny Lindbergh use of the auditorium. Lindbergh supporters protested loudly. "This council was stampeded into breaking the American principle of freedom of speech by a bunch of excited and misdirected American Legion members," said one supporter.

Although Lindbergh ultimately delivered his speech to 10,000 people in a park outside the city limits (many news accounts referred to the site as a "cow pasture"), the council's action once again propelled Oklahoma into the nation's news. Big city newspapers such as the *Milwaukee Journal*, the *New York Times*, *PM*, the *Christian Science Monitor*, the *New York Evening Sun*, and small-town newspapers such as the *Troy (New York) Morning Record*, all excoriated the Oklahoma City Council for suppressing free speech, which, to editorial writers who had been reading about the Oklahoma syndicalism trials for a year, seemed all-too-characteristic of the Sooner State officials. In his *Emporia* (Kansas) *Gazette,* William Allen White railed: Oklahoma is a state "where the Ku Klux Klan still ranges in their primordial shirt tails and . . . where they do not allow Charles Lindbergh to speak."[78]

Because Governor Phillips knew that much of the nation would be watching what happened to Lindbergh, on the morning of his speech Phillips appealed to all Oklahoma citizens "to refrain from any heckling or boisterous mob spirit." Next morning, the *Daily Oklahoman* seemed almost relieved in its lead line: "Governor Phillips can write home to the folks that Oklahoma crowds are orderly." In an editorial a week later, the *Oklahoman* complained at how widely the press had circulated the story of the cancellation of Lindbergh's use of the Municipal Auditorium, but how little it circulated "the story of the protest of more than 10,000 people who found a suitable forum for the visiting orator and who assembled in a body to show the world that the Bill of Rights is still a very vital thing in Oklahoma."[79]

Almost lost in the media cacophony was Alan Shaw's public support of the city council's decision to deny Lindbergh use of the auditorium. The CPUSA agreed with the anti-Fascist feeling that motivated council action, he told the *Oklahoma City Times.* It also understood why the people of Oklahoma City would want to deny any agent of Hitler opportunities to weaken his enemies, he told the *Daily Oklahoman.* Alan's position made transparent the control Moscow exercised over foreign policy statements articulated by any Party officials in the United States. On October 2, in fact, Alan wrote a letter to Lewis Morris on behalf of the Party calling upon the county attorney's office to investigate and prosecute the America First Committee, the KKK, and other similar groups. He sent copies of his letter to Governor Phillips and Oklahoma newspapers.[80] Between August 1939 and June 1941 the Oklahoma State Communist Party had been nearly silent on the Nazi-Soviet Pact. After Hitler invaded Russia, however, the term "imperialist war" dropped from the Communist vocabulary nationwide, including in Oklahoma.

Thus, on this issue Alan Shaw took a position to deny Charles Lindbergh's free-speech rights in concert with the American Legion and the Knights of Pythias, two organizations that later filed amicus briefs opposed to the criminal syndicalism defendants. Another irony surrounding the Lindbergh fiasco was that many Oklahoma papers protesting ACLU participation in the syndicalism trials now supported the ACLU's defense of Lindbergh's free-speech rights.

During the summer, defendant Elizabeth Green took up her pen to further advertise the plight of the Oklahoma syndicalism defendants. In a *Protestant Digest* article titled "I Face an Oklahoma Prison," she described the effects of Oklahoma's suppressive tactics. "And now there are private book-burnings," she claimed. Those who "cannot bring themselves to burn their books will go out in the middle of the night and dig holes in their fields and bury their books, in the hope that a better day may come when it will again be safe for a man to read what books he chooses."[81] In a *Social Work Today* article, Elizabeth focused on the difference between the working and unemployed poor and the wealthy elite who she said were largely in charge of state affairs. She peppered her narrative with statistics taken from federal government documents, and supplemented it with data obtained from the recent decennial census.[82]

As secretary of the Oklahoma Committee to Defend Political Prisoners, writer Gordon Friessen had attended the trials of the four defendants. He resented the way each was treated; he admitted to doing a lot of doodling while he was taking notes, largely to keep his hands busy and his mouth shut. During the summer he drafted a pamphlet describing events that the committee later published as *Oklahoma Witch Hunt*. It became one of many that circulated the country as part of the effort to raise funds for the defendants. Once the manuscript for the pamphlet was done, however, Friessen and Red Dust Player Sis Cunningham decided to leave the Sooner State. During the book trials, they had fallen in love and married, but by late summer 1941, "there was really nothing to keep us in Oklahoma. The Red Dust Players had been scattered to the winds, and we were pretty well blacklisted throughout the state." In October, they headed to New York City, where they joined a musical group called the Almanac Singers; other members included Pete Seeger and Woody Guthrie.[83]

Defense Attorney Stanley Belden left the state as well. Already in April 1941 he had notified the ACLU he would be moving to the West Coast in several months. "I see no way to continue here and make a living, as the present State Admin'n will do almost anything to see me destroyed," he wrote. "I realized what participating in such cases might do to my practice, and I would not hesitate to do it again, because I felt it was my duty. But when you finally come to the place where you are not making it, then it is necess'y to seek an income from other sources." By August, he was gone. Like other "Okies," Stanley Belden had been driven out of Oklahoma by dire economic circumstances; unlike other Okies, however, he had been deliberately driven away by those in power.[84]

Nonetheless, by the beginning of September, pressure applied to Governor Phillips, Attorney General Mac Q. Williamson, County Attorney Morris, and Assistant County Attorney Eberle seemed to be having an effect. The intensity with which Eberle pursued the first four cases was not evident in his latest remarks to the press. He announced that the remaining criminal syndicalism trials would not be scheduled until after the September docket. "We want to get to all the persons in the county jail first," he said. "We'll set these other cases after we clean out the jail."[85]

CHAPTER SIX

Swells of Protest, Changing Times, September 1941 – September 1943

D espite blustering threats last June that all remaining defendants . . . would go on trial on Sept. 8," the *Daily Worker* announced on September 10, 1941, "the prosecution has quietly announced that it is not proceeding with these cases as scheduled."
The International Labor Defense "ascribes the change," the paper
said, "to the increased pressure of public opinion following the
sentence of Mrs. Wood last June." In part the ILD was right; the
pressure continued. Many friends of the defendants continued to
send letters to Oklahoma.[1]

More obvious, however, were increasingly public protests. By the
fall of 1941, the Oklahoma book trials had become a cause celebre
for people who were highly concerned about civil liberties violations, no matter their politics. In its September 13 issue, *Publishers
Weekly* announced that a number of publishers and authors had
crafted a statement to Governor Phillips (later released to the press
by the National Federation for Constitutional Liberties) protesting
the convictions of the syndicalism defendants. "It is our firm belief

that such convictions, allowed to stand, such charges, allowed to be made, are a threat to our freedom to write, to publish, to sell books." Among those signing the statement were chief executives of Harcourt, Brace; Longmans, Green; Pocket Books; Viking Press; Hastings House; A. S. Barnes & Co.; Dial Press; Macrae, Smith; Holiday House; and McBride Publishing. Authors attaching their names to the statement included *Brave New World* author Aldous Huxley and internationally known journalist Edgar Snow.[2]

A number of authors, booksellers, and publishers (book, periodical, and newspaper) issued separate statements. *The Jungle* author and 1930s political activist Upton Sinclair called it "a most shocking thing." Sterling North, literary editor of the *Chicago Daily News,* declared: "I am incensed and bewildered by the idiocy of the Oklahoma officials, who are imitating Hitler by burning books and persecuting book sellers. Official degeneracy seems to have reached its nadir in Oklahoma." Representatives of Dawson's Book Shop in San Francisco and Harry W. Schwartz, Inc., in Milwaukee, Wisconsin, registered their protest, Dawson's asserting, "If the Oklahoma law had been enforced neither I nor other booksellers . . . could have continued." Schwartz wrote, "I do not believe there is a bookshop in America which will not have a large proportion of books that were seized in Mr. Wood's bookshop." C. Halliwell Duell, of the publishing company Duell, Sloane & Pearce, said that as a publisher of patriotic books, "I wish to enter my strong protest against any law in any state of this nation which makes the mere possession of any book a criminal offense." Charles Kerr of the Atlantic Monthly Press said: "I speak for myself and my associates . . . the day that such prosecutions honestly represent the will of the people, that day we abandon the principles of democracy which have made this country great." That same month the American Booksellers' Association used its monthly bulletin to condemn the "dangerous precedent" in Oklahoma. *Survey Midmonthly* expressed "outraged indignation at the outcome of the cases."[3]

In a separate action, the League of American Writers sent Governor Phillips a letter of protest on October 20. "In the present jailing of our books in Oklahoma . . . we are profoundly shocked by this aping of Hitler's attitude toward literature on the part of certain officials. . . . Truth, freely accessible to all, we hold to be the most potent antiseptic against error." The letter concluded with "a very incomplete list" of works by League members seized in the raids, including Robert Benchley's *20,000 Leagues Under the Sea, or David Copperfield,* Millen Brand's *The Outward Room,* Pietro di Donato's *Christ in Concrete,* Elliott Paul's *The Mysterious Mickey Finn,* and Tess Slesinger's *The Magnolia Tree.* The Board wanted to list more, but told Phillips "the prosecution has so far made it impossible even to enumerate all of the condemned works."[4]

In an editorial titled "Barbarism in Oklahoma," the *Dallas Morning News* condemned the four convictions as one of "this country's most disheartening assaults" on freedom of speech "in recent years." Among books stored in that jail cell, the *Morning News* noted, "which will be burned under Oklahoma law unless the convictions are reversed," were Carl Sandburg's biography of Abraham Lincoln, Marquis James's biography of Andrew Jackson, Ernest Hemingway's *Farewell to Arms,* and John Steinbeck's *The Grapes of Wrath.* The *Morning News* concluded: "The Oklahoma action is Hitlerism at its worst." When threats to civil liberties occurred elsewhere, the Oklahoma syndicalism cases often became a reference point to demonstrate the unreasonable lengths to which government could go. In an editorial addressing Martin Dies's accusations that many officials in the Federal Price Administration had Communist affiliations, the *New York Herald* warned that "the same emotional motivation, carried to a greater extreme, may be found in . . . Oklahoma."[5]

When the ILD National Board met September 26, members noted that "[t]he case has been recognized as a national issue by the press of the country" and was generating additional interest with the National Lawyers Guild, many trade unions, and (at last) the Bill of Rights Committee of the American Bar Association. In addition, the National Lawyers Guild, the ACLU, and the National Federation for Constitutional Liberties had promised to file amicus briefs. The ILD announced a series of speaking engagements when it became clear that Oklahoma authorities would not carry out their threat to revoke bail for defendants who left the state to make speeches. Although Bob Wood was still prohibited from speaking by court order, Ina Wood was to take a tour through the Midwest and Far West in October and November. Elizabeth Green would speak to groups in Massachusetts and Philadelphia in October.[6]

Board members also noted support for the Oklahoma defendants had come from three national conventions—the American Newspapers Guild; the International Union of Mine, Mill and Smelter Workers; and the National Maritime Union—and trade unions such as the Cascade County Trades and Labor Assembly of Montana, the United American Artists, and local chapters of the Furniture Workers, the Furriers Joint Council, and the Fur Floor Boys. The International Woodworkers of America had it on their conference agenda for October. Members of Local 65 of the United Wholesale and Warehouse Employees Union of the CIO had collected ten dollars for the family of one defendant.

Finally, the ILD reported it had circulated 8,000 copies of the *St. Louis Post-Dispatch* editorial, 3,000 reprints of the *PM* feature article on Ina Wood and Elizabeth Green, 5,000 reprints of the "Oklahoma" special issue of *Equal Justice*, and 10,000 copies of a new pamphlet with Ina Wood's picture on the front page. It also announced a forthcoming Oklahoma Committee to Defend Political Prisoners pamphlet by Gordon Friessen. The back cover of this five-cent, twenty-four-page pamphlet—titled *Oklahoma Witch Hunt*—recommended getting "your union, club, ladies auxiliary to pass a resolution condemning the prosecutions and sending copies to the Governor, the county attorney, and the local newspapers." Also being circulated was another ILD protest letter to Governor Phillips, this one already signed by (among others) the solicitor general of the state of New York, the executive secretary of the American Friends Service Committee, the president emeritus of Smith College, and ACLU Chairman E. A. Ross. Much had been accomplished, the ILD concluded.[7]

Opposition also grew within the Sooner State. In late September the Farmers Union of Jackson County unanimously passed a resolution denouncing the convictions as "unconstitutional and undemocratic" and asking that "the persecutions be stopped." The Union sent copies to Governor Phillips and County Attorney Morris. In an editorial titled "Aftermath of the Syndicalism Cases," the September 19 issue of the *Oklahoma Daily* cited the letter publishers had sent to Governor Phillips. "It seems to be up to democratic citizens in other sections of the country to try to save Oklahoma from getting a permanent black eye as being the worst suppressor and persecutor of civil liberties in the nation," the student newspaper commented. "We disagree in part—we believe that the democratic citizens of Oklahoma will also help to save our state from such a reputation. What have YOU done to help?"[8]

In early October, the same week both the *Times* and the *Daily Oklahoman* kicked off National Newspaper Week with an industry-sponsored set of educational programs designed around the slogan "The Newspaper Lights the Way to Freedom," the *Oklahoman* reported the discovery of a Communist book in the county jail library. Prosecutors Eberle and Morris both expressed surprise when a reporter asked about the offending book. A deputy jailer thought it somehow got into the collection as a donation from the America First Committee or some similar organization. "I agree with Lewis Morris," the jailer said. "Anybody has the right of free speech, to send any literature they want to our library, but we have the right to decide what the prisoners ought to read." No harm done, the *Oklahoman* reported. The Communist book was thrown out and "jail culture" was "again purified."[9]

By that time Ina Wood was well into her tour. The Women's League for Democratic Rights in Chicago arranged a well-attended meeting October 11; two days later she spoke at the Midland Hotel.[10] While in Chicago, she was also interviewed by Howard Vincent O'Brien of *Chicago Daily News*. "I'm sorry I met Mrs. Robert Wood," O'Brien wrote. "If I hadn't seen her and talked to her, I could have gone right on thinking that the United States really was a 'democracy.'" The woman in front of him "wears her clothes with a chic that overrides their lack of newness." Although "she smiles readily," O'Brien also saw "sadness in her eyes, a hurt look." Ina explained, "After all, three months in jail does leave a scar or two." And she was convicted, O'Brien said, for "dangerous thoughts." He added that, to someone as far away from Oklahoma City "as I am, it has a Gilbert and Sullivan sound — a comic opera. . . . If you — or the people of Oklahoma — can make sense out of this, you're a whole lot better than I am."[11]

During her tour Ina wrote Bob regularly, sometimes three times a day. In one letter she said she was having difficulty sleeping but that an occasional evening drink seemed to help. However, she noted, a local ordinance forbade women from sitting at the bar. "I had a scotch & soda, and it had to be served to me at a table. Do you think Eberle would insist upon 'equality' for me in this instance?"[12] Wherever she went, Ina took copies of Friessen's *Oklahoma Witch Hunt,* several ILD pamphlets, the *St. Louis Post-Dispatch* editorial, and the *PM* story about her and Elizabeth Green, all of which she handed out to interested reporters. Commenting on an address she gave in Seattle November 18, the *Washington New-Dealer* described her as "an attractive young housewife facing a ten year prison sentence under Oklahoma's notorious criminal syndicalism laws." After a presentation in Portland, Oregon, the *Portland Oregonian* argued that "indefensible" and "absurd" criminal syndicalism laws like those in Oklahoma "do a disservice to decent people everywhere. . . . If Oklahoma can imprison these people for possession of the books that go to make up a rounded education . . . then virtually every major library in the United States is subject to burning. The whole affair stinks." In San Francisco, Ina raised three hundred dollars above costs for the defense fund.[13]

Despite the potential impact of the cases on library services and collections, however, the nation's library community was noticeably silent. The American Library Association had approved a Library Bill of Rights in 1939, but had not yet mobilized efforts to combat censorship. A few members of the library community did protest individually, however. During the fall the Metropolitan Library Council of New York and the Chicago Public Library Employees Union passed resolutions condemning the convictions.[14] In late August, Dartmouth College's assistant librarian, Alexander Laing, sent a letter to Oklahoma Attorney General Mac Williamson. "I should be glad if you would officially verify, for our bibliographical use, the authors and particular editions of books used as evidence in prosecuting persons connected with the Progressive Book Store," he wrote. "It is already evident that this case will become an historic one . . . and we are consequently anxious to place on our open shelves—for the use of students and for the public generally—the authentic editions concerned, while they are still readily available."

Williamson (who considered the criminal syndicalism trials County Attorney Lewis Morris's "baby" that he had "no intention of nursing") immediately forwarded Laing's letter to Morris. At the same time, he told the *Daily Oklahoman* that "in as much as Laing had that attitude he was surprised he didn't have the books already." The *Oklahoma City Times,* which ran the story next to a picture of a local jailer sitting atop some of the forty boxes of materials seized in the raids, contacted Eberle for comment. Although the librarian "probably didn't know what he was doing," Eberle said, he "would be glad to send to Dartmouth College a complete list of books and authors. If Dartmouth wants them, Dartmouth can have them. I don't care who reads them in New Hampshire. I am interested in their effect in Oklahoma."[15]

In the December issue of the Dartmouth *Library Bulletin,* Laing reported that Eberle's offer to supply a bibliography of the contents of the bookstore "seems to have caused a little honest bewilderment in the offices of the defense counsel." He noted one defense lawyer wrote him: "Inasmuch as neither the defendants nor any other attorneys have been able to secure an inventory of the property seized from the Oklahoma authorities, we would appreciate it very much if when you receive this list you would send us a copy." Just why this inventory was going to be made available to Dartmouth but not to the defense counsel confused him, Laing said, but it "will probably have to be explained by someone who understands the Oklahoma legal structure better than we ever hope to."[16]

In the December issue of the *P.L.C. Bulletin* (organ of the leftist Progressive Librarians Council), Ralph T. Esterquest, of Princeton's Institute for Advanced Study, expressed his surprise at how librarians seemed "unmoved by the fact that . . . fascist methods are today the official means of suppressing a free people" in Oklahoma. "The entire case has been the most flagrant violation of the American Bill of Rights that we have witnessed during the present emergency. . . . Let us shout to our readers," he concluded, the words that Ina Wood said to the people of Oklahoma. "Read — Read — Read! Find out what the pygmy minds have forbidden you to know."[17]

The event that likely had the most impact on the trials, however, occurred on December 7, 1941, when the Japanese struck Pearl Harbor. Within days the United States declared war on Japan, Italy and Germany, which automatically made the nation an ally of the Soviet Union in the European theatre. As war mobilization became the nation's highest priority, attitudes toward Communists shifted rapidly in some places, not so rapidly in others. Oklahoma fit the latter category, but although Oklahoma officials did not abandon their attitudes, the war certainly muted their criticism. Because the criminal syndicalism trials had been part of the voice through which they had expressed that criticism, the appeals process was directly influenced by this turn of events. Advocates for the defendants pressed forward; forces behind the prosecutions slowed matters to a crawl.[18]

In an appeal for support for the Oklahoma defendants, the ILD mailed out 10,000 copies of the Bill of Rights printed up in red, white, and blue for the Bill's 150th anniversary. The circular quoted President Roosevelt's proclamation designating December 15 as Bill of Rights Day: "We . . . who have seen these privileges lost . . . in other countries can now appreciate their meaning to those people who enjoyed them once. . . . And by that realization we have come to a clearer conception of their worth to us, and to a stronger and more unalterable determination that here in our land they shall not be lost or weakened or curtailed." In an editorial titled "Keep America Free," *Woman's Home Companion* acknowledged the importance of Bill of Rights Day and worried that "the ugly tread of intolerance is shaking the ground beneath us." As evidence, the *Companion* cited treatment of the Oklahoma defendants.[19] Bill of Rights Day came and went without much notice in Oklahoma.

At its December conference, the United Christian Council for Democracy (a federation of twelve Protestant denominations) unanimously passed a resolution protesting the Oklahoma convictions as "an attack on the Bill of Rights and the rights of every man to hold an opinion of his own and to know the opinions of others." The Council forwarded a copy to Governor Phillips. On December 22 the American Committee for Democracy and Intellectual Freedom released to the Associated Press a letter to Phillips signed by 279 social scientists from 74 universities arguing that if the books in the Oklahoma cases were outlawed in their states they would have to close their classes.[20] That same day the weekly University of Chicago Round Table sponsored a radio discussion of "Civil Rights and Public Danger." Guest speakers included Harvard law professor Zechariah Chafee, who, referring to the *Communist Manifesto,* commented: "It would be rather ridiculous if we put people in jail for publishing the basic document of our ally, Russia."[21]

In her November 10, 1941, *Tulsa Tribune* "A Woman's View" column, Mrs. Walter Ferguson reported a conversation she recently had with a large group of Oklahoma City friends—none of whom, she said, were Communists or Fascists, all of whom deplored the treatment meted out to the criminal syndicalism defendants. "Yet, by their own confessions, none had protested against something they believed to be wrong, unjust, and undemocratic going on in their state. They had not raised their voices for the right of free speech or fair trial." Ferguson urged her readers to ask themselves: "How much would I do to defy the rise of vicious tyranny and injustice at home, and if I will do nothing, do I in truth love and serve democracy?"[22]

And in its January bulletin, the Oklahoma Committee to Defend Political Prisoners wrote, "We ... work and pray for a victory of the United Nations," but "we [also] wish that the time and effort now devoted to seeing that justice is done to the twelve Americans that we represent could be spent more directly in helping to win the war. The convictions are holding back the enlistment in the army of several of the defendants." Editors also noted that *Oklahoma Witch Hunt,* which John Eberle had called a "new and expensive book" about the trials, was enjoying brisk sales (at five cents each) to libraries across the nation.[23]

On January 8, 1942, the *Tulsa Tribune* thought it caught "a hint" that the criminal syndicalism convictions might be reversed. On that day the Criminal Court of Appeals declared that distributing literature by Jehovah's Witnesses on the streets of Oklahoma City constituted an act of free speech, and thus the municipal ordinance prohibiting it was "invalid on its face." The *Tribune* quickly connected the decision to the syndicalism defendants and noted that the evidence in their cases had "consisted simply of proof that they offered for sale the works of Karl Marx and other Russian writers, works which are to be found on the shelves of most public libraries."[24]

In early January Governor Phillips received a petition signed by 145 social workers urging him to halt all the book trials until higher courts could decide appeals of those already convicted. When asked about the petition by the *Daily Oklahoman,* Phillips said: "When I get any of that Communist or pink stuff I never read it. It goes into a special box where I put it and turn it over to the FBI." When told by the *Oklahoman* that the petition had even been signed by Mary Anderson, head of the Women's Bureau of the United States Department of Labor, Phillips responded: "I don't give a damn if she is queen of Portugal." Phillips was true to his word. He turned the letters over to the FBI.[25]

By January 1942, eight organizations had filed appellate briefs. Briefs for the prosecution were filed by the American Legion and the Knights of Pythias; briefs for the defense were filed by the ACLU, National Lawyers Guild, National Federation for Constitutional Liberties, American Newspaper Guild, League of American Writers, and Book and Magazine Guild of the United Office and Professional Workers of America. Barefoot told all organizations that their briefs would apply to all companion cases, and that oral argument would be set by agreement of counsel, probably for late spring.[26]

But on January 24, 1942, John Eberle announced he would be resigning as assistant county attorney to go into private practice. "Well hold on to your seats!" Nena Beth Stapp wrote a friend at the ILD. "Would like to know just how much the pressure and adverse publicity had to do with this." She saw it as a good sign. "Getting him out of the way, and speculations about his successor, seem to open up new possibilities and hopes for us, I think." The *Oklahoma*

City Times thought Eberle was following the example of two other lawyers from the county attorney's office, who in previous years had used their experiences there to move into more lucrative private practices. "Eberle said he has no political ambitions and wants to get out of the prosecutor's office in the interest of a life career." Although his resignation would not be effective for several weeks, he told the *Times,* he nonetheless promised he would complete his briefs in the criminal syndicalism appeals and argue them before the appellate court.[27]

By this time it had become apparent that the prosecution would not initiate new trials and was reconciled to weathering the appeals process. It was also apparent that the county attorney's office was dragging its feet—appeals would not be heard until the fall, for reasons defense lawyers and supporters initially could not quite understand. In February John Eberle moved into private practice and was no longer initiating activity. Lewis Morris had not been successful in his bid for a gubernatorial nomination and seemed less willing to try the cases in the press. Some speculated he was looking for another position. Although the country's attention had decidedly turned toward the war effort, the criminal syndicalism cases would not go away.

Defense supporters across the political spectrum kept the criminal syndicalism trials before the public by comparing Oklahoma's record on civil liberties to the rhetoric used to justify war. If Americans were being asked to wage war to defend basic freedoms, this argument went, those same freedoms had to be afforded to citizens at home. And the president of the United States gave them ample ammunition. In a "Message to the Booksellers of America" for their annual banquet on May 6, Roosevelt wrote: "It is more important that your work should go on now than it has ever been at any other time in our history." Although "books burn," they "can not be killed by fire. . . . In this war, we know, books are weapons. And it is a part of your dedication always to make them weapons for man's freedom."[28] Now petitioners and protestors could quote the president; Governor Phillips's "special box" continued to fill with petitions and protests.

On February 7, the ILD held a book sale in New York City, asking authors whose works were known to be locked in the Oklahoma County jail to donate the original manuscripts or autographed duplicate copies of the books in order to raise funds for the Oklahoma defendants. The first sale was so successful that a second (this one cosponsored by the League of American Writers) was held March 8. For it, organizers issued a catalog. "In Oklahoma," an introduction noted, "twelve American men and women face 10 years in the penitentiary and a $5,000 fine each because Oklahoma County prosecutors hate and fear what is written in some of the books in this catalogue." Evidence for their crimes, the catalog said, was 10,000 volumes confiscated from a bookstore, all of which "ARE STILL IN JAIL."

Among items offered was a bound volume of 110 messages protesting the "Oklahoma Witch Hunt" sent to Oklahoma officials from literary luminaries like Theodore Dreiser, Dorothy Parker, and Clifford Odets, a final draft manuscript of *All Out on the Road to Smolensk* that author Erskine Caldwell autographed, an original corrected typescript of *America Organizes to Win the War* autographed by Dorothy Canfield Fisher, the typescript of *The Thin Man* autographed by author Dashiell Hammett, the original typescript of the play *Don't You Want to Be Free?* autographed by playwright/poet Langston Hughes, and the original corrected typescript of *American House of Lords: An Inquiry into the Freedom of the Press* signed by Secretary of the Interior Harold L. Ickes. William Saroyan sent the original corrected typescript of his play, *The Man With the Heart in the Highlands,* along with a note to the buyer. "I cannot be generous by giving it to you," he said, because the money was going to the Oklahoma victims. "The hero is yourself. Give them all you can." Also offered for sale were seven volumes of the original stenographic transcripts of the Scottsboro trials, and a two-volume transcript of Ina Wood's trial. The prize of the collection, however, was the original corrected typescript of Joseph E. Davies's best-selling *Mission to Moscow* autographed by its author. It was purchased for one hundred dollars. Numerous authors, including Dashiell Hammett and Erskine Caldwell, also donated autographed copies of their books.

After the sale concluded, several people requested copies of the catalog as souvenirs of Oklahoma's censoring practices.[29]

While the appellate process dragged on, the defendants received permission to leave the state several times. Bob Wood made attempts to join the army (thoughts of what was happening to Sherishevsky relatives his family had left behind in Bialystok in 1917 must have crossed his mind), but he was rebuffed by Oklahoma City local Draft Board No. 5 because of his conviction. On May 5, the *Daily Oklahoman* reported on page one that he had hitchhiked from New York to appear before the Board. "I came all the way down here to get in the army," he told a reporter. "After all, Russia is fighting for us now, and they convicted me because I was accused of saying nice things about Russia." He also spoke for Alan Shaw and Eli Jaffe, he said. "What harm would it do for Lewis Morris to go before the court of appeals and dismiss the cases so I can fight for the United States?" When the reporter ran to Morris for comment, the county attorney was quick to respond. "That's just cheap patriotism," he said. "They could have joined the army a long time ago. Sure, we weren't fighting then, but England needed some help. That's what they call chauvinism in the books — I don't know how you spell it." Although Bob Wood was not allowed to join the army, defense attorney George Croom was. He announced in early June that he was leaving the case.[30]

All the while, protests continued to pour in to Governor Phillips. At its annual conference April 23–25, the National Executive Board of the State, County and Municipal Workers of America unanimously adopted a resolution protesting the prosecutions. On May 5, members of the Atlantic District Local Two, American Communications Association of the CIO, unanimously adopted an almost identical resolution. Both sent copies to Governor Phillips.[31] At the behest of the editor of the *Churchman,* 176 clergymen from thirty-three states signed a letter to Phillips expressing concern at the continued prosecutions. Among those signing were Roland Bainton of the Yale Divinity School, Daniel J. Fleming and Reinhold Niebuhr of the Union Theological Seminary, and editors of *The Christian Leader* and *The Emancipator.* In early June the ILD drafted a boilerplate resolution on the Oklahoma cases that it sent by the hundreds to local unions. The results of these efforts were obvious, and in part made more effective by the antilabor legislation the Oklahoma Legislature had passed in January 1941. Not a few labor leaders noticed that the same people who had spearheaded the Little Dies Committee had also been integral to this legislation.[32] Within months Governor Phillips had nearly forty newly passed resolutions move through his "special box" from local union chapters that represented college teachers, leather workers, butchers, miners, autoworkers, jewelers, furriers, carpenters, architects, steelworkers, bakers, the International·Ladies Garment Workers Union Locals 45, 84, and 95 in Los Angeles and San Francisco, and 500,000 organized workers represented by the New York Industrial Union Council.[33]

All this time, however, defense counsel could not understand why the prosecution was so slow in responding to the appellate brief Bob Wood's attorneys filed on June 20, 1941. Month after month passed, and still the state had not acted. On May 28, 1942, however, U.S. Attorney General Francis Biddle issued an opinion on efforts to deport Harry Bridges, an Australian citizen who came to the United States in 1920 and had a long career in San Francisco as president of the International Longshoremen's and Warehouse Union. Bridges was suspected of being a member of the Communist Party. In his opinion, Biddle argued that Communists advocated the overthrow of government by force and violence, which meant that Bridges had violated the Alien Registration Act of 1940. Eberle quickly seized upon it. Here was the chief law officer in the country making an argument that seemed to parallel the point Oklahoma officials were pursuing against the criminal syndicalism defendants. "Mr. Biddle handed the Oklahoma prosecution 7,000 words of inspiration," the ILD reported, "and in less than three weeks their Robert Wood brief was written, printed, and filed."[34]

The brief contained eight propositions and concluded with references to Biddle's findings of fact and conclusions of law in the Bridges case that the Oklahoma prosecutors considered relevant to their cases. In its brief the state contended that the criminal syndicalism law was constitutional, that freedom of speech and press were limited and subject to punishment when exercised outside proper bounds, that evidence introduced in the case was legal, competent, and properly received, and that "opening and closing arguments to the jury were proper reading of exhibits and comments thereon, and were properly made in answer to defense arguments."[35]

Three weeks later the American Legion filed its amicus brief, focusing primarily on Communism, not the trials' merits. "In fairness to the boys of America who fight unceasingly on the hot sands of the desert, amidst the mysticism of India, in the ancient land of the Chinese, in the shadow of the Pyramids, on land and sea and island, in the air, under the sea," said the final paragraph, "who as their white faces are turned to the sky for the last time and who with failing breath ask their God to let this government of the people continue, we ask that the conviction of one who sought to undermine it and overthrow it be upheld and that Robert Wood be required to serve his sentence as fixed by the jury."[36]

In late July Judge B. B. Barefoot set September 9, 10:00 A.M. for hearing oral arguments in the appeals. The ILD announced that Congressman Marcantonio planned to travel to Oklahoma to participate in oral arguments with ILD attorney Sam Neuberger and local attorney Stanley Belden (who had returned from California to Oklahoma to enter the military).[37] *Publishers Weekly* reported the appeals date and expressed amazement that "the temper of the prosecution is as full of venom as if nothing had happened in the two years since the raid took place, as if national sentiment has not been aroused, or as if the world situation were quite as it was when the shop was raided." Again *Publishers Weekly* appealed to its readers to write Governor Phillips.[38]

If people expected the atmosphere at the appeals hearing to be different from the original four cases, they were quickly disappointed. When defense lawyers requested on September 8 that the hearing be delayed by a day so Marcantonio could make several important roll call votes in Congress and still attend final arguments in Oklahoma City, Judge Doyle announced he would refuse to attend the oral arguments. "If they were local attorneys, I'd know how to take care of them," he later told reporters. "If I were presiding judge, they wouldn't be permitted to appear at all in this case." Doyle made no secret that he was especially irritated with Marcantonio's characterization of the original prosecution as "fascist" and prosecutors as "fascist-minded." That, Doyle said, was an insult. "They have reflected on the patriotism of the people, the conduct of the courts and as far as I am concerned, they have forfeited their right to be heard by any court of which I am a member." Although he refused to listen to out-of-state defense lawyers, he told reporters, he still intended to participate in the decision.[39] Earlier defense concerns about Doyle's neutrality appear to have been well founded.

Presiding Judge Barefoot and Judge Dick Jones quickly put distance between themselves and Doyle. "We are not concerned with statements made outside the record by anybody," they said. "All parties to these appeals are entitled to a fair and courteous hearing in open court." Defense lawyers also refused to comment directly on Doyle's statements. "We are highly appreciative of the courtesy extended by the court in permitting us as members of the bar of another state to appear before it in this case." Ultimately defense lawyers decided to substitute Herman Rosenfeld of New York for Marcantonio, rather than antagonize Doyle further by pressing their case. In reporting Doyle's remarks, the *Daily Oklahoman* referred to the dispute as an "unprecedented division among judges of the high court." But defense counsel still had not met the last obstacle suddenly placed in their way to interfere with their strategy. Twenty minutes before the appeal hearing was opened the state finally filed briefs in the cases of Ina Wood, Alan Shaw, and Eli Jaffe. Defense counsel had little time to read them before oral arguments started.[40]

As the parties took their places at 10 A.M. on September 9, they played to a packed courtroom. In the audience were Clarence and Hulda Lewis, Nena Beth Stapp, Alan Shaw, and Roscoe Dunjee, armed with pen and notebook to record for the next issue of *Black Dispatch* "a courtroom drama, which bids fair to become a classic in judicial and intellectual circles." Neither Eli Jaffe nor Bob and Ina Wood attended. For two days the two sides laid out their cases.[41]

Stanley Belden opened for the defense by reviewing the facts. He especially attacked the legality of the search warrants and condemned the treatment meted out to defendants while they were in custody. Sam Neuberger addressed the legal questions. Holding opinions or possessing books did not constitute a clear and present danger to the state of Oklahoma, nor a violation of the state's criminal syndicalism law. "I still want to know what these defendants did in Oklahoma County in violation of the law," he said. "If you convict these defendants, I pity the man in this state who in future years has any book in his home other than the Holy Bible."[42]

John Eberle was chief spokesman for the prosecution; Lewis Morris sat to his left. All the state had to prove, Eberle said, was that defendants "had the intent to bring about the overthrow of the government. . . . When we prove they have books advocating things prohibited by the legislature, that's all we have to do." One justice asked: "Did anyone identify Alan Shaw's signature on his membership card, or was it admitted solely on circumstantial evidence?" Eberle replied: "Your Honor, Judge, everybody knows Alan Shaw is a Communist. . . . We did not have any evidence, but I have a case I will read to the court which will settle that point." Judge Barefoot interrupted: "Does the legislature have the right to say a man cannot be a member of the Communist Party?" "I don't think the legislature has the right to say a man cannot be a Republican, a Democrat, or a member of any political party," Eberle replied, "but I want to read you an opinion recently made by United States Attorney General Francis Biddle." He then quoted from Biddle's statement that Communists advocated the overthrow of government through force and violence. "That's why they scattered literature saying 'The Yanks Are Not Coming,' and . . . they sang songs such as the 'Internationale.' . . . You see, a Communist never goes to take a drink without he makes a memorandum, and we have all of their memorandums." But was there a clear and present danger shown in state's evidence? Justice Jones asked. "If you can't show this, in my judgment the defendants should be discharged." "We don't have to prove they had the fuse lit, rifles stacked or the dynamite ready," Eberle replied. "We only have to prove that they possessed books that taught the overthrow of the government in a manner prohibited by the legislature."[43]

Eberle appeared oblivious to changes that had been taking place in free speech jurisprudence over the past fifteen years. In a series of cases favoring the protection of free speech — some involving state criminal syndicalism laws and Communist Party members — the U.S. Supreme Court had adopted the "clear and present danger" test to expand free speech protection. Under this standard, "The question in every case is whether the words used are used in such circumstances and are of such a nature as to create a clear and present danger that they will bring about the substantive evils that Congress has a right to prevent. It is a question of proximity and degree." Without this protection, the Court had said, state statutes might serve as a "dragnet which may enmesh anyone who agitates for a change of government if a jury can be persuaded that he ought to have foreseen his words would have some effect in the future conduct of others." Eberle's views reflected the superpatriotic World War I fervor that led to free-speech restrictions, not the Supreme Court's subsequent concern for civil liberties that occurred thereafter.[44]

A local attorney representing the Knights of Pythias followed Eberle. "They're trying to take our loyal Negroes and make them believe they should form a separate nation within the United States," he argued. The attorney representing the American Legion rose next and looked at Neuberger and Rosenfeld. "I take it that the men on the other side of this table represent some organization. An age old civilization is dying in Europe, but even though that be true, representatives of that social order have no right to come into our hemisphere and attempt to overthrow our form of government." Judge Jones interrupted him. Did you attend the original trials? The Legion attorney said he did not. Jones continued: "Our problem here is how to save civil liberties. Liberties are not absolute, and we know the government has a right to draw a line somewhere." Judge Barefoot wanted to know about the books impounded by the state. He asked Lewis Morris: "Were all of the books seized Communist books?" Morris fudged: "They sought to show that copies of the

same books seized were in the library of the University of Oklahoma, but the court would not permit the introduction of this
testimony."[45]

Local press coverage of the hearing varied. The *Oklahoma City
Times* hoped the "East's radical centers" did not affect local opinion. "The work of four Oklahoma juries . . . will get the fishy eye
from a large assortment of representatives of recognized radical
groups." The *Oklahoman* chose not to editorialize, but did note
"lawyers argued and judges sizzled without precedent as Oklahoma's Red cases were paraded before the criminal court of appeals." National press coverage was more generous and included
lengthy articles in the *Christian Science Monitor, Chicago Tribune,* and
Washington Post.[46]

When Neuberger, Belden, and Rosenfeld reported to the ILD
Board on September 14, they noted that "with the exception of the
fascist-minded prosecution clique which is determined to continue
its railroading," sentiment in the state had turned in their favor.
The *St. Louis Post-Dispatch* editorial, they acknowledged, had been
especially effective. When Board members heard that a quick fund-
raising campaign initiated several weeks earlier netted $2,254.85
and a lot of publicity across the nation, they decided to host another
New York City dinner dedicated to "Defending the Home Front"
on October 9. They also agreed to send defendants out on another
speaking tour, ask Roscoe Dunjee "to assume leadership of publicity
for the cases in the Negro press," and initiate "the widest possible
letter writing and resolutions campaign from trade union organizations, individuals, and groups of prominent people" directed to
Oklahoma Attorney General Williamson.[47]

Three hundred fifty people attended the October 9 dinner, at
which African American Chicago Alderman Earl B. Dickerson discussed discrimination as a deterrent to a national unity essential to
win the war, and CPUSA General Secretary Earl Browder argued that
the Oklahoma cases were examples of disunifying influences in the
United States. Also speaking were Carol King, who defended Harry
Bridges in the case upon which Oklahoma prosecutors relied so
heavily; New York City Council member Adam Clayton Powell; and

ILD President Vito Marcantonio. Sam Neuberger gave an auto-biographical account of his experiences representing the defendants in Oklahoma City. Numerous trade union organizations reserved tables for their groups; all proceeds above costs were donated to the Oklahoma defense fund.[48]

The letter-writing campaign moved quickly. The ILD distributed thousands of leaflets titled "An Open Letter to the Attorney General," which condemned the trials and provided space for petitioners to sign their names and identify organizations they represented. Many sympathizers wrote their own letters to the Oklahoma attorney general. One of the most colorful came from Comfort A. Adams, well-known Harvard emeritus professor of engineering and at the time employed in war-industry research. "I have followed with interest" the Oklahoma syndicalism cases, he began, but "after careful study of all the facts available to me" concluded no evidence existed to justify guilty verdicts against the four defendants. The source of Oklahoma's problem, Adams surmised, was a "stupid and almost superstitious fear of socialism or communism, as fostered by the propaganda of a very powerful and highly organized financial group, and supported by millions of innocent and unthinking victims of that propaganda." Conduct of Oklahoma officials was "more dangerous to our highly cherished rights and freedoms" than anything done by the defendants. "How can we ask respect for these rights when they are utterly disregarded by some of our courts and other Government agents?"[49]

Others joined Adams in the letter-writing campaign, including the 500,000 CIO members of the Greater New York Industrial Council; Plymouth Local Union No. 51, United Auto Workers in Detroit; and Local 623 (New York) of the AFL's Amalgamated Meat Cutters Union.[50] In a two-week period Williamson was contacted by the Cook County (Chicago) Industrial Union Council; the Construction and General Laborers Local 273 from Great Falls, Montana; Machinists Local 79 from Seattle; the State CIO Board of Arkansas; the Teachers' Union Local at MIT in Cambridge, Massachusetts; Local 9 of the Marine and Shipbuilding Workers of America in San Pedro, California; the Mississippi Delta Organizing Committee of United Cannery

locals from Truman, Arkansas, and Greenville, Mississippi; Local 9 of
the Miners Union in Mullan, Idaho; Local 4427 of the United Mine
Workers of America in Purseglove, West Virginia; the United Shoe
Workers of America in Philadelphia; the Social Services Employees
Union from Baltimore, Maryland; the United Furniture Workers
Local 450 from Cleveland; and the Cleveland and Seattle Industrial
Union Councils. The president of the American Communications
Association of the CIO wrote Williamson, "[A]t a time when we are
fighting to rid the world of fascism . . . it is shocking to find a State
Government in the conduct of a fascist-like witch-hunt."

By the end of November one hundred presidents and secre-
taries of state and regional CIO and AFL councils formed themselves into a Labor Committee on the Oklahoma Criminal Syndicalism Cases to monitor the situation. In December, officers from the
International Union of Fishermen and Allied Workers of America,
the United Office and Professional Workers of America, and the
United Farm Equipment and Metal Workers of America joined the
Committee. Even the Ellis County (Oklahoma) attorney joined the
chorus. "Were I not prohibited by my official obligations," he wrote
Williamson, "I would volunteer to defend them so far as my poor
ability might permit; not so much for the sake of these individuals,
but for the cause of human liberty."[51]

In the midst of this national campaign, the defendants tried to
resume normal lives. After graduating from high school in May,
Wilma Lewis left for a National Youth Administration training
school in Wichita to learn sheet metal work. Thereafter she returned to Oklahoma City and, although she scored extremely well
in an exam for a sheet metal worker position at nearby Tinker Air
Force Base, she was not offered the job. In the meantime Eli had
been courting her in love letters he sent in red, white, and blue
special-delivery airmail envelopes from New York, where he had
been living since being permitted to leave the state in October 1941.
One letter popped the question: Would she marry him? Ask my
parents, she responded. He did. They said yes, she said yes, and in
mid-September she bought a one-way ticket to New York City. After
both a rabbi and a minister refused to marry a Jewish man and

Gentile woman, they were married in a civil ceremony on September 26, 1942, by a member of the Ethical Culture Society. He contributed his fee to the Oklahoma defense fund. Although few attended the ceremony, a celebratory party thereafter drew many friends, including playwright Arthur Miller, Eli's old friend since college days. Eli reminisced to Miller some years later: "I still recall you playing (?) the guitar and literally whipping up and making like a raging storm." "A romance which flowered in the midst of Oklahoma's syndicalism trials led Saturday to the marriage license bureau in New York," reported the *Daily Oklahoman* in its September 27 edition.[52]

Wilma quickly took a job in a New York aviation plant while Eli made twenty-five dollars a month working as managing editor for the *Weekly Review*. In its October 18 issue, *PM* published an interview with Wilma and Eli carrying the headline "Overnight They Put My Family In Jail . . . It Was a Nightmare." In the interview Wilma recounted the August 17 "nightmare" from her perspective and in picturesque detail. When asked why she was working in the defense industry given her experiences, she responded: "I saw what Fascism could be like in this country. Now I know what the fight is about." Asked why he left Brooklyn for Oklahoma in 1938, Eli responded, "I went out there to get material for a book I was writing, a sort of *Grapes of Wrath*. Well, I got the sour grapes — and most of the wrath!"[53]

In late October 1942, the Oklahoma Criminal Court of Appeals ordered the four convicted defendants to return to Oklahoma City by December 1 and remain there until it handed down its decision. Judge Barefoot indicated that the court might not issue its decision until February 1943, "at the earliest." The ILD argued that "this constituted clear persecution of the defendants." All four had to leave jobs in the New York City area and remain in Oklahoma City, where they were unlikely to get employment. Board members tried unsuccessfully to convince the court of appeals to relax restrictions on their travel in order to use them as much as possible for fund-raising events.[54]

Between November 5 and November 28, Ina Wood traveled through cities in the East, including Newark, New Haven, Boston,

Philadelphia, Baltimore, and Washington, while Wilma and Eli Jaffe traveled through Midwest cities, including Cleveland, Akron, Toledo, Detroit, Chicago, Milwaukee, Indianapolis, and St. Louis, before returning to Oklahoma City on November 29. At each site they spoke to union and civil liberties groups. In Detroit Eli addressed Local 51 of the United Automobile Workers, where a young African American man sporting a UAW pin on his lapel approached him. "You ain't just batting your gums," he told Eli. He knew Jim Crow life as a youth in the South, he said, and racism in the industrial North. "If you folks in Oklahoma win your fight against those fascists down there, it'll help us up here and the same thing around."[55] Wilma and Eli also went through St. Louis, where a local *Post-Dispatch* reporter interviewed them. "With so many Americans fighting for world freedom, liberty must not be strangled at home," Wilma told the reporter. A picture of the couple accompanied the story, all located on page one, above the fold.[56]

The *Daily Oklahoman* also noted the defendants' return on page one, and on page seven ran a picture of them all plus Wilma. The paper was careful to mention that all of the defendants had been living in New York City. There Ina Wood had been employed as a clerk in a private library, Eli Jaffe as an editor of "a weekly youth magazine," and Bob Wood as a truck driver until a bout with arthritis confined him to a hospital in recent weeks. Only Alan Shaw, who was now state secretary of the Communist Party, had remained in Oklahoma City. "If there is a chance for an early decision, I would just as soon wait here until then," Bob told the *Oklahoman*. "Otherwise I would like to return to the east for additional medical treatment."[57]

While in Oklahoma, the defendants tried to make good use of their time. Shortly after their return to Oklahoma City, Bob and Ina hosted a party at a local hotel. FBI agents lingered outside, taking down license plate numbers. Among those invited was an informant for the Intelligence Office at Will Rogers Air Field. "Robert and Ina Wood are the real leaders and the party whips," the informant reported, "experienced and well traveled and slick as ice." Alan and Eli were "mere babes in arms" next to Bob Wood, "who keeps them going through flattery and bombast." The informant was especially taken with Ina, "who is very dark, poised, beautiful, educated and practically worshipped by the whole group." Bob Wood and Eli Jaffe, he observed, "are quite Jewish . . . and therefore doubly opposed to the Axis." The informant concluded his report by noting all the defendants "and their wives are now primarily concerned with soliciting funds by which to advertise and thereby gain sympathy in Oklahoma. They are all making trips around the state, dunning friends who can afford to contribute."[58]

This was not the only intelligence the FBI gathered against the defendants. Postal officials assisted the FBI in intercepting the defendants' mail as early as March 1941, and within the year the Bureau had imposed a "mail cover" on all the defendants' correspondence. Their phones were also tapped. In September 1942, the FBI learned that Alan Shaw would be out of town and J. Edgar Hoover recommended "a technical surveillance on [his] residence" during his absence, including the installation of listening devices. Alan and Nena Beth's neighbors reported they could hear "the clattering of typewriters and the rustling of papers" late at night; their landlord offered to furnish the FBI "with information of any activities" and "would cooperate . . . in any and every way possible." Agents and their informants regularly attended Communist Party meetings, reporting events in great detail, and for a while FBI agents filed reports every two weeks. Informants reported that Bob continued to hold meetings in Oklahoma, "chiefly to discuss race discrimination." The FBI noted with concern that Bob had successfully "recruited at least ten new members and probably more in Tulsa, and has revived interest among heretofore lackadaisical members."[59]

But defendants nonetheless struggled between December 1 and the unpredictable day the decision would be handed down. They dined several times with defense attorney George Croom and his family as they waited. Most were unable to obtain employment except for part-time jobs. Alan received some income as state secretary of the Oklahoma Communist Party, but at times he and Nena Beth also minimized expenses by staying with her mother. Because he had been denied gasoline rationing cards, Alan had to take the train or bus to perform Party work. Ina worked part-time at the

Black Dispatch for Roscoe Dunjee, who was criticized by some members in the African American community for hiring a white woman. Bob eventually got a job as a "warehouse man" at a Tulsa tire company. Eli and Wilma Jaffe stayed with her parents on their small farm outside Oklahoma City. Wilma tried to get a job, but no one would hire her. Eli got part-time work helping with the wheat harvest.[60]

At last, on February 17, 1943, the three-judge panel of the Oklahoma Criminal Court of Appeals handed down a decision. Two-and-a-half years after their arrests, the convictions of three of the defendants—Alan Shaw, Eli Jaffe, and Ina Wood, those charged solely with Communist Party membership—were reversed and their cases remanded. Judge Dick Jones wrote a 41-page opinion, in which Judge Barefoot concurred. Judge Doyle did not participate; local papers cited "health reasons."[61] The decision upheld the constitutionality of the criminal syndicalism law, but also held that "the books, pamphlets and other written material" should not have been admitted "without evidence . . . to show that the statements therein made were in truth and fact statements representing the true position of the Communist Party."[62] Furthermore, the court cited a U.S. Supreme Court case for the proposition that "[n]o inference can be drawn from the possession of the books mentioned, either that they embodied the doctrines of the Communist Party or that they represented views advocated by the appellant."[63]

Unlike the district court judges who presided over the three original cases, the opinion stated, the court had actually read most of the books introduced into evidence. The court quoted Thomas Jefferson: "I hold a little rebellion now and then is a good thing and as necessary in the political world as storms in the physical." The court held that a jury could find a defendant guilty only if it found that the defendant by his or her "individual action" advocated "the overthrow of our government by the bullet instead of the ballot," and that such advocacy presented a "clear and present danger." Upholding the convictions "could only be because there is popular demand for it and this, in effect, would mean a substitution of mob rule for that of courts of law." And in commenting on the civil liberties of the three defendants the court ruled: "If we were to deny any one of these any one of the guaranties provided by our constitution it would establish a precedent that might in the future cause the arrest and confinement of thousands of our citizens and would more surely result in a violent revolution and overthrowing of our government than these alleged statements of a puny few."[64]

Alan Shaw was sitting with his wife in a downtown drugstore when he received the news. His first reaction was to kiss Nena Beth, "as other customers watched and wondered." He called the decision an "affirmation of the principles of democracy which we are fighting to defend." He predicted that Bob Wood's conviction would also be overturned because the jury in his case received the same "faulty instructions." Ina Wood, now "an expectant mother," said she was "very happy" about the reversals and wanted "to thank all of the people in Oklahoma and over the nation who put up the money for bonds and bail." Eli and Wilma Jaffe were sitting on the front porch of Wilma's parents' home when they heard the news. Eli "was gleeful," the *Oklahoman* reported. "I guess we're going to be in the army," he said. "They've got us 4-F now because of the convictions, but maybe this'll make us 1-A again." The *Daily Oklahoman* carried the story on page one above the fold.[65]

In a *Weekly Review* interview, Wilma said, "This is a real victory . . . for national unity and against the home-spun fascists Oklahoma seems plagued with." She hoped the decision would enable her to harness her skills and training and get a job in one of Oklahoma City's aircraft factories, "where I can do the most good making nails for Hitler's coffin." Eli echoed her sentiments. "This decision is a kick in the face of the red-baiters and the fascist-minded prosecutors, who thought they could tell people what books they could read, what thoughts they could think, what political party they could belong to."[66]

When asked about the opinion, John Eberle — now in private practice — declined comment. Lewis Morris — who had recently become a district judge — said: "I believe in the American judicial system and the opinion speaks for itself." New County Attorney George Miskovsky, who had fifteen days to seek a rehearing, was undecided about his next move. "I want an opportunity to examine the opinion and familiarize myself with the facts and circumstances before making any decisions." The FBI did not have much confidence in Miskovsky. "It is known by this office that the Communist Party sponsored Miskovsky in his campaign for County Attorney," an agent reported. He told J. Edgar Hoover that Miskovsky had promised the ILD he would dismiss indictments against all defendants who had not yet been brought to trial.[67]

In the *Tulsa World*'s Sunday edition, Capital Bureau correspondent Lorren Williams noted how much had changed between August 1940 and February 1943. If the trials were held again, he said, it would be in a vastly different setting, locally, nationally, and internationally. "Gone would be most of the principals and much of the background trappings which made the trials a Roman Holiday which drew attention from coast to coast." Judge Ben Arnold had been elevated to the state Supreme Court, partly because of the publicity he received in the trials. Lewis Morris had been elevated to the district court, partly for the same reason. John Eberle was now in private practice, and Morris's successor "won the office over the opposition of most of the old courthouse crowd." Because state Senator Paul Stewart had been elected to Congress in 1942, "his voice is lost from the legislative halls of Oklahoma." And former-governor Phillips, like Stewart a "ponderous individual" who "had no sympathy with 'Reds' or with labor agitators," had yielded the office of governor to Robert S. Kerr, who deliberately abstained from "Red Hunts." And of course, in 1943, Russia was an ally. "Writers who two years before were denouncing 'the Bear that walks like a man,' are finding in Stalin a genius, both of civil and military operations." New trials, Williams concluded, were highly unlikely.[68]

In an ILD press release, Congressman Marcantonio characterized the decision as "a powerful blow to reaction, and the first important victory on the road to finally wiping out the Oklahoma criminal syndicalism cases." He warned, however, that "until the conviction against Robert Wood is also reversed, and until the three cases which have been sent back for new trials, and the eight untried cases, are finally dismissed, the victory is not complete." Bolstered by "the magnificent response of the American people in expressing its opposition to these prosecutions and supporting the defense," the ILD was inspired to continue its campaign "without abatement."[69]

Publishers Weekly reported the news in a matter-of-fact manner without celebration. Similar stories appeared in the *Washington Post, Wall Street Journal,* and *Chicago Tribune.* In contrast, the *Daily Worker* celebrated the victory over "the fascist gentry who originated the cases," and *New Masses* pronounced the reversal "a real victory for civil liberties and national unity." On February 23, the *Saturday Evening Post* published on its front cover Norman Rockwell's "Freedom of Speech" painting, one of the "four freedoms" pieces he did to remind Americans what they were fighting to defend.[70]

Oklahoma City Communists planned a victory rally at the Shrine Auditorium for the evening of March 1, but that afternoon Judge Barefoot called defense lawyers into his chambers and warned against it. "Such actions on the part of the Party . . . will in no way help" Bob Wood's appeal, he said. In response, plans shifted. "The party decided to make the meeting strictly a women's affair," the FBI reported, and especially featured Nena Beth Stapp. Two hundred people attended. A similar rally was held in Tulsa the next day. Except for these two rallies, however, state Party response to the decision was deliberately muted.[71]

Soon after the appellate court rendered its decision, John Eberle filed a petition and brief criticizing the Criminal Court of Appeals and asking for a rehearing. In a split decision rendered May 19 (Judge Doyle dissenting), the appellate court denied the request. Judge Jones, who wrote the opinion, was obviously miffed at the prosecution. "In view of the extraordinary length of the brief and of some of the extravagant statements used by counsel in challenging the conclusions reached by a majority of this court . . . we feel a further statement of the issues should be made." In his petition Eberle argued that the court was obligated to Oklahoma citizens to make sure the Communist "menace to our government is checked." Jones, however, emphasized that "we intend to dispose of the issues" raised by Eberle "solely upon what we determine to be the applicable law and without any consideration of extrajudicial matter." Eberle had clearly met his match. To Eberle's argument that the court's decision nullified the criminal syndicalism act, Jones replied "This is not true." The Court of Appeals only wanted to "establish certain legal principles" to "govern its future application" and guard against the kind of violations of civil liberties evident in these cases that the Supreme Court had already addressed in similar "clear and present danger" cases. "If we let down the bars to make it easier to convict Communists, then the bars will be down as to all other citizens. All people benefit when courts insist on the maintenance of free speech and other constitutional liberties for men we dislike."[72]

"Okla. Court Ruling Blow to Witch Hunters," teased the *Daily Worker.* "Communism Ruling in Oklahoma Stands," reported the *Christian Science Monitor.* "Judge Chides State, Upholds Red Decisions," the *Daily Oklahoman* told its readers on page one. The next day, County Attorney Miskovsky dismissed all charges based solely on membership in the Communist Party. Charges were still pending against some defendants for selling literature in violation of the criminal syndicalism law. Except for Bob Wood, the court also released all prisoners from bail; in early June $44,500 was returned to the ILD.[73]

Not until September 15 — nearly thirty-seven months after the original raids on the Progressive Book Store — did the Criminal Court of Appeals render its opinion in Bob Wood's case. As with previous decisions, the court upheld the constitutionality of the state's criminal syndicalism law, and the three-man panel split 2–1, with Judge Doyle dissenting. In his opinion, Judge Barefoot made only passing reference to rhetorical excesses in the prosecution's case, and primarily addressed himself to the issue of whether selling and distributing literature seized in the August 17 raid constituted a violation of the law. He declared that limitations upon individual liberty must have appropriate relations to the state's safety. "When the legislative act exceeds the need, the principles of constitutional freedom are violated." Although a statute may be "perfectly legal," if its "application is such that one is deprived of personal constitutional liberty, a conviction must be set aside as violate of due process."[74]

Barefoot quoted at length a recent Supreme Court decision articulating the "clear and present danger" test: "There is a material difference between agitation and exhortation calling for the present violent action which creates a clear and present danger," he said, "and mere doctrinal justification or prediction of the use of force under hypothetical conditions at some future time — prediction that is not calculated or intended to be presently acted upon."[75] The court criticized the way the trial court had interpreted the law in its instructions to the jury. "This construction and application of the statute amounted to holding that anyone who at any time and for any reason displayed or sold books of this character is presumed to have advocated the doctrines therein announced. Under this construction, any bookstore owner or manager, or librarian selling or circulating such a book would be guilty of violation of the statute. . . . This was clearly error, and denial of a fundamental right." Because the jury in the Robert Wood case was not told that to find the defendant guilty it was necessary to prove he "had an unlawful intent" to violently and forcefully overthrow government by selling and distributing literature, and that the sales and distribution of this literature were "reasonably likely to result within the immediate future, in the commission of a crime," Barefoot said, the Criminal Court of Appeals had no choice but to reverse the trial court's decision.

Upon hearing of the reversal, Bob asked through his lawyer if he could return to his old job in New York City, where his wife and six-week-old son Timothy were now living. County Attorney Miskovsky immediately endorsed the request, the court issued the order, and Bob Wood announced plans to leave the state. To close friends, he said he "never wanted to see Oklahoma again." Before leaving, however, Bob met with Communist colleagues, nominated a small group of the faithful to carry on Party activities in Oklahoma, and announced he would be joining the military.[76]

When news of Bob's release was wired to New York, a *Daily Worker* reporter quickly went to Ina's west-side apartment for her reaction. Ina was bathing Tim, who, his mother swore, "smiled outright" when told his father was soon coming home. "I'd somehow like to say thanks to all the people and publications who really helped us," she said. "Everywhere I went I found people who were not only interested in the case but terribly angry about it—and many of them were editors who used the columns of their papers to show how they felt." Accompanying the article was a photo of Ina holding her smiling "chunk of humanity."[77]

Although the International Labor Defense crowed that the decision "is a victory for all people in America," and especially the "millions" who "joined with us in fighting against . . . domestic fascists who are playing Hitler's game of disunity and persecution of all minorities," the ILD fully expected Eberle to seek a rehearing. Defense attorneys promised to move in district court for final dismissal of the case against Bob Wood and the book possession charges still stemming against Ina Wood, Eli Jaffe, Alan Shaw, Elizabeth Green, and Max Sparer.[78] But County Attorney Miskovsky commented that it would be "silly" to retry the remaining cases if they led to the same result.[79]

On September 19, the *Daily Oklahoman* carried a letter to the editor from W. J. "Bill" Loe, who said he was glad the "red cases" were finally dismissed. "These cases have not only cost the taxpayers thousands of dollars," he said, "but one only has to read the editorial comments on these cases to know that Oklahoma has been made the laughing stock of the intellectual world."[80] The letter was unique for the local dailies; for the previous three years the *Oklahoman* and the *Times* chose not to print scores of letters to the editor sent by people across the state and the country criticizing Oklahoma's prosecution of the cases. It is also highly probable that many Sooner State residents who disagreed with the editorial positions these newspapers consistently took chose not to write public letters of protest for fear of retaliation against them and their families by organizations like the County's Civil Guards or the City's Emergency Defense Battalion. The trials had certainly provided plenty of evidence to justify those fears.

On October 5, the Oklahoma County District Court dismissed all remaining charges for selling or possessing books against the last six defendants. The next day Miskovsky told the judge he would be glad to return the books and pamphlets still occupying a county jail cell to their rightful owners "if each defendant would establish which book he owned. . . . If no one calls for them soon, we'll probably look the stock over and dump the pamphlets on the trash heap and then find a way to make legal disposition of all the better volumes." Alan Shaw told the *Daily Oklahoman* that evening that he planned to claim the materials.[81]

"Finis," the ILD announced in an October 9 press release. A week later Bob Wood, Alan Shaw, and Eli Jaffe had their draft status changed from 4-F to 1-A and were ordered to appear before their draft boards. "All three," the *Daily Worker* reported, "welcomed the opportunity they had previously sought in vain to serve with the armed forces of our country." At the end of the year, when the *Daily Oklahoman* celebrated the 151st anniversary of the Bill of Rights, it warned readers in an editorial of extending too much power to government, and especially the president. "We shall do well to take notice of the rock from which we are hewn. Here in the Bill of Rights is the source of our liberties. Here also is the source of genuine Americanism."[82]

CHAPTER SEVEN

Aftermath

Defendants

Eli Jaffe

On a clear frosty January morning in 2004, Wilma Jaffe stood along a narrow country road in Hyde Park, New York, eagerly awaiting her visitor. The rustic wood home she and Eli had begun building in 1993 was set back far from the road; she worried her visitor might not be able to find it. She was a small woman, smaller than I expected, and older too.[1] Perhaps I had become too used to identifying her name with a much younger person whose photo I had repeatedly seen in microfilmed newspapers from the 1940s. She stood there bundled in a brown wool coat and hat with a warm smile on her now-wrinkled face. When I arrived, Wilma got in the car and directed me down a deeply rutted dirt driveway to the home back among the trees. She was eager to talk as I explained the book project that had brought me to New York.

On August 17, 1940, sixteen-year-old Wilma Lewis had been left alone on an Oklahoma City street as her parents and older brother were hauled off to jail. Now she was an energetic, politically active seventy-nine-year-old widow fully engaged in the present by attending antiwar protest rallies and lobbying politicians. Her ninety-four-year-old friend, Sis Cunningham, formerly a member of the Red Dust Players, lived in a nursing home in nearby New Paltz. (Sis has since died.) Wilma was one of the few living participants in the book trials who had kept in touch with all four defendants after they were finally freed from Oklahoma's control. From memory, she easily supplied much of the biographical information we had not uncovered in our research.

In the fall of 1943, when all charges were finally dismissed, Eli and Wilma headed to Los Angeles to pursue his dream of becoming a Hollywood screenwriter. Wilma took a job as a tool and die maker while Eli tried to break into the business. By the end of that year, Eli had finished "Full Is the Earth," the novel that sent him to Oklahoma. It was never published. Eli's attempts to launch a screenwriting career ended when Uncle Sam called. He entered the military in January 1944, leaving a pregnant Wilma behind. That pregnancy ended in miscarriage, however, and Wilma continued working as a tool and die maker during Eli's service in the Army Signal Corps, where he was the news editor of *Maptalk,* a magazine distributed to soldiers. Once Eli returned from the military in March 1946, he and Wilma stayed in California until 1947, when they returned to New York. By that time he was thirty-four years old, she twenty-four; they were finally about to begin a "normal" life together. Several years later Eli gave up on Communism. He informed his friend, *Letters from the Dust Bowl* author Caroline Henderson, that "now, instead of knowing all the answers" he hardly knew the questions.[2]

The next forty years brought Eli and Wilma regular paychecks and four children (one of whom died in a bicycle accident at the age of ten; they adopted another son shortly thereafter). Eli began work in New York City, first with the garment workers union, then, upon discovering his talent as a public speaker, as a public relations officer and fund-raiser for hospitals and other medical institutions. One such job took them to Denver from 1958 to 1959, but they again returned to Manhattan and spent most of Eli's remaining working years there. In the meantime, Wilma entered college and in 1974 earned a master's degree in education.

In 1978 Wilma and Eli left Manhattan for Hyde Park, where they bought a modest older home in the country. Eli took a job as fundraiser for nearby Vassar Brothers Hospital. Wilma dusted off her skills as a metal worker and laid a concrete foundation and built a porch on their home. She later added a greenhouse. In the 1980s, Eli joined the antinuclear movement, starting a Dutchess County "Committee of 1000 for a Nuclear Freeze" (Eli always "thought big," Wilma said). He also founded the Eleanor Roosevelt Chapter of Veterans for Peace, so named after receiving permission from Mrs. Roosevelt's family to honor her in this way. Perhaps this was some form of acknowledgment for Roosevelt's politically courageous twenty-five-dollar donation in September 1940.

Eli retired in 1987 to pursue his writing and step up his political activism. Wilma chuckled as she recalled his retirement: "He gave all his ties away and began to wear only bolos around his neck." Wilma worked as an educator in a variety of adult education jobs and in 1990 was recognized as New York State's "Adult Teacher of the Year." In January 2001 she suffered an aneurysm and retired at the age of 76.

In 1991 the *Hyde Park Townsman* reported that the Jaffes were mobilizing local opposition to the Bush (I) administration's invasion of Iraq, rejecting Bush's comparison of Saddam Hussein to Hitler. "Those who liken Saddam Hussein to Hitler don't understand that history," said Wilma. Though he fully supported World War II once the United States had entered it, Eli argued that "wars since have been dividing, not uniting." He and Wilma called on Dutchess County residents to speak out against the war. The *Townsman* noted their longtime involvement in peace efforts. Eli added, "We're as patriotic as anyone else, but our vital interests start at home. . . . The homeless, the starving kids, the unemployed — that's our vital interest."[3] His words echoed positions he took in Oklahoma between 1938 and 1943. In retirement, Eli was a frequent writer of "Letters to the Editor" in local newspapers, generally advocating for peace and social justice. Wilma served as chair of the Dutchess County Democratic Committee for six years.

Although Eli continued to write creatively, he never produced a magnum opus to bring him fame and fortune. In all, he wrote over a dozen plays (some of which were performed in local venues) and dozens of short stories (most of which were never published). All, however, drew from his past; several connected in some way to the criminal syndicalism trials. One, "The Story of a Sad, Sad Old Man: A Fairytale for Children Between the Ages of Six to Two," was modeled on prosecutor John Eberle, and "The Iron Room," a purportedly fictional work, clearly describes his time in the Oklahoma County jail. Longtime friend and playwright Arthur Miller informed Eli in 1947 that "The Iron Room" was "by far the best thing you'd ever done." Wilma later recalled Miller bringing a beautiful platinum blonde on a visit to the Jaffes' Long Island vacation cottage in the early 1950s. Initially, neither she nor Eli knew who Marilyn Monroe was, although Wilma later remembered she seemed "very sympathetic" when the discussion turned to blacklisting.[4]

Decades later, as Eli readied a memoir titled *Oklahoma Odyssey* for self-publication, he again consulted Miller. After reading the manuscript, Miller felt compelled to comment: "[T]he terrible thing about it all to me is the contrast between your ideals, so pure and rather naïve, and the vileness taking place in the Soviet Union at the very same time—Stalin was slaughtering 'kulaks' just about then, I think." Miller raised the issue, he said, because the book "lacks a certain philosophical distance. In short, how do you feel now about what you went through? Were you tricked, conned, betrayed? And if so, where does that leave the whole question of ideals now?"[5]

Eli resisted Miller's approach. "Why can't it simply be the odyssey of a man who 50 years ago 'saw the heartlands and learned the minds of many distant men,' as Homer wrote." Eli said his form of "Communism" was a "socialism which I thought existed in the Soviet Union." Yes, he ignored Stalin's "excesses . . . because that was secondary to my concern for the unemployed and hungry. The issue for me was not Stalin and the kulaks; the issue was Oklahoma people struggling for bread and jobs." He admitted that he was "condemned by my own 'romanticism' about the movement and by my own 'purity' (or naivite) [*sic*]," but concluded that his ideal now, as then, "is the struggle for a peaceful world."[6]

Eli believed throughout his life that "marrying Wilma made me the luckiest man in the world." She, on the other hand, vividly remembers that he was "the most exciting thing to come along" in her life, in an "intellectually stimulating" way. Eli died on September 22, 2001, at the age of 88. His last "Letter to the Editor" appeared in the *Poughkeepsie Journal* several weeks earlier. Characteristically, it was about peace. In his last public talk a few days before his death, he told the Unitarian Universalist Fellowship in Poughkeepsie that the September 11 attacks in New York City should not be allowed to rush the United States into war. First, he said, "give peace a chance."[7]

I had spent several days with Wilma as she reminisced over the past fifty-three years. She cooked several meals we shared at her simple kitchen table. She had enjoyed the time, she said. It forced her to organize the file drawers and desks full of materials that dominated the first floor of her home. It had been a good visit. But as I left, she was eager to get back to her computer so she could catch up on the latest peace protests and letter-writing campaigns and resume her lifelong quest for peace and justice.[8]

Alan Shaw

Of all the convicted criminal syndicalism defendants, only Alan Shaw remained in Oklahoma after the criminal charges were dismissed. He had ties to the Sooner State through Nena Beth, whose family continued to live in the area. In 1943, he replaced Bob Wood as Communist Party leader for both Oklahoma and Arkansas. He was also paid to serve as a *Daily Worker* correspondent. Unlike Bob Wood and Eli Jaffe, however, Alan did not serve in the military. He tried to enlist, but was rejected for "chronic neurosis." He was convinced his Communist ties were the real reason he was not allowed to serve.[9]

Until September 1950, Alan and Nena Beth lived in Oklahoma

City. The FBI continued its surveillance, including intercepting personal letters between them.[10] Both of their children were born there (Judy in 1943, Toni in 1948), and all experienced cruelties of many kinds. Several times, for example, crosses were burned on their lawn. On July 23, 1950, the *Daily Oklahoman* published an article in its Sunday edition titled "Tomorrow's Commissar? He Lives in Frame House." The article included a photograph of their residence and identified their home address. Shortly thereafter, just as Wisconsin Senator Joseph McCarthy was about to transform national paranoia about Communism into a witch-hunt of another kind on a national scale, the family disappeared. On October 6, the *Daily Oklahoman* reported their sudden mysterious departure in a front-page article titled "Communist Gone! But Is It for Good?" that also included a large picture of Nena Beth and two-year-old Toni.[11] In the article, Nena Beth's mother stated that the Shaws had moved to Chicago, but neighbors reported that they had relocated to New Mexico, or to New York, or that they were simply on vacation.

In truth, the Shaw family relocated to Milwaukee, Wisconsin (ironically, McCarthy's home state), where they remained for the rest of their lives. It is likely that the CPUSA supported Alan's move, perhaps even initiated it, because Alan continued to work for the Party for years thereafter. Alan hoped to avoid in Milwaukee what his family experienced in Oklahoma City, but life was not easy in the Midwest. The Party valued Alan's work and, as a result, he was often sent to other states for months. But federal officials "tailed" him round the clock wherever he went, and the family's phones were routinely tapped, their mail regularly intercepted and read. Because high visibility curtailed his effectiveness, he took an assumed name and devised elaborate plans to see his wife and children clandestinely. In a conversation with a close friend, Alan's daughter Toni recalled one particular scheme. Someone — not a member of the family — would take the children to a grocery store where another would meet them. They were then placed in a car and taken to their father in a secret location. The children were also given assumed names. Toni remembered an incident when a stranger innocently asked, "What's your name, little girl?" She blurted out her real rather than her assumed name, and immediately became frightened she had betrayed the family secret. Not only did the children live for long periods without their father, they also grew up in a climate of fear and secrecy. Police questioned their teachers, and parents urged their children not to play with "those Commie girls."

Lack of money was also a pervasive problem. Alan's CPUSA support was insufficient to sustain the family, and Nena Beth had difficulty finding a job except for temporary work like "slinging hides at the tannery." Although she began drinking heavily in Oklahoma, Alan's long absences exacerbated the problem and close friends knew her to be an alcoholic. Nevertheless, when Alan ended his underground existence in the late 1950s, Nena Beth earned a master's degree and began a career as a social worker. Alan began work in the flooring business, starting as a linoleum and carpet layer and eventually working his way up to store manager. People respected his judgment, and trusted the estimates he gave them. Eventually he earned a good living, much of which he gave away.

From the late 1950s, Alan and Nena Beth largely lived the life of ordinary American citizens. They raised their children as best they could and participated in community life. A lifelong learner, Alan took courses at local colleges. He also loved to play bridge. According to friends, his concern for social justice never diminished. He made several trips to Washington, D.C., to participate in social justice demonstrations and was present in the crowd that heard Dr. Martin Luther King deliver his "I Have a Dream" speech. Alan continued to attend state Party meetings in Milwaukee and enjoyed discussing political theory, especially Marxism. But many of the younger members at the meetings considered him too conservative, too cautious. Several wanted action "now." Only years later did the more-tempered Party members learn that those most vociferous for quick action were in fact police informants.

Older daughter Judith spent the summer of 1964 working with civil rights groups in Mississippi, then in 1967 met John Wheeldon, a member of the Australian Parliament, while he was in Milwaukee speaking against the war in Vietnam. They soon married, and she moved to Australia in 1968. Eventually she became headmistress of an Anglican boarding school for girls near Sydney, a position she still holds. Younger daughter Toni became a nurse, married, then divorced. In October 2002, she committed suicide at the age of fifty-four.

In 1986, Nena Beth suffered a debilitating stroke that left her unable to speak or care for herself. For a while, Alan became her caregiver, but in 1988 he was forced to move his wife of nearly fifty years into a nursing home. She died there in January 1989. Alan lived another ten-and-a-half years, playing bridge, traveling the world, and participating in half a dozen elder hostels. He died in Milwaukee of a heart attack on September 13, 1999, at the age of eighty. To his death, his daughter Judith says, he "was an unreconstructed Stalinist. He could never accept that history had marched on." Still, until his death, he called his daughter Toni before every election to remind her to vote. Alan's obituary asked that donations in his name be given to the Milwaukee Hunger Task Force.[12]

Bob Wood

Charles Sherin assumed the name "Robert Wood" when he became active in CPUSA affairs. FBI sources speculated throughout his life about his true identity, asserting at times that he had sneaked into the United States on a false passport, or that he was a labor organizer from Detroit. Other sources identify him with other names.[13] We finally learned his identity by connecting a few key facts, finding a few key people, and utilizing a variety of sources.

I first met Robert's son Timothy in New York City in January 2004. Wilma Jaffe had given me his telephone number, and I was eager to meet him. Timothy had earned degrees from Cornell and Princeton, served one year as a Fulbright scholar in London and, when I met him, was Special Lecturer of Architecture at the New Jersey Institute of Technology. I knew little of his parents' life after they left Oklahoma in 1943, the year Tim was born. He had invited me to his Upper East Side apartment, where he and his wife, Ruth, met me at the door. Their son Michael, a young man now, also introduced himself. He was eager to learn more about his grandparents. Tim had organized a number of photographs and other material for my review, and he, like Wilma, seemed eager to talk. Ruth supplied us with cold drinks and pastry as we sat at the dining room table, chatting about her husband's parents.

What Tim did not know is that FBI surveillance of his parents continued after the convictions were reversed. In October 1943 an informant reported to the FBI that Bob and Ina's apartment "contained such books as 'Our Latin American Neighbors' . . . 'Main Currents in American Thought' . . . 'The Fall of Paris' . . . and 'Mission to Moscow.' " It was clear that the informant had searched the apartment and reported on other items, including tickets to "the Fall dance of the Veterans of the Lincoln Brigade" and a "note to look up WATSON's pamphlet on how to write for a union paper." When Bob and Ina named their son "Timothy Daniel," the FBI noted, it was to honor Tim Worth, "alleged Communist Party agent and former Communist Party member . . . who was killed acting as a bodyguard for Trotsky," and Dan Garrison, "deceased Party member in Oklahoma."[14]

Bob joined the army in early 1944 and was assigned to serve as company clerk at bases in Texas and Kansas. He also served in the "Information & Education" section (a job that ironically required him to explain Fascism and lecture the officers on the war itself), and wrote articles for *Stars and Stripes*. He never hid his Communist Party affiliation and, as a result, he failed to rise in the ranks. In 1945 he was shipped to Europe, where he saw action in Germany with the 13th Armored Division. He returned to the United States with a Bronze Star in late 1945.[15]

Upon his return, Bob went back to work for the Party in New York as secretary of the state chapter; Ina edited the CPUSA-supported *Balkan Review*. But their thirteen-year marriage dissolved in 1947, a breakdown that had begun while he was in the military. That same year, Bob married Mayflower descendant Jane Kauffman, the only daughter of a wealthy St. Louis banker and his socialite wife, who had moved to New York City in the early 1930s, was appalled by the poverty she saw, and became a lifelong activist. Ironically, Jane had been the lover of artist Joe Jones when he urged Eli Jaffe to move to Oklahoma in 1938 to research his novel. What attracted Bob to Jane was not her pedigree but her political activism.

Bob's association with the Communist Party ended in March 1951, when he was expelled "for various violations of Party discipline," the *Daily Worker* reported, "for acts of white chauvinism, and for conduct unbecoming and inconsistent with his post of Party leadership." Bob had for some time "conducted a struggle against the policies of the Party."[16] Hardly surprising, given his greater concern for social justice than Party ideology. The "white chauvinism" charge stemmed from Bob's assertion that an African American Party member had been elevated to a position he did not deserve and for which he was not qualified. But Bob believed his dismissal was less about policy and more about image. In the late 1940s, Bob and Jane began vacationing in Cuba, where Bob got to know the owners of Jose Piedra Cigars. Bob always loved good cigars, or "ceegars," as he often called them, and was fluent in Spanish. Soon thereafter he became Jose Piedra's sole agent in the United States. He was so successful that his capitalist venture quickly became embarrassing to the Communist Party leadership, despite the fact that Bob shared his profits generously with his workers in Cuba and the United States. It was because of his unwillingness to relinquish his import business, he believed, that the Party decided to expel him. The FBI subsequently interviewed Bob in the hope that he would turn on the Party and become an informant. Bob refused.[17]

Between the time Fidel Castro took power, in 1959, and the trade embargo imposed by the Kennedy administration in 1961, Bob's company was the sole U.S. import agent for all Cuban cigar brands. He and Jane continued to travel to Cuba, and on at least one occasion met the Cuban dictator. After the U.S. embargo, Bob visited other countries and imported their cigars and goods. But his business success did not temper his social activism. He and Jane became advocates for Hispanic peoples in the Chelsea section of New York, fighting to defend their right to housing. Often he would break locks installed by landlords to deny tenants access to their possessions.[18] Despite his break with the Communist Party, FBI surveillance did not diminish in the 1950s. Because he knew his line was tapped, Bob told family members to call him only from pay phones.

Although he was told in his fifties that he had heart disease, he refused to change his behavior. He continued to smoke "ceegars" until he died of a massive heart attack on Memorial Day, 1963, a week shy of his fifty-sixth birthday. Like Eli Jaffe and Alan Shaw, Bob was a lifelong learner; when he died, he was teaching himself Portuguese. Jane placed flowers on his grave every Memorial Day until her own death, in 2004, but even without Bob she continued her social activism. Five days after Bob died, Jane's landlord asked when she would be vacating the rent-controlled apartment they shared. She stayed and, even at ninety-three, staged "what may have been her most colorful protest: sleeping in the lobby of her apartment building to pressure the landlord to hasten the replacement of the elevator, which at that point had been out of service for months. She installed an air mattress in the lobby and went to bed there in a nightgown and nightcap."[19]

Ina Wood

Ina's 1947 divorce from Bob changed her life in significant ways. She never remarried. Initially she practiced law part-time. She and Tim lived just a few blocks from Vito Marcantonio's political headquarters, where she regularly volunteered. Ina was active in her son's life, including his public school PTA. Tim vividly recalls, however, the time she was denounced at a PTA meeting because of her Communist Party affiliation. Her Party ties affected her in other ways as well. She received referrals from the Marcantonio headquarters and represented a number of clients before the Workman's Compensation Board. However, her Party membership eventually led to the revocation of her license to practice before the Board, and she was out of a job. Unable to find another, in 1954 she returned to Massachusetts, where she had family. When she moved, she and Bob agreed it would be better if their son stayed in New York with Bob and Jane. It was one of the most difficult decisions Ina ever made.

Ina moved into her brother's home in Andover after his wife died. She kept house for him and practiced law there part-time. Described by many as a "very private person," Ina lacked the optimism of her Oklahoma codefendants; her cup was generally "half empty," said a friend. But she loved books, and while in New York City applied for various jobs in libraries. Although she served briefly as a library clerk, none offered her a real job, one library telling her she was "overqualified." Columbia University rejected her application to enroll in its Master of Library Service program (probably because she lacked an undergraduate degree), but she finally did serve as an assistant to a law librarian at Boston University.[20] This "Union Maid" died in Andover at the age of eighty-six.

Defense Attorneys and Prosecutors

George Croom

George Croom died of a heart condition at the age of fifty in Richmond, California, on February 18, 1952. He had volunteered for the Army in 1943, and when he was discharged, in 1945, he moved his family to Richmond. Initially he began study for the California bar exam but four days before taking it suffered a serious heart attack. Because his doctor advised against taking the exam, Croom worked for a while as an income tax consultant and car salesman. He also owned and managed a launderette. As McCarthyism rippled through the country in the early 1950s, Croom often worried he would be arrested and jailed for his associations with the Oklahoma defendants; he seldom talked about his participation in the trials for fear that California red-baiters would persecute him and his family. He and his wife, Willie Etta, had four children.[21]

Stanley Belden

Stanley Belden left for California in 1941, where he married Gladys Biram, who with her young daughter had moved there with him. Gladys first met Stanley in Oklahoma when her father heard him speak at a union rally and brought him home for dinner. Initially he planned to practice law in California, but in August told the ACLU he could "not get the necessary recommendations from Oklahoma."[22]

Shortly thereafter he returned to Oklahoma, having been ordered to report for military duty. He completed basic training, but was discharged for medical reasons, likely because of his flat feet. Stanley and Gladys had their first child in Oklahoma while he was in the service. Once discharged, they moved to Albany, Oregon, where Stanley found a job in a sawmill. Another daughter was born, and the family moved to the state of Washington. After two more children, the family returned to Oklahoma, where a friend promised Stanley employment with an oil company. For a while he also practiced law, but when the oil company folded, Stanley took a job on a chicken farm. After eighteen months in Oklahoma, the family left for good and returned to Oregon, where Stanley tried to obtain a law license. He was not permitted to take the bar exam, however, ostensibly because he had earned his law degree from a two-year law school in Tennessee; he always blamed Oklahoma officials. Eventually he developed skills as a reflexologist and physical therapist. He and Gladys joined the Unitarian Church and became active in a number of peace and justice efforts. During the Vietnam War, Stanley counseled conscientious objectors. In 1987 he stood with Martin Sheen, Carl Sagan, Daniel Ellsberg, and Kris Kristofferson to protest nuclear bomb testing at the Nevada test site. He died in Eugene, Oregon, in 1993 at 95, until his death a peace activist.[23]

John Eberle

In 1942, John F. Eberle began private law practice with the law firm of Looney, Watts, Fenton & Eberle. By the 1950s he decided to go it alone and spent the rest of his professional life in solo practice. His son, John T. Eberle, born in 1952, also became a lawyer and at this writing continues his solo practice in Oklahoma City. Eberle and his wife of forty-four years, Helen, also had two daughters. Eberle died on January 12, 1990, at eighty-six. His official obituary included no reference to the 1940–43 trials, but it is clear he held to his beliefs all his life. At the time of his death, two billboards Eberle erected stood boldly next to Interstate 40. One read: "God Bless America, President George Bush, Senator Don Nickles [a conservative Republican]"; the other, "Had Enough Ted Kennedy, Jessie Jackson, Jim Barker, Jim Wright? Switch to Republican." His father "felt pretty strongly," Eberle's son said in a *Daily Oklahoman* interview about the billboards. Eventually, "one was burned," his son said, "another was chainsawed down."[24]

Lewis Morris

County attorney Lewis Morris's professional career also fared well after the convictions. In 1943 he became district court (state trial court) judge, a position he occupied until his death of a heart attack in 1949 at the age of fifty-five. His obituary called him not only a "distinguished" jurist but also a "brilliant prosecutor" who served in that position for twelve years.[25]

Epilogue
Taking Measure

The books on trial, and the people who sold them, became mirrors that reflected the chauvinism, insecurity, and racism of people across the country in general, and Oklahoma in particular. The anti-Communist attitudes that John Eberle and Lewis Morris displayed (and the prejudices they exploited to perpetuate them) long outlasted the trials themselves. The racist nature of the testimony they used to inflame public opinion anticipated the tactics used in the Deep South in the 1950s and 1960s to smear civil rights activities as Communist inspired.

In Oklahoma, state politicians seldom had second thoughts about bird-dogging Communists. In 1945, the State Senate voted to repeal the law that Communists could not hold public office. During the debate, one senator jokingly noted that the "Communist Party had dissolved and its members had joined the Democratic Party." Another displayed a newspaper headline that read: "Red Army only thirty-nine miles from Berlin." "That's my speech," he said. A third senator stated: "We are rubbing out something we did here inadvisedly. We know we went on a witch-hunt." The House, however, was not willing to concede. When a bill finally passed the full legislature, Communists were still excluded from public office, and all public employees were required to swear that "they were not Communists, that they did not advocate violent revolution, and that they would take up arms in case of emergency."[1]

In the early 1950s Oklahoma passed another law that required all public employees to swear they had not belonged to the Communist Party or other subversive organizations during the past five years. It passed without a single negative vote in either chamber. The U.S. Supreme Court ultimately held this (and other laws like it) unconstitutional. Excluding "persons solely on the basis of organizational membership, regardless of their knowledge concerning the organizations to which they had belonged," violates due process. "During periods of international stress, the extent of legislation with such objectives accentuates our traditional concern about the relation of government to the individual in a free society," the Court noted. "The perennial problem of defining that relationship becomes acute when disloyalty is screened by ideological patterns and techniques of disguise that make it difficult to identify. Democratic government is not powerless to meet this threat, but it must do so without infringing the freedoms that are the ultimate values of all democratic living."[2]

Oklahoma law still declares the Communist Party "illegal and not entitled to any rights, privileges, or immunities" and makes it "unlawful for such Party . . . to exist, function, or operate in the State of Oklahoma."[3] And the criminal syndicalism law that "justified" the book trials remains in effect, ever at the ready for the next set of zealots more concerned about imagined threats to social order than to violations of civil liberties.

Although Communism in the United States is no longer considered a danger to homeland security, threats from non-Communist sources have now taken center stage. The 1995 bombing of the Alfred P. Murrah federal building in Oklahoma City by a misguided citizen on the extreme right prompted President William Jefferson Clinton to sign sweeping antiterrorism legislation into law, despite strong opposition by both the American Civil Liberties Union and the National Rifle Association. The 2001 attacks on the World Trade

Center and the Pentagon, as well as the downing of United Airlines Flight 93, led to the passage of the USA PATRIOT ACT (Uniting and Strengthening America by Providing Appropriate Tools Required to Intercept and Obstruct Terrorism Act of 2001). This act, too, faced strong and vocal opposition, but passed the House and Senate just six weeks after the attacks, and was immediately signed by President George W. Bush. John Ashcroft, his attorney general, promised that "within an hour" of Bush's signature he would "direct federal investigators across the United States to exercise their newly expanded powers to wiretap, search, detain and deport suspected terrorists." An executive order signed shortly thereafter permits foreigners charged with terrorism to be tried in secret courts outside the United States. Ironically, a powerful voice from the Sooner State protested. "This is a time when people who believe in the worth of an individual need to stand up for individual liberties," Republican Oklahoma Governor Frank Keating said. "[N]o matter how wicked" the noncitizen, he or she "should get the due process protections provided in the Constitution." Revelations in late 2005 that President Bush authorized the National Security Agency to engage in warrantless telephone and e-mail searches within American borders serve as a reminder that an undeclared war on terrorism, like a military war, can also serve as a catalyst for civil liberties restrictions.[4]

In the 1940s, Oklahoma officials and their allies and sympathizers showed a vengeful streak in the book trials that accelerated an already greatly exaggerated sense of threat to national security, and brought with it a flagrant disregard for basic civil liberties. But parallels clearly exist between Oklahoma at midcentury and the paranoid politics of various periods — before and after — in American history. When viewed from a historical perspective, these campaigns of "preventive justice" constitute a chain of civil liberties violations with links that connect events centuries ago to the present. Over the generations, government officials have regularly (sometimes deliberately) overimagined threats to the country from alien sources, and then violated citizens' civil liberties clearly enumerated in the Bill of Rights.[5] Particular groups or associations have been presumed guilty based on a belief that what they said rather than what they did justified acts of censorship and suspension of due process. Individuals often suffered imprisonment without due process for "supporting" the enemy, just as the book trial defendants went to jail because Oklahoma officials thought that all members of the CPUSA were conspiring to violently overthrow the government. Multiple examples punctuate American history, beginning in the 1790s with America's near-war with France, and reemerging in the Civil War, World Wars I and II, throughout the Cold War, and in the Vietnam era. The 1930s' and 1940s' expansion of free speech protection reflected in the 1943 opinions of the Oklahoma Criminal Court of Appeals could not withstand McCarthyism in the 1950s. In times of national crisis, free speech often suffers.[6] Inevitably, the state's response to each perceived threat is significant and constitutes an overreaction that leads to legislation and law enforcement that strengthens the government's hand while weakening individual liberties.

Public opinion, however, can have an effect, as this book clearly demonstrates. Between 1940 and 1943, Oklahoma's excesses in the book trials accelerated and intensified a nation's response by creating a target that actually brought left and right together to defend civil liberties. Protests from thousands (if not tens of thousands) of private citizens poured into the offices of the county attorney, the state attorney general, and the governor. On issues of civil liberties, the Oklahoma Federation for Constitutional Rights and many University of Oklahoma students and faculty acquitted themselves admirably during the hysteria, although many also paid a price. Except for the two Oklahoma City dailies and most small-town Sooner State weeklies, much of the nation's publishing industry (book, periodical, and newspaper) rallied behind the book trial defendants. Labor responded loudly, and many academic and literary luminaries protested. And although dissent from the nation's library community was muted and highly localized, the fact that many of the books on trial were easily accessible on library shelves was cited repeatedly by the media to demonstrate the absurdity of the trials.

All too often when the state exceeds its authorized power and engages in witch-hunts, the public servants through whom it works are not held accountable, except by history. In the Sooner State, prosecutors John Eberle and Lewis Morris, State Senator Paul Stewart, and Governor Red Phillips (among others) continued to lead prosperous lives in powerful public and private positions after the book trials concluded. Instead, the price for government excesses is usually paid by the individuals against whom they are directed. Historical perspective and document declassification eventually identify at least some of the excesses brought by national, state, and local hysterias, but those ·caught in the middle cannot appreciate the triumph of reason at some later date. None of our Oklahoma book trial defendants or their lawyers will ever read this book.

Although Eli Jaffe, Alan Shaw, and Bob and Ina Wood chose to affiliate with the Communist Party, Oklahoma's response surely influenced their lives forever after. Each of them spent several months in jail and experienced unfair trials. For much of their lives, the FBI kept them under surveillance, opened their mail, tapped their phones, followed them from state to state, planted informants in their meetings, and collected inventories of the books in their own homes. At one point, in an attempt to charge Eli Jaffe with a federal crime, the FBI contacted his local draft board to see if he had notified authorities of his change of address. He had. The FBI even monitored Eli and Wilma's marriage ceremony, noting the marriage license number and dutifully reporting the names and addresses of the minister and the two witnesses. It also reported the progress of Eli's novel.[7]

Ironically, although FBI files on the four defendants are voluminous, much of the information contained therein is unreliable, or simply false. Most of it was supplied by informants, much of it consisting of little more than speculation. At one point, the defendants were deemed so dangerous the FBI classified them with hundreds of others elsewhere in the country as "Group A" — "individuals believed to be the most dangerous and who in all probability should be interned in event of War." But a July 1943 memorandum from the U.S. attorney general to J. Edgar Hoover argued that the system "is inherently unreliable," the evidence "inadequate; the standards applied to the evidence . . . defective; and . . . the notion that it is possible to make a valid determination as to how dangerous a person is in the abstract and without reference to time, environment, and other relevant circumstances, is impractical, unwise, and dangerous." Such classifications, he ordered, should be "cancelled, and should not be used as a determination of dangerousness or of any other fact." Hoover ignored the order, simply telling his subordinates to rename the project and keep it secret.[8] Nowhere in the FBI files or anywhere else is there one iota of evidence that any of the book trial defendants ever initiated or advocated violence. In fact, they were only the objects of violence exercised by others, many of whom were government officials.

Although most of the book trial defendants eventually broke with the Communist Party (Alan Shaw excepted), they never abandoned a visceral commitment to reduce poverty, fight racism, and advocate social justice that bound them together in the first place. In all cases, their lives after 1943 demonstrate that Party membership was only a temporary platform for their lifelong activism on behalf of poor people and against war. Oklahoma officials were philosophically and culturally too blindered to see any altruism or patriotism in the nonviolent behaviors of the book trial defendants; all they could see was conspiracy, and somehow they managed to find "evidence" of that conspiracy in books that were also on the shelves in public and academic libraries throughout the country. Although officials' civil liberty violations did not measurably improve Oklahoma's domestic security, they presaged the tactics implemented on a national scale less than a decade later.

While the Oklahoma defendants were certainly infected by Party rhetoric and regularly parroted a Party line passed from Moscow through the New York headquarters of the Communist Party of the United States of America, at the same time they were made to suffer unjustly for believing in, and acting upon, the principles the Party espoused and for subversive activities carried on elsewhere in the country by a few hundred Soviet agents. They were the unfortunate (albeit not entirely innocent) subjects of a witch-hunt in the

Sooner State because there was no one else Oklahoma officials could reach in their backyard to fight a ghost they feared but could not see. Public and private sector powerbrokers in general, and John Eberle, Lewis Morris, and their associates in particular, vastly overestimated any threat posed to the social order by the Oklahoma chapter of the Communist Party. In fact, the effects of poverty, unemployment, and racism were much greater threats, but Oklahoma leaders largely chose to ignore them.

At the very least, one can say that the four defendants—and undoubtedly a nation—emerged from the experience with a good dose of cynicism. That, too, is not an isolated response. The true measure of a strong democratic government is how it responds during the most difficult of times. When a government—local, state, or federal—responds to fear of an outside threat (perceived or real) by restricting the protections offered by its own laws, when it exercises a "with us or against us" mentality that is incapable of accommodating a multiplicity of political activities, then it demonstrates that its protection is conditional only. The arrogance of power is the enemy of civil liberties. And individuals are not the only ones who suffer when civil liberties are shortchanged. Such government oppression alienates those who are oppressed and others who observe the oppression. It diminishes respect for a democratic form of government. It also results in self-censorship, the discouragement of dissenting voices, and ultimately the limitation of social reform.

Like accounts of other violations of civil liberties in American history, this book demonstrates how a coalition of superpatriotic forces led by government officials acted against particular groups of people who, they thought, constituted threats to domestic security and were conspiring to attack the social order. And like other incidents, this one shows how a few courageous people stood up against these attacks, and how their fight rallied others in a grassroots effort to reverse their effects. *Books on Trial* is a story of egregious civil liberties violations by government officials during a time of national insecurity. It can serve as one more example to cite against present and future mistakes brought about by the arrogance of power.

Abbreviations

ACLU MSS. Papers of the American Civil Liberties Union, Seeley G. Mudd Library, Princeton University, Princeton, New Jersey.

American Legion Brief, Robert Wood. Brief of the American Legion as Amicus Curiae, *Robert Wood v. Oklahoma,* A-10046.

Bizzell MSS. Papers of William Bennett Bizzell, Western American History Collection, University of Oklahoma, Norman, Oklahoma.

Defendant's Brief, Eli Jaffe. Brief of Defendant in Error, *Eli Jaffe v. Oklahoma,* A-10185.

Defendant's Brief, Ina Wood. Brief of Defendant in Error, *Ina Wood v. Oklahoma,* A-10199.

Defendant's Brief, Robert Wood. Brief of Defendant in Error, *Robert Wood v. Oklahoma,* A-10046.

Defendant's Reply Brief, Robert Wood. Defendant's Reply Brief, *Robert Wood v. Oklahoma,* A-10046.

HLS Special Collections. Special Collections, Langdell Hall, Harvard Law School. Harvard University, Cambridge, Massachusetts.

ILD MSS. Papers of the International Labor Defense, Microfilm Collections, Law Library Reading Room, Library of Congress, Washington, D.C.

Ina Wood app. rec. Ina Wood v. Oklahoma, A-10199, Case Made. Appellate records, Oklahoma Department of Library and Archives, Oklahoma City, Oklahoma.

Ina Wood FOIA File. Freedom of Information Act files obtained from U.S. Department of Justice, Washington, D.C.

Ina Wood Trial Record. Oklahoma v. Ina Wood, No. 14494. Oklahoma County Courthouse, Oklahoma City, Oklahoma.

Jaffe app. rec. Eli Jaffe v. Oklahoma, A-10185, Case Made. Appellate records, Oklahoma Department of Library and Archives, Oklahoma City, Oklahoma.

Jaffe FOIA File. Freedom of Information Act files obtained from U.S. Department of Justice, Washington, D.C.

Jaffe MSS. Eli Jaffe Papers, Western American History Collection, University of Oklahoma, Norman, Oklahoma.

Jaffe Trial Record. Oklahoma v. Eli Jaffe, No. 14492. Oklahoma County Courthouse.

Knights of Pythias Brief, Robert Wood. Brief of Knights of Pythias as Amicus Curiae, *Robert Wood v. Oklahoma,* A-10046.

LAW MSS. Papers of the League of American Writers, Bancroft Library, University of California-Berkeley, Berkeley, California.

McCoy MSS. Papers of Ralph E. McCoy. Special Collections, Morris Library, Southern Illinois University, Carbondale, Illinois.

NAACP MSS. Papers of the National Association for the Advancement of Colored People, Manuscripts Division, Library of Congress, Washington, D.C.

NFCL Brief, Robert Wood. Brief of the National Federation for Constitutional Liberties as Friend of the Court, *Robert Wood v. Oklahoma,* A-10046.

NLG Brief, Robert Wood. Brief of the National Lawyers Guild as Amicus Curiae, *Robert Wood v. Oklahoma,* A-10046.

OSR MSS. Oklahoma School of Religion Papers, Western American History Collection, University of Oklahoma, Norman, Oklahoma.

Personnel Files. Basement, Evans Hall, University of Oklahoma, Norman, Oklahoma.

Phillips MSS. Papers of Governor Leon Chase Phillips, State Archives, Oklahoma Department of Libraries, Oklahoma City, Oklahoma.

Plaintiff's Brief, Alan Shaw. Brief of Plaintiff in Error, *Alan Shaw v. Oklahoma,* A-10083.

Plaintiff's Brief, Eli Jaffe. Brief of Plaintiff in Error, *Eli Jaffe v. Oklahoma,* A-10185.

Plaintiff's Brief, Ina Wood. Brief of Plaintiff in Error, *Ina Wood v. Oklahoma,* A-10199.

Plaintiff's Brief, Robert Wood. Brief of Plaintiff in Error, *Robert Wood v. Oklahoma,* A-10046.

Robert Wood app. rec. Robert Wood v. Oklahoma, A-10046, Case Made. Appellate records, Oklahoma Department of Library and Archives, Oklahoma City, Oklahoma.

Robert Wood et al. Trial Record. Oklahoma v. Robert Wood, Ina Wood, Alan Shaw, Eli Jaffe, Elizabeth Green, No. 14490. Oklahoma County Courthouse, Oklahoma City, Oklahoma.

Robert Wood FOIA File. Freedom of Information Act files obtained from U.S. Department of Justice, Washington, D.C.

Robert Wood Trial Record. Oklahoma v. Robert Wood, No. 14497. Oklahoma County Courthouse, Oklahoma City, Oklahoma.

Ross MSS, WHS. E. A. Ross Papers, Archives Division, Wisconsin Historical Society, Madison, Wisconsin.

Shaw app. rec. Alan Shaw v. Oklahoma, A-10083, Case Made. Appellate records, Oklahoma Department of Library and Archives, Oklahoma City, Oklahoma.

Shaw FOIA File (Army). Freedom of Information Act files obtained from U.S. Department of the Army, Fort George G. Meade, Maryland.

Shaw FOIA File. Freedom of Information Act files obtained from U.S. Department of Justice, Washington, D.C.

Shaw Trial Record. Oklahoma v. Alan Shaw, No. 14493. Oklahoma County Courthouse, Oklahoma City, Oklahoma.

Student Handbill Collection, BC Archives. Student Handbill Collection, Brooklyn College Archives and Special Collections, Brooklyn, New York.

Wood MSS. Correspondence and miscellaneous materials in the possession of Timothy Wood, New York City.

Notes

Chapter One

1. Shaw app. rec., 459.

2. Compiled from the following sources: *Shaw v. Oklahoma*, 134 P.2d 999 (Okla. Crim. App. 1943); Shaw app. rec., 459–60, 1008; Defendant's Brief, Robert Wood, 5, 75; Plaintiff's Brief, Ina Wood, 3; NFCL Brief , Robert Wood, 5; *Daily Oklahoman*, November 26, 1940; *Daily Worker,* November 29, 1940; *Tulsa Tribune,* June 13, 1941; *New Masses* 39 (February 25, 1941): 17.

3. Interview with Eli and Wilma Jaffe, *PM,* October 18, 1942. See also "An Oklahoma Story," by Wilma Lewis Jaffe [Wilma wrote this in early 1943, just before appellate decisions to convictions resulting from these arrests were handed down, and probably in anticipation of interviews to follow]; Jaffe MSS, Box 1; telephone interview with Wilma Jaffe, November 15, 2003; interview with Wilma Jaffe, January 9, 2004; interview with Orval Lewis, September 25, 2004; *PM,* October 18, 1942; Elizabeth Green, "I Face an Oklahoma Prison," *Protestant Digest* 4 (August–September 1941): 29–30. See also untitled pamphlet issued in 1941 by the International Labor Defense in New York City, copy located in McCoy MSS.

4. Plaintiff's Brief, Eli Jaffe, 2–6. See also Eli Jaffe, *Oklahoma Odyssey: A Memoir* (Hyde Park, N.Y.: Eli Jaffe, 1993), 96–97; Sasha Small, "Oklahoma Fascists Jittery as ILD Rallies People," *Daily Worker,* August 20, 1941.

5. Search warrant dated August 17, 1940 can be found in Robert Wood et al. Trial Record. See also Green, "I Face an Oklahoma Prison," 30.

6. *Daily Oklahoman,* August 29, 1940; Robert Wood app. rec., 1002, 1187; NFCL Brief, Robert Wood, 7.

7. Robert Wood app. rec., 1035; Penn Kimball, "New York Gets a Look at Two Oklahoma 'Criminals,' " *PM*, July 29, 1941.

8. See Jaffe app. rec., 7–8; NLG Brief, Robert Wood, 11–12; Plaintiff's Brief, Robert Wood, 57; Elizabeth Green, "Oklahoma Ordeal," *New Masses* 39 (August 19, 1941): 17.

9. Sasha Small, "Oklahoma Okays Hitler," *New Masses* 43 (October 22, 1940): 16; Small, "Oklahoma Fascists."

10. Interview with Wilma Jaffe, January 9, 2004. She also related parts of this story in a letter to the International Labor Defense, which Elizabeth Green quoted in "Oklahoma Ordeal," 17.

11. Interview with Wilma Jaffe, January 9, 2004. See also Owen Knox, *Oklahoma Story* (Washington, D.C.: National Federation for Constitutional Liberties, 1940), 6; Madeline B. Rose, "Sis Cunningham: Songs of Hard Times," *Ms.* 2 (March 1974): 29–32; and Agnes "Sis" Cunningham, "The Red Dust Players," *Cimarron Review* 38 (January 1977): 38–43.

12. See "Action Letter," National Federation of Constitutional Liberties, October 9, 1940, OSR MSS, Box 4. See also untitled undated pamphlet, Jaffe MSS, Box 1; *Daily Oklahoman*, August 29, 1940; and Small, "Oklahoma Okays Hitler," 16–17.

13. Gordon Friessen, *Oklahoma Witch Hunt* (Oklahoma City: Oklahoma Committee to Defend Political Prisoners, 1941), 10; Green, "I Face an Oklahoma Prison," 30; Jaffe, *Odyssey*, 97. Orval Lewis describes the jailers as "nasty acting" and describes some of the other prisoners as "pretty bad characters." Interview with Orval Lewis, September 25, 2004.

14. Jaffe, *Odyssey*, 97; Defendant's Brief, Eli Jaffe, 2–3; Jaffe app. rec., 737–78.

15. *Oklahoma City Times*, August 19, 1940; *Daily Oklahoman*, August 20, 1940.

16. See Howard K. Berry, Sr., *He Made It Safe to Murder* (Oklahoma City: Oklahoma Heritage Association, 2001). See also *Daily Oklahoman*, August 20, 1940.

17. Jaffe, *Odyssey*, 98. See also *Oklahoma City Times*, August 20, 1940; *Daily Oklahoman*, August 21, 1940.

18. Robert Wood Trial Record; *Daily Oklahoman*, August 21, 1940. See also Press Release, Oklahoma Committee to Defend Political Prisoners, November 28, 1940, 1 (as found in Wood MSS); and "Fascism: Oklahoma Brand," *New Masses* 39 (December 10, 1940): 18.

19. Green, "Oklahoma Ordeal," 15; *Daily Oklahoman*, August 21, 1940; August 22, 1940.

20. *Daily Oklahoman*, August 21, 1940; August 22, 1940.

21. Jaffe, *Odyssey*, 97.

22. Interview with Wilma Jaffe, January 9, 2004; Jaffe, *Odyssey*, 100–103.

23. See, for example, *Wisconsin Rapids* (Wis.) *Daily Tribune*, August 21, 1940; *Fresno* (Cal.) *Bee*, August 21, 1940; *Chillicothe* (Mo.) *Constitution-Tribune*, August 21, 1940; and the *Galveston* (Tex.) *Daily News*, August 24, 1940.

24. Hays to Phillips, August 21, 1940, copy in Ross MSS, Box 23. See also *Los Angeles Times*, August 21, 1940.

25. *Daily Oklahoman*, August 23, 1940.

26. *Daily Oklahoman*, August 23, 1940; August 24, 1940; August 27, 1940.

27. Open letter, Marcantonio to Attorney General Jackson, September 25, 1940, Ross MSS, Box 23; *Daily Oklahoman*, August 24, 1940; August 25, 1940.

28. Interview with Orval Lewis, September 25, 2004; *Daily Oklahoman*, August 26, 1940; *Daily Worker*, October 24, 1942.

29. Friessen, *Oklahoma Witch Hunt*, 13; Letter from Pauline Marriott (held as a material witness on $2,000 bond, later reduced to $1,000) to ACLU General Counsel Arthur Garfield Hays, August 27, 1940, ACLU MSS, reel 190, v. 2241. The inscription over the courthouse door remains today.

30. *Oklahoma City Times*, August 29, 1940; "Communist's $9,000 Is Traced," *Daily Oklahoman*, August 29, 1940. See also Plaintiff's Brief, Robert Wood, 91.

31. *Daily Oklahoman*, August 30, 1940.

32. *Daily Oklahoman*, August 30, 1940. Ironically, the Oklahoma Bar Association had also suspended George Croom's license to practice in 1935, not reinstating it until 1943 (e-mail from Oklahoma Bar Association, August 26, 2004). The Bar said nothing about Croom, however.

33. These events recounted in Jerome M. Britchey (ACLU N.Y. office) to Ira Latimer, October 16, 1940, copy in Ross MSS, Box 23; Britchey to Belden, September 6, 1940, ACLU MSS, reel 209, v. 2422; Belden to Britchey, September 11, 1940, ACLU MSS, reel 190, v. 2241. See also Belden to Hayes, September 30, 1940, ACLU MSS, reel 209, v. 2422. When Marshall was in Oklahoma, Belden regularly "invited him to eat carry-out chicken in his law office because Cushing restaurants wouldn't serve blacks through the front door." See Carl T. Rowan, *Dream Makers, Dream Breakers: The World of Justice Thurgood Marshall* (Boston: Little, Brown & Co., 1993), 96–97. See also David Arnold, "Stanley Belden: Veteran of Protest," *Northwest Magazine* (1987): 6.

34. *Daily Oklahoman*, August 30, 1940; September 4, 1940; September 6, 1940; NLG Brief, Robert Wood, 11–12; Plaintiff's Brief, Ina Wood, 11–12; Ina Wood app. rec., 1040. Unbeknownst to the defendants and their lawyers, Judge Mills often reported to the FBI the names of any individuals coming through his courtroom he suspected of being a Communist. Dillard, Memo for the File, August 15, 1942, Shaw FOIA File.

35. *Daily Oklahoman*, September 7, 1940.

36. Jaffe, *Odyssey*, 104–106; Belden to Unger, September 19, 1940, Ross MSS, Box 23; Oscar Ameringer to Baldwin, August 28, 1940, ACLU MSS, reel 190, v. 2241.

37. Information gleaned from Robert Wood Trial Records; *Oklahoma City Times*, September 7, 1940; September 5, 1940; September 17, 1940; *Daily Oklahoman*, September 17, 1940; September 18, 1940. In a biography based on his own

version of events, Pruiett spun the story differently. "When he rose to defend the owner of a Communist bookstore in an unpopular 1940 case, his popularity plummeted as did his finances." See Berry, *Safe to Murder,* 657.

38. Britchey to Belden, September 6, 1940, ACLU MSS, reel 209, v. 2422; Belden to Hays, September 3, 1940, ACLU MSS, reel 209, v. 2422. Months later the CPUSA agreed to pay Belden a "modest" fee (see Baldwin to Robert Minor, March 10,1941, ACLU MSS, reel 209, v. 2422), although it insisted the ACLU should contribute, since Belden represented the ACLU's position. See Minor to Baldwin, March 11, 1941, ACLU MSS, reel 209, v. 2422. Eventually, the ACLU did contribute to the fee. See Baldwin to Belden, April 17, 1941, ACLU MSS, reel 209, v. 2422.

39. Belden to Unger, September 19, 1940, Box 23, Ross MSS.

40. Belden to Unger, September 19, 1940, copy in Ross MSS, Box 23; *Daily Oklahoman,* September 19, 1940; September 20, 1940; Motion and Affidavit, September 18, 1940, Robert Wood Trial Record, copy also found in Ross MSS, Box 23.

41. Open letter, Marcantonio to AG Jackson, September 25, 1940, copy in Box 23, Ross MSS.

42. Interview with Orval Lewis, September 25, 2004; *Oklahoma City Times,* September 21, 1940; Typed essay by Wilma Jaffe, Jaffe MSS, Box 1.

43. Copy of the open letter and press release dated September 28, 1940, in Ross MSS, Box 23. See also Ross to Jackson, October 7, 1940, in which Ross argues, as ACLU chairman, that Jackson needs "to uphold the constitutional rights of minority groups to a place on the official ballot." Ross to Jackson, October 7, 1940, Ross MSS, Box 23. Marcantonio served Congress for seven terms and was also chairman of the American Labor Party. See also Michael J. Ybarra, *Washington Gone Crazy: Senator Pat McCarran and the Great American Communist Hunt* (Hanover, N.H.: Steerforth Press, 2004), 669.

44. *Daily Oklahoman,* August 29, 1940.

45. *Daily Oklahoman,* October 4, 1940. See also *Norman Transcript,* September 29, 1940.

Chapter Two

1. Michal R. Belknap, *Cold War Political Justice: The Smith Act, the Communist Party, and American Civil Liberties* (Westport, Conn.: Greenwood Press, 1977), 10–12.

2. See Debs to Belden, October 26, 1918, copy supplied by his daughter, Candy Wilcott. For more information on Belden as a conscientious objector, see *Oklahoma City Times,* January 24, 1919.

3. See Von Russell Creel, "Socialist in the House: The Oklahoma Experience, Part I," *Chronicles of Oklahoma* 70 (Summer 1992): 144–83; "Part II," 70 (Fall 1992): 258–301. See also Sherry Warrick, "Radical Labor in Oklahoma: The Working Class Union," *Chronicles of Oklahoma* 52 (Summer 1974): 180–95.

4. *Daily Oklahoman,* August 17, 1917. Background information on the Green Corn Rebellion taken from Charles Bush, "The Green Corn Rebellion" (master's thesis, University of Oklahoma, 1932); Virginia Pope, "The Green Corn Rebellion: A Case Study in Newspaper Self-Censorship" (master's thesis, Oklahoma A&M, 1940); and James Morton Smith, "Criminal Syndicalism in Oklahoma: A History of the Law and Its Application" (master's thesis, University of Oklahoma, 1946), 9–17. See also William Cunningham, *The Green Corn Rebellion* (New York: Vanguard Press, 1935) for a fictionalized account of these events.

5. See James H. Fowler II, "Tar and Feather Patriotism: The Suppression of Dissent in Oklahoma During World War I," *Chronicles of Oklahoma* 56 (Winter 1978–79): 409–430; James H. Fowler II, "Creating an Atmosphere of Suppression, 1914–1917," *Chronicles of Oklahoma* 59 (Summer 1981): 202–223; and O. A. Hilton, "The Oklahoma Council of Defense and the First World War," *Chronicles of Oklahoma* 70 (Winter 1992–93): 394–415. See also Wewoka *Capital-Democrat,* August 9, 1917; and *Daily Oklahoman,* February 11, 1919. This was not the first time state or federal lawmakers addressed this issue. On March 3, 1903, Congress passed an immigration law that excluded "anarchists or persons who believe in or advocate the overthrow by force of the government of the United States." See Ted Morgan, *Reds: McCarthyism in Twentieth-Century America* (New York: Random House, 2003), 57.

6. Robert J. Goldstein, *Political Repression in Modern America from 1870 to the Present* (Cambridge, Mass.: Schenkman Publishing Co., 1978), 126.

7. *Daily Oklahoman,* February 11, 1919.

8. 21 Okla. Stat. sec. 1261, 1263; *Session Laws,* 1919, chapter 70, 110. See also Smith, "Criminal Syndicalism in Oklahoma," 41–52; Morgan, *Reds,* 70. See also *Daily Oklahoman,* August 21, 1940, in which the paper quotes Harrison on the law's origins; and Nigel Anthony Sellars, *Oil, Wheat & Wobblies: The Industrial Workers of the World in Oklahoma, 1905–1930* (Norman, University of Oklahoma Press, 1998), 133–35. Sellars refers to Harrison as "a well known racist and Red baiter" who all his life "urged the deportation of leftists."

9. See Sheldon Nuringer, "Governor Walton's War on the Ku Klux Klan, 1923–24," *Chronicles of Oklahoma* 45 (Summer 1967): 153–79.

10. Smith, "Criminal Syndicalism in Oklahoma," chapters 5 and 6; *Berg v. State,* 233 P. 497 (Okla. Crim. App. 1925); *Wear v. State,* 235 P. 271 (Okla. Crim. App. 1925).

11. For more detail, see David M. Kennedy, *Freedom from Fear: The American People in Depression and War, 1929–1945* (New York: Oxford University Press, 1999).

12. Leonard Arrington, "The New Deal in the West: A Preliminary Statistical Inquiry," *Pacific Historical Review* 38 (August 1969): 314.

13. Caroline Henderson, "Letters from the Dust Bowl," *Atlantic Monthly* 157 (May 1936): 540–51. See also Caroline Henderson (Virginia C. Purdy, ed.), " 'Dust to Eat:' A Document from the Dust Bowl," *Chronicles of Oklahoma* 58 (Winter 1980–81): 440–54; and Caroline Henderson (Alvin O. Turner, ed.), *Letters from the Dust*

Bowl (Norman: University of Oklahoma Press, 2001). See also *Daily Oklahoman,* March 5, 1939.

14. *Oklahoma City Times,* July 16, 1937, quoted in Elizabeth Green, "God Made Oklahoma Rich—II," *Social Work Today* 8 (December 1941): 19. See also Robert K. Carr, *State Control and Local Finances in Oklahoma* (Norman: University of Oklahoma Press, 1937), where he elaborates these conclusions.

15. The Works Progress Administration was founded in 1935. In 1939 its name was changed to the Work Projects Administration.

16. Green, "God Made Oklahoma Rich—II," 18; U.S. House of Representatives, *Interstate Migration of Destitute Citizens,* 67th Cong., 3rd sess. (Washington, D.C.: Government Printing Office, 1940), 2783; Elizabeth Green, "God Made Oklahoma Rich—I," *Social Work Today* 8 (November 1941): 14; "This Week Throughout Oklahoma," *Harlow's Weekly* 50 (August 20, 1938): 2–3.

17. Jaffe, *Odyssey,* 52, 88; *Daily Oklahoman,* April 22, 1939; Green, "I Face an Oklahoma Prison," 26–33; Green, "God Made Oklahoma Rich—II," 17–19; Sis Cunningham, *Red Dust and Broadsides: A Joint Autobiography* (Amherst: University of Massachusetts Press, 1999), 180. The lawyer's letter to the mayor quoted in Clifford Trafzer, "Harmony and Cooperation: Robert M. Hefner, Mayor of Oklahoma City," *Chronicles of Oklahoma* 62 (Spring 1984): 70–85.

18. *Daily Oklahoman,* April 22, 1939. See also W. Richard Fossey, " 'Talkin' the Dust Bowl Blues': A Study of Oklahoma's Cultural Identity During the Great Depression," *Chronicles of Oklahoma* 55 (Spring 1977): 12–33. For a good summary of Oklahoma's attitude toward New Deal legislation and funding opportunities for states, see Keith L. Bryant, "Oklahoma and the New Deal," in *The New Deal: The State and Local Levels, Vol. II,* in John Braeman, Robert H. Bremmer, and David Brody, ed., (Columbus: Ohio State University Press, 1975), 166–97.

19. *Daily Oklahoman,* April 25, 1939.

20. Green, "God Made Oklahoma Rich—II," 17; *Interstate Migration of Destitute Citizens,* 2028–30. See also Phillips MSS, Box 1, Folder 4.

21. Lyle H. Boren, "The Grapes of Wrath: Extension of Remarks," *Congressional Record,* 76th Cong., 3rd sess. 1940, pt. 13, LXXXVI, 139–40; *Oklahoma City Times,* August 5, 1939; *Interstate Migration of Destitute Citizens,* 1759. For a good summary of the mixed reaction to *The Grapes of Wrath* (book and movie versions) in the Sooner State, see Marsha L. Weisger, "The Reception of *The Grapes of Wrath* in Oklahoma: A Reappraisal," *Chronicles of Oklahoma* 70 (Winter 1992–93): 394–415. See also correspondence in ACLU MSS, reel 179, v. 2158 for another perspective on the reception Oklahoma gave *The Grapes of Wrath.*

22. For a good summary of how Communists found jobs in Washington-based New Deal agencies, see Ybarra, *Washington Gone Crazy,* especially chapters 6–8. See also Morgan, *Reds,* chapter 6.

23. Morgan, *Reds,* 133–43, 168–69.

24. Harvey Klehr, John Earl Haynes, and Kyrill M. Anderson, *The Soviet World of American Communism* (New Haven: Yale University Press, 1998). This book is part of the Yale University Annals of Communism Project, a series based on manuscripts from recently opened Russian state and party archives.

25. Defendant's Brief, Robert Wood, 4, referencing Report No. 290 of the U.S. Congress, January 17, 1931, "Investigation of Communist Activity"; Louis Adamic, "What the Proletariat Reads: Conclusions Based on a Year's Study Among Hundreds of Workers Throughout the United States," *Saturday Review of Literature* 1 (December 1934): 321; Philip Rahv, "Where the News Ends," *New Leader* (October 12, 1938): 8. See also Morgan, *Reds,* chapter 7; Henry Hart, "Contemporary Publishing and the Revolutionary Writer," *American Writers' Congress* (New York: International Publishers, 1935), 159–62.

26. See David Roediger, "Foreword," in Jessie Lloyd O'Connor, Harvey O'Connor, and Susan Bowles, *Harvey and Jessie: A Couple of Radicals* (Philadelphia: Temple University Press, 1988), x. See also Michael Denning, *The Cultural Front: The Laboring of American Culture in the Twentieth Century* (New York, N.Y.: Verso, 1996), especially chapters 2 and 8. The blindered idealism that drew many of these social activists to the Communist Party in the 1930s is obvious in the comments of people interviewed for the documentary, *Seeing Red.*

27. *Daily Oklahoman,* January 30, 1932. See Roger W. Cummins, " 'Lily White' Juries on Trial: The Civil Rights Defense of Jess Collins," *Chronicles of Oklahoma* 63 (Summer 1985): 168–69; "Oklahoma Senate Votes Measure to Ban Ballot to Communist Party," *Daily Worker,* March 11, 1935 (found in ACLU MSS, reel 122, v. 670); Edgar Clemons to Roger Baldwin, March 4, 1935, ACLU MSS, reel 126, v. 854.

28. Details about Charles Sherin's family and early life supplied in telephone interview with Ed Sherin, March 21, 2005. See also "Random Thoughts from a Factory Roof," an essay about "Magnes Brothers Silk Co., Mill Street, Paterson, N.J., Summer of 1927," written by Charles Sherin in February 1932; and "Your Uncle Bob" to "Eddie," February 1, 1951, copies provided by Ed Sherin.

29. "Tulsa-Bob," Jaffe MSS, Box 2. See also Robert Wood, *To Live and Die in Dixie* (New York: Southern Workers Defense Committee, 1935) 20–21; FBI Report by Ralph T. Hood, July 1, 1940, Robert Wood FOIA File. Other biographical data offered by Wood himself at the Little Dies Committee hearings. See *Oklahoma City Times,* February 5, 1941; Jaffe, *Odyssey,* 5; interview with Wilma Jaffe, October 1, 2004; interview with Timothy Wood, March 11, 2005. See also Ybarra, *Washington Gone Crazy,* 203–204, and Robin D. G. Kelly, *Hammer and Hoe: Alabama Communists During the Great Depression* (Chapel Hill: University of North Carolina Press, 1990), 121. Kelly mistakenly identified Wood's original name as "Charles Sherrill." Elizabeth Gurley Brown describes Wood's tendency to fill his pockets with news clippings and use them in public speeches in "Life of the Party," *Daily Worker,* June 22, 1950.

30. *Daily Oklahoman,* May 27, 1938. See also Denning, *Cultural Front,* 226; and

Douglas Warren, "Red Pens from the Village: *The Anvil* and *The Left,* Midwestern Little Magazines of the Early 1930s," *Mid-America: An Historical Review* 11 (1984): [49].

31. Alonzo Poling related this story to the Oklahoma Senate Committee on Privileges and Elections on February 5, 1941. See *Daily Oklahoman,* February 6, 1941.

32. According to its stationery letterhead, *Black Dispatch* was the "Largest Circulated Negro Journal in the South Read in Every State in the Union." See letter from Roscoe Dunjee to Walter White, August 14, 1941, NAACP MSS, Box C157.

33. Cunningham, *Red Dust,* 174–75. See also "Official Program of the Oklahoma Conference of Branches, N.A.A.C.P., First Baptist Church," Muskogee, May 28 & 29, 1938, Reference Center for Marxist Studies, New York City. Wood addressed the conference on "The Scottsboro Case."

34. We were unable to verify the marriage time and location, but the FBI included it in a November 25, 1942, report. See Report by Jack H. Dillard, Robert Wood FOIA File.

35. Plaintiff's Brief, Ina Wood, 3–4, 7–8; Ina Wood app. rec., Exhibit B-5, 1943; Defendant's Brief, Ina Wood, 4. See also Jaffe, *Odyssey,* 32–33; Friessen, *Oklahoma Witch Hunt,* 4; *Tulsa Tribune,* October 6, 1941. Timothy Wood shared details of his mother's physical features in letters to us dated April 28, 2005 and May 4, 2005.

36. *Brooklyn College Vanguard,* October 18, 1940; Jaffe, *Odyssey,* 5–12.

37. Jaffe, *Odyssey,* 5–19. See also "Workers Alliance Plans Sit-Down on Relief Cuts," *Daily Oklahoman,* July 20, 1937.

38. Jaffe, *Odyssey,* 21–22; *Daily Oklahoman,* March 23, 1938.

39. *Tulsa World,* March 13, 1938; March 28, 1938; *Claremore Messenger,* March 30, 1938; Jaffe, *Odyssey,* 18, 24–26.

40. C. H. Henderson to Jaffe, May 3, 1941, Jaffe MSS, Box 1.

41. See Henderson, *Letters from the Dust Bowl,* 22–23, 172, 178. Eli also tried to recruit Henderson for the Workers Alliance, but was unsuccessful. Caroline Henderson to Eli Jaffe, December 14, 1939, in *Letters from the Dust Bowl,* 175.

42. *Brooklyn College Vanguard,* October 18, 1940; Jaffe app. rec., 122. See also Jaffe, *Odyssey,* 93–95. Information about his name change from family friend Jo Powers Biddle, interview June 14, 2004.

43. See James A. Robinson, "Loyalty Investigations and Legislation in Oklahoma," (master's thesis, University of Oklahoma, 1955), chapter 2; and Harvey Klehr, *The Heyday of American Communism* (New York: Basic Books, 1984), 275.

44. Quoted in Mary Ann Slater, "Politics and Art: The Controversial Birth of the Oklahoma Writers' Project," *Chronicles of Oklahoma* 68 (Spring 1990): 72–89.

45. *Seminole Producer,* February 3, 1939; February 10, 1939.

46. *Daily Oklahoman,* May 27, 1938.

47. *Daily Oklahoman,* December 6, 1938; Herbert L. Brannon, "Portrait of Governor Leon C. Phillips," *Chronicles of Oklahoma* 46 (Summer 1968): 122–26. See

also *Black Dispatch,* December 14, 1940, in editorial titled "Criminal Syndicalism," where Dunjee quotes from undated copy of *Oklahoma City Times.*

48. H.B. No. 78, Okla. H.R. January 19, 1939. See also Charles M. Perry to ACLU, February 9, 1939, ACLU MSS, reel 177, v. 2137.

49. "No Bombs Nor Beards, Red Rally Not Even Pink," *Daily Oklahoman,* February 23, 1939.

50. T.T. Johnson, Municipal Auditorium Manager, to Alan Shaw, August 22, 1939, ACLU MSS, reel 177, v. 2137; *Daily Oklahoman,* August 15, 1939, August 23, 1939.

51. "We Might Be Next," *Daily Oklahoman,* August 16, 1939; Alan Shaw v. T.T. Johnson, No. 99537, Okla. Co. Dist. Ct., cited in Robinson, "Loyalty Investigations," 45–46. See also *Daily Oklahoman,* March 12, 1940; March 17, 1940; "Communist Criticizes Hecklers, Accuses City Police of Violence," *Oklahoma City Times,* August 26, 1939.

52. Ina Wood Trial Record, 2, 7. See also Shaw app. rec., 59; "State of the Nation," *New Masses* 38 (March 26, 1940): 17; *Daily Oklahoman,* August 24, 1939; August 26, 1939; Press Release, Oklahoma Committee to Defend Political Prisoners, November 18, 1940 (which quotes Loe's testimony at Shaw trial), copy found in Wood MSS. The meeting is described in *Daily Oklahoman,* September 11, 1939.

53. FBI report by Ralph T. Hood, July 1, 1940, Robert Wood FOIA File. See also Jaffe, *Odyssey,* 90–92; *Daily Oklahoman,* December 18, 1939. After the Soviet Union invaded the Baltic States and Finland, Caroline Henderson wrote Eli. "I respect the constancy of your faith in Russia, even though I can no longer share it." Henderson to Jaffe, in *Letters from the Dust Bowl,* 177.

54. *Daily Oklahoman,* December 31, 1937.

55. Interview with Orval Lewis, September 25, 2004; *Daily Oklahoman,* December 31, 1937; December 31, 1939.

56. *Daily Oklahoman,* December 30, 1939.

57. Picture and copy of OYL program in Exhibit D-28, Shaw app. rec. Stapp quotation taken from Robert C. Cottrell, *The Social Gospel of E. Nicholas Comfort: Founder of the Oklahoma School of Religion* (Norman: University of Oklahoma Press, 1997), 218. See also *Chicago Defender* (national ed.), January 6, 1940. In early 1940 the OYL asked attorney Stanley Belden to investigate whether the new group could incorporate under state law. Belden was not optimistic. "The Legion is the most un-American organizations [*sic*] that we have to contend with here," he wrote the ACLU. The Legion-sponsored Oklahoma Junior Legislature continued its organizing efforts. Letter, Belden to ACLU, February 21, 1940, ACLU MSS, reel 190, v. 2241; *Oklahoma Daily,* December 5, 1940; *Black Dispatch,* December 14, 1940.

58. *Daily Oklahoman,* January 1, 1940; January 7, 1940; April 1, 1940; April 19, 1940; May 17, 1940; *Oklahoma City Times,* January 9, 1940.

59. "Okay KKK," *New Masses* 35 (February 20, 1940): 17.

60. *Daily Oklahoman,* March 12, 1940; March 13, 1940; March 17, 1940. Letter of March 16, 1940, is Exhibit D-16, Shaw app. rec.

61. *Daily Oklahoman,* March 16, 1940. See also August 21, 1940, where Harrison is interviewed by the *Oklahoman* after the raids had taken place, and Eberle invoked the criminal syndicalism law. Survey in ACLU MSS, reel 209, v. 2422.

62. *Daily Oklahoman,* March 21, 1940; Cunningham, *Red Dust,* 193.

63. Sis Cunningham, "Red Dust Players," attached to Peter Seeger to Sis, July 20, 1948, copy in possession of Ronald D. Cohen.

64. Green, "I Face an Oklahoma Prison," 26–33. Eberle later claimed the list of WPA workers Green and Jaffe compiled for the Food Stamp Office was used for recruitment purposes. See Plaintiff's Brief, Robert Wood, 91. Bank book incident is in *PM,* July 29, 1941. See also Green, "God Made Oklahoma Rich — I," 13.

65. Governor's speech reported in *Daily Oklahoman,* June 1, 1940.

66. See pamphlet found in Jaffe MSS, Box 1; Shaw app. rec., 56, 59, 67, 143–47; *Oklahoma City Times,* November 18, 1940. See also "Press Release," International Labor Defense, November 23, 1940 (copy found in Wood MSS) for Civil Guard quote. Statement about city clerk taken from Shaw app. rec., 114.

67. *Daily Oklahoman,* June 9, 1940. See also June 4, 1940. Quote about illegality of these two organizations in Shaw app. rec., 156, in which Croom questioned Goff and quoted Attorney General Robert Jackson.

68. See also *Union Maids,* a documentary about 1930s female labor activists, produced by Julia Reichert and James Klein.

69. The account of Guthrie and Seeger taken from the following sources: Joe Klein, *Woody Guthrie: A Life* (New York: Alfred A. Knopf, 1980), 159–63; Jaffe, *Odyssey,* 85–89; David Dunaway, *How Can I Keep From Singing* (New York: McGraw Hill, 1981), 68–69; Woody Guthrie, *American Folksong* (New York: Oak Publications, 1961), 5; and Pete Seeger, "Woody Guthrie, Songwriter," *Ramparts* 7 (November 30, 1968): 29–30. See also *Tulsa World,* July 9, 2000, reporting an interview with Seeger about the visit to Oklahoma.

70. *Shaw v. State,* 134 P. 2d 999, 1012 (Okla. Crim. App. 1943); Jaffe, *Odyssey,* 93–95; FBI report by Jack H. Dillard, February 3, 1943, Shaw FOIA Files.

71. *Tulsa Daily World,* June 13, 1940.

72. *Daily Oklahoman,* June 10, 1940; June 17, 1940; Friessen, *Oklahoma Witch Hunt,* 9; Ruth McKenney, "Law in the Dust Bowl," 17. See also *Oklahoma City Times,* November 18, 1940; and Denning, *Cultural Front,* 355–56.

73. Motion for a Change of Venue, Ina Wood Trial Record, 2; Green, "Fascism: Oklahoma Brand," 18. Evidence for song at book burning in "Oklahoma Story," by Wilma, Jaffe MSS, Box 1. Comment about Russians eating their own children from clipping found in Jaffe MSS, Box 1, titled "Bookburning in Oklahoma." See also McKenney, "Law in the Dust Bowl," 17; *Daily Oklahoman,* December 28, 1938. The leader of the Silver Shirts, William Dudley Pelley, was imprisoned during World War II for sedition. For more information, see Esther Rosenfeld, "Fatal Lessons: United

States Immigration Law During the Holocaust," 1 *U.C. Davis J. Int'l & Pol'y* 249, 262–63 (1995). See also Webber's obituary, *Daily Oklahoman,* August 22, 1959, and E. F. Webber, *The Man Everyone Ought to Know* (Oklahoma City, n.p., 1942), 4. Comment about Webber being "an organizer" for the Silver Shirts can be found in Donald S. Strong, *Organized Anti-Semitism in America: The Rise of Group Prejudice in the Decade 1930–1940* (Washington, D.C.: American Council on Public Affairs, 1941), 53.

74. See Christine A. Jenkins, " 'The Strength of the Inconspicuous': Youth Services Librarians, the American Library Association, and Intellectual Freedom for the Young, 1939–1955," (Ph.D. diss., University of Wisconsin-Madison, 1995), 187.

75. *Norman Transcript,* September 26, 1940.

76. The Smith Act can be found in 18 U.S.C. 2385. See also Samuel Walker, *In Defense of American Liberties: A History of the ACLU* (New York: Oxford University Press, 1990), 123; Belknap, *Cold War Political Justice,* 25.

77. Walker, *In Defense of American Liberties,* chapters 6 and 7.

78. FBI report by Ralph T. Hood, July 1, 1940, Robert Wood FOIA File; *Daily Oklahoman,* June 17, 1940; June 24, 1940; June 26, 1940; June 30, 1940; July 6, 1940.

79. Open letter to Attorney General Jackson by Vito Marcantonio, September 25, 1940, copy found in Ross MSS, Box 23.

80. Jaffe, *Odyssey,* 92; Defendant's Brief, Robert Wood, 2, 82; *Daily Oklahoman,* August 18, 1940; Hollywood actor story in August 15, 1940. See also pamphlet, "10 Years and $5,000 Fine For 'Dangerous Thoughts' " (New York: International Labor Defense, 1941). Story of buried books in interview with Wilma Jaffe, January 10, 2004. To our knowledge, the books are still buried there.

81. "10 Years and $5,000 Fine"; interview with Wilma Jaffe, January 9–11, 2004; interview with Orval Lewis, September 25, 2004.

Chapter Three

1. David M. Rabban, *Free Speech in Its Forgotten Years* (Cambridge, U.K.: Cambridge University Press, 1997), 2, 14–16, 373–75. See, e.g., Fiske v. Kansas, 274 U.S. 380 (1927); DeJonge v. Oregon, 299 U.S. 353 (1937); Herndon v. Lowry, 301 U.S. 242 (1937).

2. "Ben Arnold," *Daily Oklahoman,* April 23, 1939.

3. *Oklahoma City Times,* January 24, 1942; *Daily Oklahoman,* December 12, 1938. Eberle's out-of-court reference to "Jews" relayed in interview with Orval Lewis, September 25, 2004. See also J. A. O'Brien, "Communism and Religion: A Struggle Unto Death," *Catholic Digest* 4 (August 1940): 69–73. See also "De Communismo Atheo; Encyclical Letter Divini Redemptoris, March 19, 1937," *Christian Social Action* 7 (November 1941): 276–88. In a section subtitled "Shrewd and Widespread Propaganda," Pius notes how "Communism . . . makes use of pamphlets"

and other printed materials. "Little by little it penetrates all classes of the people . . . with the result that few are aware of the poison which increasingly pervades their minds and hearts." And especially he warned Catholics around the world that "the preachers of Communism are also proficient in exploiting racial antagonisms and political divisions and opposition."

4. *Oklahoma Daily,* September 30, 1941; "Judge Morris' Rites Incomplete," *Daily Oklahoman,* January 5, 1949; untitled article in *Sooner Magazine,* February 1939 (clipping found in Jaffe MSS, Box 2).

5. Jaffe, *Odyssey,* 26; Friessen, *Oklahoma Witch Hunt,* 4; interview with Wilma Jaffe, January 10, 2004; Jaffe app. rec., 256; *Tulsa Tribune,* February 19, 1952; telephone interview with Margaret (Croom) Gandy, August 21, 2005, who as an 8-year-old attended most of the trials with her mother.

6. *Daily Oklahoman,* October 1, 1940.

7. *Daily Oklahoman,* October 1, 1940. See also *Daily Worker,* October 3, 1940.

8. "Storm Troop Spirit at Okla. Trial," *Daily Worker,* October 5, 1940. One letter recipient later reported to staff that when he tried to raise funds for the defense by showing the letter to several people on the streets of Durant, Oklahoma, he was nearly "run out of town." Report by J. B. Gray, January 12, 1942, Shaw FOIA File.

9. Appeal from Nena Beth Stapp, Secretary, Oklahoma Committee to Defend Political Prisoners, n.d., included with letter to ACLU's Baldwin, September 17, 1940, ACLU MSS, reel 1900, v. 2241; *Oklahoma Daily,* September 29, 1940; *Daily Oklahoman,* October 1, 1940.

10. Wood to Elizabeth Green, Goldie Lewis, and Ina in jail, 5:00 p.m., September 30, 1940, Wood MSS. Eberle's comment quoted in "Action Letter," October 9, 1940, National Federation for Constitutional Liberties, OSR MSS, Box 4.

11. *Daily Oklahoman,* October 2, 1940; *Oklahoma City Times,* October 1, 1940; Small, "Oklahoma Okays Hitler," 1.

12. *Oklahoma City Times,* October 1, 1940; October 3, 1940.

13. Small, "Oklahoma Okays Hitler," 1. "Militant" comment in pamphlet in Jaffe MSS, Box 1.

14. These events compiled from *Daily Oklahoman,* October 2, 1940; *Oklahoma City Times,* October 3, 1940; and Bob Wood to "Dear Folks," October 1, 1940, Wood MSS.

15. Bob Wood to "Dear Folks," October 1, 1940, Wood MSS.

16. *Daily Oklahoman,* October 3, 1940.

17. *Daily Oklahoman,* October 4, 1940. See also Martin Dies, *The Trojan Horse in America* (New York: Dodd, Mead & Company, 1940).

18. *Daily Worker,* October 4, 1940; October 5, 1940; *Daily Oklahoman,* October 4, 1940; October 7, 1940.

19. Records obtained through FOIA requests verify that no formal investigation was underway, but the FBI was tracking the individual defendants and receiving information about the trials. These records also show, however, that Eberle regularly shared information with the FBI.

20. *Daily Oklahoman,* October 5, 1940.

21. *Daily Oklahoman,* October 5, 1940; October 7, 1940.

22. *Daily Oklahoman,* October 8, 1940; *Daily Worker,* October 9, 1940.

23. *Daily Oklahoman,* October 8, 1940.

24. *Oklahoma Daily,* October 10, 1940.

25. *Daily Oklahoman,* October 9, 1940.

26. *Daily Oklahoman,* October 9, 1940.

27. *Oklahoma City Times,* October 9, 1940; *Daily Oklahoman,* October 10, 1940; Plaintiff's Brief, Robert Wood, 93–102.

28. *Daily Oklahoman,* October 11, 1940; *Oklahoma City Times,* October 11, 1940.

29. *Daily Oklahoman,* October 11, 1940.

30. Plaintiff's Brief, Robert Wood, 103–111.

31. Plaintiff's Brief, Robert Wood, 103–111; NFCL Brief, Robert Wood, 35; *PM,* November 12, 1940.

32. Arnold's address to courtroom in Petition for Change of Venue, Ina Wood Trial Record, 3–4.

33. Interview with Wilma Jaffe, January 10, 2004; see also Friessen, *Oklahoma Witch Hunt.*

34. *Daily Oklahoman,* October 12, 1940.

35. Robert Wood to "Ina, Eliz, and Mrs. Lewis," October 11, 1940, Wood MSS.

36. See, for example, *Port Arthur* (Tex.) *News,* October 12, 1940; *Hammond* (Ind.) *Times,* October 13, 1940; October 13, 1940; and *Syracuse* (N.Y.) *Herald-Journal,* October 12, 1940, each of which included a picture of Wood in his jail cell.

37. *New York Times,* October 12, 1940; *Oklahoma Daily,* October 11, 1940.

38. "Vigilante Justice," *New Masses* 43 (October 15, 1940): 16.

39. *Daily Worker,* October 12, 1940. See also October 14, 1940; October 15, 1940.

40. Nick Comfort to Amy Comstock of the *Tulsa Tribune,* November 7, 1940, OSR MSS, Box 4; "Action Letter," October 9, 1940, National Federation for Constitutional Liberties, OSR MSS, Box 4. See also Wayne A. and Shirley A. Wiegand, "Sooner State Civil Liberties in Perilous Times, 1940–1941, Part 1," *Chronicles of Oklahoma* 84 (Winter 2006–2007): 444–63.

41. Hugh Fisher to Mrs. Robert Wood, October 10, 1940, Wood MSS.

42. Bob Wood to Ina, October 12, 1940, Wood MSS.

43. *Norman Transcript,* October 18, 1940; *Oklahoma Daily,* October 17, 1940; October 20, 1940.

44. Robert Wood's grandson, Michael Wood, spotted the song listed in Chuck Mancuso, *Popular Music and the Underground: Foundations of Jazz, Blues, Country & Rock, 1900–1950* (Kendall/Hunt Publishing Co., 1996). Michael's father, Timothy, contacted Nora Guthrie at the Woody Guthrie Archives, and she sent the song to him. To our knowledge, the song was never recorded.

45. Bob to Ina, October 21, 1940, Wood MSS.

46. Bob to Ina, October 23, 1940, Wood MSS.

47. Jaffe, *Odyssey,* 113–14.

48. ILD Newsletter, ACLU MSS, October 25, 1940, reel 190, v. 2241; Small, "Oklahoma Okays Hitler," 20.

49. *Daily Oklahoman,* October 20, 1940; October 25, 1940; November 2, 1940.

50. *Daily Worker,* October 26, 1940; *Equal Justice* (Autumn 1940): 3–4.

51. Minutes, ILD National Board, November 15, 1940, ILD MSS, reel 1; *Daily Oklahoman,* November 5, 1940; November 8, 1940.

52. *Daily Oklahoman,* November 8, 1940. See also "News Release," International Labor Defense, November 12, 1940, Wood MSS; *Publishers Weekly* 140 (July 5, 1941): 22; Roosevelt's response to the press also quoted in Brief of the NFCL Brief, Robert Wood, 23; *Norman Transcript,* November 10, 1940; undated Newsletter, Oklahoma Committee to Defend Political Prisoners, Wood MSS. A brief article in *The Nation* noted that Stapp had not received permission to make public Mrs. Roosevelt's private donation. See *The Nation* 151 (November 23, 1940): 505.

53. *Daily Oklahoman,* November 9, 1940. See also *Daily Worker,* November 9, 1940; November 12, 1940.

54. *Daily Oklahoman,* November 9, 1940.

55. Undated newspaper clipping in Wood MSS (dated by reference to the 1940 election and reference to Bob Wood's release from jail).

56. See "News Release," ILD, November 12, 1940, Wood MSS; *Daily Oklahoman,* November 13, 1940.

57. *PM,* November 14, 1940.

58. *PM,* November 13, 1940.

59. *Oklahoma City Times,* November 20, 1940; November 23, 1940.

60. *Daily Oklahoman,* November 23, 1940.

61. Shaw Trial Record, November 14, 1940.

62. Minutes, ILD National Board, November 15, 1940, ILD MSS, reel 1.

63. *Daily Worker,* November 16, 1940.

64. *Daily Oklahoman,* November 16, 1940; November 18, 1940; November 19, 1940; *Daily Worker,* November 19, 1940; Press Release, Oklahoma Committee to Defend Political Prisoners, November 18, 1940; November 23, 1940, Wood MSS. Loe's comment about Jesus Christ taken from Shaw app. rec., 109.

65. *Oklahoma City Times,* November 22, 1940. See also Jaffe, *Odyssey,* 107; and untitled pamphlet, Jaffe MSS, Box 1.

66. *Norman Transcript,* November 21, 1940; *Daily Oklahoman,* November 21, 1940.

67. *Daily Oklahoman,* November 23, 1940; November 24, 1940. See also *Daily Worker,* November 29, 1940.

68. *Daily Worker,* November 25, 1940.

69. *Daily Oklahoman,* November 26, 1940.

70. *Daily Oklahoman,* November 26, 1940; November 27, 1940; Press Release,

November 28, 1940, Oklahoma Committee to Defend Political Prisoners, Wood MSS.

71. *Oklahoma City Times,* November 27, 1940. In his master's thesis, James Morton Smith recounts in a footnote that he had interviewed Newman on June 7, 1942. Newman said he appeared in the Shaw case without a subpoena only after Eberle had said he would use one if necessary. Newman said he felt that his testimony was introduced for its emotional worth. " 'The cases were wholly emotional, without a shred of justice in them,' he asserted." See Smith, "Criminal Syndicalism in Oklahoma," 115.

72. Belden wrote to the ILD on October 28, "I am personally of the opinion that it might be well for Mr. Shaw to take the stand (since they have the proof that he was a member of the Communist Party)." See ACLU MSS, reel 2241. See also Plaintiff's Brief, Alan Shaw, 4.

73. *Daily Worker,* November 29, 1940.

74. Jaffe, *Odyssey,* 107–111.

75. Jaffe, *Odyssey,* 117–18, 124–25; interview with Wilma Jaffe, January 9, 2004; January 11, 2004.

76. Interview with Wilma Jaffe, January 10, 2004.

77. Press Release, November 28, 1940, Oklahoma Committee to Defend Political Prisoners, Wood MSS.

78. *Daily Worker,* November 29, 1940. See also Circular, "ILD Christmas Drive, 1940," in ILD MSS, reel 1.

79. *Daily Oklahoman,* December 3, 1940; December 4, 1940; *Daily Worker,* December 6, 1940; ILD Minutes, National Board, December 11, 1940, ILD MSS, reel 1.

80. Shaw app. rec., 576; Plaintiff's Brief, Alan Shaw, 107–111.

81. Oklahoma v. Shaw, A-10083, Case Made, 576; *Daily Oklahoman,* December 3, 1940; December 4, 1940; *Daily Worker,* December 6, 1940. See also *Black Dispatch,* December 21, 1940.

82. Shaw app. rec., 706–18.

83. Shaw app. rec., 706–54.

84. *Miami Daily News Record,* December 10, 1940. See also an article by Robert Wood describing Morris's courtroom behavior in *Daily Worker,* December 11, 1940; "Another Kind of Violence," *Black Dispatch,* December 21, 1940; Plaintiff's Brief, Alan Shaw, 113; Shaw app. rec., 730; Smith, "Criminal Syndicalism in Oklahoma," 118.

85. Shaw app. rec., 755; Smith, "Criminal Syndicalism in Oklahoma," 119. See also *Brooklyn College Vanguard,* December 6, 1940.

86. *Daily Oklahoman,* December 10, 1940.

87. *Daily Oklahoman,* December 10, 1940; *Daily Worker,* December 11, 1940. By this time, Belden's Jehovah's Witness clients had fired him, because they were unwilling to associate with a lawyer representing Communists. Letter from Belden to Roger Baldwin, Director, ACLU, November 16, 1940, ACLU MSS, reel 190, v. 2441.

88. *Daily Oklahoman,* December 10, 1940; *Cushing Daily Citizen,* December 10, 1940; *Miami Daily News Record,* December 10, 1940; *Norman Transcript,* December 10, 1940; December 11, 1940.

89. *Black Dispatch,* December 14, 1940; December 21, 1940.

90. *Tulsa Tribune,* December 11, 1940

91. *Miners' Voice* quoted in Smith, "Criminal Syndicalism in Oklahoma," 136; *Daily Oklahoman,* December 11, 1940; *Daily Worker,* December 11, 1940; *Nation* 151 (December 28, 1940): 647; *New York Times,* December 10, 1940; *Capital Times,* December 12, 1940; *American Guardian,* January 3, 1941. See also *Chicago Tribune,* December 11, 1940; *Christian Science Monitor,* December 20, 1940; *Los Angeles Times,* December 20, 1940; *Oshkosh* (Wis.) *Daily Northwestern,* December 10, 1940; *Sheboygan* (Wis.) *Press,* December 10, 1940; and *Fresno* (Calif.) *Bee,* December 11, 1940.

92. ILD Minutes, December 11, 1940, ILD MSS, reel 1; *Daily Worker,* December 9, 1940.

93. *Daily Oklahoman,* December 4, 1940; December 5, 1940; December 7, 1940; and December 9, 1940 See also H. G. McGinnis, "Must the Constitution Protect Those Who Would Destroy It?" *America* 64 (December 7, 1940): 230–31.

94. *Daily Oklahoman,* December 14, 1940; December 18, 1940.

95. See *Tulsa World,* February 18, 1943; Jaffe, *Odyssey,* 130–33; *Daily Worker,* December 18, 1940.

96. Shaw app. rec., 779–80.

97. *Daily Oklahoman,* December 20, 1940; *Oklahoma City Times,* December 19, 1940. See also *New York Times,* December 20, 1940; and Green, "Fascism: Oklahoma Brand," 18. Shaw's courthouse quote was slightly inaccurate, but he nonetheless captured the sentiment. The sign above the east entrance reads: "Equal and exact justice to all men, of whatever state or persuasion, religious or political."

Chapter Four

1. See letter, Streeter Stuart to U.S. Representative Wilburn Cartwright, August 9, 1940; Letter from Southeastern State College President T. T. Montgomery to Streeter Stuart (termination letter), August 31, 1940; Letter from Cartwright to Streeter Stuart (responding to Stuart's letter of August 9 calling for him to vote against conscription), August 27, 1940; all found in Ross MSS, Box 23.

2. *Norman Transcript,* October 17, 1940; Letter, Sec., OU AAUP chapter to Bizzell, October 19, 1940, Bizzell MSS, Box 152, 9439.1. Ten days later the OU chapter approved action of the national AAUP to investigate Stuart's dismissal. See *Norman Transcript,* October 29, 1940.

3. Copy of telegram, dated October 19, 1940, in Wood MSS.

4. Letter, Belden to ACLU Staff Counsel Britchey, October 23, 1940, ACLU MSS, reel 190, v. 2241. Thompson, Comfort and Wright each gave accounts to a

Daily Oklahoman reporter after the session. See *Daily Oklahoman,* October 20, 1940. See also *Seminole Producer,* October 20, 1940.

5. *Daily Oklahoman,* October 20, 1940. See also *Norman Transcript,* October 20, 1940.

6. *Daily Oklahoman,* October 21, 1940; October 23, 1940; October 25, 1940. See also *Black Dispatch,* February 15, 1941.

7. Circular from "Oklahoma Committee on Constitutional Rights" to "Dear Friend," dated October 22, 1940, copy found in OSR MSS, Box 4; and Ross MSS, Box 23. See also *Black Dispatch,* February 15, 1941; and John Thompson to Ira Latimer, October 22, 1940, copy found in Ross MSS, Box 23.

8. Copy of "A Call to the People of Oklahoma" found in Wood MSS.

9. *Oklahoma Daily,* October 29, 1940.

10. *Norman Transcript,* November 12, 1940; November 13, 1940; *Oklahoma Daily,* November 14, 1940. See also ILD Press Release, November 23, 1940, copy found in Wood MSS.

11. Baldwin to Ross, November 14, 1940, Ross MSS, Box 23. See also Goldstein, *Political Repression,* 262.

12. *Oklahoma City Times,* November 16, 1940; *Black Dispatch,* November 23, 1940; and *Daily Oklahoman,* November 16, 1940. See also September 21, 1942.

13. *Norman Transcript,* November 15, 1940; *Daily Oklahoman,* November 16, 1940.

14. Resolution reprinted in "Press Release," ILD, November 23, 1940, Wood MSS. See also "Resolutions Passed by the Recent Oklahoma Federation for Constitutional Rights," *Black Dispatch,* November 30, 1940.

15. *Daily Oklahoman,* November 16, 1940; *Black Dispatch,* November 23, 1940.

16. Lewis Morris quoted in *New Masses* 39 (November 26, 1940): 20. See also *Oklahoma City Times,* November 22, 1940; *PM,* November 14, 1940; Bizzell to Memminger, December 3, 1940, Bizzell MSS, Box 160, 9443.3.

17. *Daily Oklahoman,* November 16, 1940.

18. ILD Press Release, November 23, 1940, in Wood MSS; undated editorial quoted in *Oklahoma City Times,* November 28, 1940, and found in Jaffe MSS, Box 1.

19. *Black Dispatch,* November 23, 1940. See also Robert Wood, "Peace Advocacy Is Crime in Eyes of Okla. Authorities," *Daily Worker,* November 25, 1940. At a meeting of Southwestern Regional Conference of the Oklahoma Conference of Branches, NAACP, in Watonga on December 6, John Thompson said in a keynote address, "We have drifted off to a dangerous place where we have become extremely intolerant." See *Black Dispatch,* December 7, 1940.

20. *Oklahoma Daily,* November 17, 1940.

21. Copy of this pamphlet found in Jaffe MSS, Box 1; and ACLU MSS, reel 201, v. 2340.

22. *Daily Oklahoman,* November 18, 1940; November 21, 1940. Historian Mi-

chael Ybarra notes Dilling used her husband's money to self-publish *Red Network.* He also concludes that "Dilling was, to put it mildly, insane." See *Washington Gone Crazy,* 225.

23. *Norman Transcript,* November 18, 1940. See also Press Release, Oklahoma Committee to Defend Political Prisoners, November 28, 1940, Wood MSS; and "Adams Flays Subversive Actions," *Oklahoma Daily,* November 19, 1940. See also *Daily Oklahoman,* October 14, 1940.

24. *Oklahoma City Times,* December 28, 1940.

25. *Oklahoma City Times,* December 28, 1940; Jaffe, *Odyssey,* 138–39; *Norman Transcript,* December 29, 1940. See also *Daily Oklahoman,* December 28, 1940.

26. *Brooklyn College Vanguard,* October 8, 1940; *Oklahoma City Times,* November 22, 1940.

27. *Brooklyn College Vanguard,* December 6, 1940; December 20, 1940; *Daily Oklahoman,* December 7, 1940.

28. *Brooklyn College Vanguard,* January 10, 1941; January 17, 1941. See also flyer, Student Handbill Collection, BC Archives. For an account of the New York committee, see Walker, *In Defense of American Liberties,* 125–26.

29. *Daily Worker,* January 6, 1941; January 11, 1941; *New Masses* 38 (January 14, 1941): 1. For an account of Blitzstein's important role in the larger Popular Front movement of the 1930s, see Denning, *Cultural Front,* 285–95.

30. *Daily Worker,* January 10, 1941; January 16, 1941; January 19, 1941; January 22, 1941; January 24, 1941. See also *Daily Oklahoman,* January 19, 1941, for a brief notice that the rally was taking place.

31. Copy of this letter in Ross MSS, Box 23.

32. *Daily Oklahoman,* January 16, 1941. See also *Daily Worker,* January 30, 1941.

33. *Daily Oklahoman,* January 19, 1941; *Norman Transcript,* January 24, 1941.

34. For a briefer account of these hearings from a University of Oklahoma perspective, see George Lynn Cross, *Professors, Presidents, and Politicians: Civil Rights and the University of Oklahoma, 1890–1968* (Norman: University of Oklahoma Press, 1981), 122–27.

35. *Norman Transcript,* January 23, 1941; January 24, 1941; *Daily Oklahoman,* January 24, 1941. See also Press Release, May 8, 1941, Oklahoma Federation for Constitutional Rights, OSR MSS, Box IV.

36. Flyer reproduced in Shaw app. rec., Exhibit No. 3.

37. Pamphlet found in Shaw Trial Record. Pamphlet also reproduced in Shaw app. rec., Exhibit No. 2.

38. "A Statement of Principles," *Social Work Today* 3 (January 1941), 4–5.

39. *St. Louis Post-Dispatch,* January 26, 1941.

40. Phillips's statement quoted in *Black Dispatch,* February 15, 1941. See also *Daily Oklahoman,* January 27, 1940; January 28, 1941; and *Norman Transcript,* January 28, 1941.

41. *Daily Worker,* February 2, 1941.

42. *Oklahoma City Times,* January 28, 1941.

43. *Daily Oklahoman,* January 29, 1941; *Norman Transcript,* January 28, 1941; *Oklahoma City Times,* January 28, 1941.

44. Descriptions of these events in *Norman Transcript,* January 28, 1941; *Daily Oklahoman,* January 29, 1941.

45. *Norman Transcript,* January 29, 1941; *Oklahoma Daily,* January 30, 1941. The *Daily* was probably referring to Trinity Baptist Church.

46. *Daily Oklahoman,* January 30, 1941; *Norman Transcript,* January 30, 1941.

47. Eli Jaffe, "Oklahoma 'Plain Folks' Aid Communists' Fight Against Ban," *Daily Worker,* February 2, 1941.

48. *Norman Transcript,* February 4, 1941; *Daily Oklahoman,* February 4, 1941.

49. *Daily Oklahoman,* February 6, 1941; *Oklahoma City Times,* February 5, 1941.

50. *Daily Oklahoman,* February 6, 1941; *Oklahoma City Times,* February 6, 1941. The Associated Press circulated a picture of Wood taking an oath before the Senate Committee. See *Oelwein* (Iowa) *Daily Register,* February 11, 1941; *Kansas City Star,* February 12, 1941; and *Nevada State Journal,* February 18, 1941.

51. *Daily Oklahoman,* February 6, 1941; *Oklahoma City Times,* February 5, 1941; February 6, 1941.

52. *Daily Oklahoman,* February 6, 1941; *Oklahoma City Times,* February 6, 1941.

53. *Norman Transcript,* February 6, 1941.

54. *Daily Oklahoman,* February 7, 1941. The Little Dies Committee hearings also drew national attention. See, e.g., *Christian Science Monitor,* January 31, 1941.

55. *Black Dispatch,* February 15, 1941; *Oklahoma Daily,* February 15, 1941. Story of "Communist Code" in Jaffe, *Odyssey,* 144.

56. *Black Dispatch,* February 15, 1941. See also *Chicago Defender* (national ed.), February 22, 1941.

57. *Norman Transcript,* February 11, 1941.

58. *Black Dispatch,* February 15, 1941; *Daily Oklahoman,* February 12, 1941. See also Cortez A. M. Ewing, "Nick Comfort's Attitude Toward Public Affairs," Memorial Service Transcript, OSR MSS, 4; Ken Lowe, "Broken Images," July 30, 1961, OSR MSS, Index, 2.

59. *Daily Oklahoman,* February 12, 1941.

60. *Oklahoma City Times,* February 12, 1941; *Tulsa World,* February 13, 1941.

61. *Daily Oklahoman,* February 13, 1941.

62. *Tulsa World,* February 13, 1941; *Daily Oklahoman,* February 13, 1941.

63. *Black Dispatch,* February 22, 1941; March 1, 1941; *Norman Transcript,* February 13, 1941.

64. Minutes, ILD National Board, January 17, 1941; February 14, 1941, ILD MSS, reel 1.

65. ILD Press Release, February 1, 1941, ACLU MSS, reel 2; *Daily Worker,* January 16, 1941.

66. Belden to Baldwin, March 17, 1941, ACLU MSS, reel 209, v. 2422; Belden to Unger, March 31, 1941, ACLU MSS, reel 201, v. 2340; Minutes, ILD National Board, March 7, 1941, ILD MSS, reel 1. See also *Daily Oklahoman,* April 11, 1941.

67. *Brooklyn College Vanguard,* March 28, 1941.

68. Abraham J. Isserman, *Investigating Committees and Civil Rights* (Washington, D.C.: National Federation for Constitutional Liberties, 1941), 8–10.

69. Edward S. Smith, *Civil Liberties in the Present Crisis* (Washington, D.C.: National Federation for Constitutional Liberties, 1941).

70. See Baldwin to Belden, November 26, 1940; Baldwin to Haight (ABA), December 30, 1940; Lerch (ABA) to Baldwin, January 13, 1941; Belden to Baldwin, April 19, 1941; Ewing to Forster (ACLU), August 7, 1942, ACLU MSS, reel 209, v. 2422.

71. Chief Reed wrote a memorandum about the events and later provided a copy to the FBI, found in Robert Wood FOIA File. See also *Kansas City Star,* April 25, 1941; April 26, 1941; *Kansas City Times,* April 25, 1941; April 26, 1941; *New York Times,* April 27, 1941; *Daily Worker,* April 28, 1941; memorandum from P. E. Foxworth to FBI Director, May 8, 1941, Robert Wood FOIA File.

72. Newsletter, Oklahoma Committee to Defend Political Prisoners, May 2, 1941, copy found in Jaffe MSS, Box 1.

73. *Kansas City Journal,* April 26, 1941; April 28, 1941; *Kansas City Star,* April 25, 1941; April 26, 1941; *Oklahoma City Times,* April 26, 1941; *Daily Oklahoman,* April 26, 1941; *Norman Transcript,* April 28, 1941. The *Journal* proved correct about Reed's actions making headlines across the country. See, e.g., *Los Angeles Times,* April 26, 1941; *Christian Science Monitor,* April 29, 1941, and subsequent condemnatory editorial on April 30, 1941.

74. *Daily Oklahoman,* April 30, 1941. See also Order Granting Permission to Leave State, Robert Wood app. rec., April 29, 1941.

75. Frederick Simpiels, "So Oklahoma Grew Up," *National Geographic* 79 (March 1941): 269–314.

76. *Norman Transcript,* February 25, 1941.

77. Dreiser's statement quoted in Newsletter, Oklahoma Committee to Defend Political Prisoners, April 26, 1941, copy found in Jaffe MSS, Box 1.

Chapter Five

1. Pamphlet found in Jaffe MSS, Box 1.

2. Jaffe, *Odyssey,* 146–47.

3. *Daily Oklahoman,* April 27, 1941; Jaffe app.rec., 409–453; *Enid News,* April 25, 1941; *Oklahoma City Times,* April 26, 1941; Jaffe, *Odyssey,* 147.

4. *Oklahoma City Times,* April 25, 1941; April 26, 1941; *Enid News,* April 25, 1941.

5. Jaffe, *Odyssey,* 149.

6. *Daily Oklahoman,* April 29, 1941; Jaffe app. rec., 855–56.

7. *Daily Oklahoman,* April 29, 1941; Jaffe, *Odyssey,* 148; Jaffe app. rec., 840.

8. Newsletter, May 2, 1941, Oklahoma Committee to Defend Political Prisoners, copy found in Jaffe MSS, Box 1; Jaffe, *Odyssey,* 149; *Daily Oklahoman,* April 30, 1941.

9. *Daily Oklahoman,* April 30, 1941.

10. *Daily Oklahoman,* May 1, 1941; *New York Times,* May 1, 1941; Jaffe, *Odyssey,* 149. Jaffe comment to reporters in Newsletter, May 2, 1941, Oklahoma Committee to Defend Political Prisoners, copy found in Jaffe MSS, Box 1.

11. These communications reprinted in Newsletter, May 2, 1941, Oklahoma Committee to Defend Political Prisoners, copy found in Jaffe MSS, Box 1. See also *New York Times,* May 1, 1941; *Christian Science Monitor,* May 2, 1941; and *New York City Post,* April 29, 1941, and *Daily Kennebec Journal* (Augusta, Maine), May 9, 1941.

12. *Oklahoma City Times,* May 7, 1941.

13. See *Special Committee Report,* Committee on Privileges and Elections, Senate Resolution No. 15, 1941. The Committee's assessment did not match FBI observations, which numbered 146 Communists in Oklahoma (the Bureau had files on 72), led by a Party constantly in search of contributions to cover its meager costs. See W. H. Erwin (Special Agent in Charge, Little Rock, Ark.) to FBI Headquarters, October 18, 1942, Shaw FOIA File.

14. See James A. Robinson, *Anti-Sedition Legislation and Loyalty Investigations in Oklahoma* (Norman: University of Oklahoma Bureau of Government Research, 1956), 30; *Daily Oklahoman,* May 8, 1941; *Norman Transcript,* May 8, 1941.

15. These events described in Robinson, *Loyalty Investigations and Legislation in Oklahoma,* 82–83.

16. "Newsletter," May 20, 1941, Oklahoma Committee for the Defense of Political Prisoners, copy found in Jaffe MSS, Box 1. See also Paul Wellman, "Oklahoma Hears Some Back Talk," *Kansas City Star,* May 4, 1941.

17. Minutes, May 9, 1941, ILD MSS, reel 1. The National Lawyers Guild, founded in 1937, "was the nation's first racially integrated bar association." See National Lawyers Guild, www.nlglorg/about/history.htm.

18. *Daily Maroon,* May 2, 1941; May 9, 1941.

19. Jaffe, *Odyssey,* 150–51, 152–53; *Daily Worker,* May 23, 1941; May 27, 1941; *Daily Oklahoman,* May 23, 1941. Jaffe's remarks were reprinted in *The Weekly Review* and Jaffe's own *New Appeal to Reason.* See *The Review* (June 1941): 6; and *New Appeal to Reason,* June 1941, 4. In his summary of the trial, Jaffe also referred to Eberle as "Little Caesar."

20. Quoted in Ina Wood Trial Record, June 1, 1941. See also *Oklahoma City Times,* June 3, 1941; and Jaffe, *Odyssey,* 152–53. Caroline Henderson sent a check for Eli's defense fund on May 26, 1941. See Caroline Henderson to Eli Jaffe, May 26, 1941, *Letters From the Dust Bowl,* 180.

21. Kenneth Lowe, Administrative Secretary, OFCR, to Baldwin, June 5, 1941, ACLU MSS, reel 209, v. 2422. Trooper quote relayed by George Croom to his son,

Bobby Gene. Telephone interview with Bobby Gene Croom, April 20, 2005. See also Report, Jack H. Dillard (Oklahoma City FBI Agent) to FBI Headquarters, January 13, 1943, Shaw FOIA File.

22. *Oklahoma City Times,* June 2, 1941; *Daily Oklahoman,* June 1, 1941.

23. *Duluth* (Minn.) *Herald,* June 19, 1941; *Calumet* (Mich.) *New Herald,* June 23, 1941; *New Republic* 104 (June 30, 1941): 892.

24. Clarice F. Brows, ACLU Acting Staff Counsel, to George T. Haight, June 11, 1941, ACLU MSS, reel 201, v. 2340; Eugene P. Ledbetter to Charles H. Lerch, June 19, 1941, ACLU MSS, reel 201, v. 2340.

25. *Daily Worker,* June 2, 1941; *Daily Oklahoman,* June 1, 1941; June 3, 1941; June 4, 1941; June 8, 1941; Ina Wood Trial Record, June 1, 1941.

26. *Daily Worker,* June 6, 1941.

27. *Oklahoma City Times,* June 6, 1941.

28. *Tulsa Tribune,* June 6, 1941.

29. *Daily Worker,* June 9, 1941; *New Masses* 39 (April 25, 1941): 22; (June 3, 1941): 23; (June 17, 1941): 9. See also Report of Franklin Folson, National Executive Secretary, League of American Writers, June 6, 1941, Box 5, and Resolution No. 7, Box 5, LAW MSS. See also *Bulletin of the League of American Writers,* September 1941: 1, and January 19, 1942: 11, copies found in Box 1. The organization dissolved in 1942.

30. Kenneth Lowe, Oklahoma Federation for Constitutional Rights Administrative Secretary, observed the trial. His fifteen-page summary can be found in ACLU MSS, reel 209, v. 2422, quote here taken from p. 2. Because Ina Wood seldom wore hats, Wilma Jaffe guesses Elizabeth Green lent Ina this outfit. Interview with Wilma Jaffe, January 10, 2004.

31. *Tulsa Tribune,* June 10, 1941. Unlike other Oklahoma newspapers, the *Norman Transcript* gave no coverage to Ina's case.

32. *Daily Worker,* June 10, 1941; June 11, 1941; June 14, 1941; *New Masses* 39 (June 10, 1941): 21. Lowe summary in ACLU MSS, reel 209, v. 2422, 4. Biographical sketch of Hunt in *Daily Oklahoman,* April 23, 1939.

33. *Daily Oklahoman,* June 12, 1941.

34. *Tulsa Tribune,* June 13, 1941.

35. Copy of trial transcripts outlining these objections can be found in ILD MSS, reel 22. See also *Daily Oklahoman,* June 13, 1941.

36. ACLU MSS, reel 209, v. 2422, 6–7. See also Ina Wood app. rec., 1149.

37. ACLU MSS, reel 209, v. 2422, 8–9.

38. ACLU MSS, reel 209, v. 2422, 8–9.

39. *Daily Oklahoman,* June 13, 1941; June 14, 1941; *Daily Worker,* June 13, 1941.

40. *Oklahoma City Times,* June 16, 1941.

41. Lowe summary in ACLU MSS, reel 209, v. 2422, 9–10. See also *Oklahoma City Times,* June 6, 1941; and *Daily Oklahoman,* June 17, 1941.

42. Ina Wood, app. rec., 1364–71; 1450–51.

43. Quotes taken from Ina Wood app. rec., 1454–55; *Equal Justice* 14 (Spring 1941): 3; and *Daily Worker,* September 20, 1943.

44. *Daily Worker,* June 17, 1941; *Equal Justice* 14 (Spring 1941): 3; *Oklahoma City Times,* June 16, 1941.

45. Lowe summary in ACLU MSS, reel 209, v. 2422, 12, 14.

46. *Equal Justice* 14 (Spring 1941): 3; *Black Dispatch,* June 21, 1941.

47. *Equal Justice* 14 (Spring 1941): 3; *Daily Oklahoman,* June 19, 1941; *Black Dispatch,* June 21, 1941; Lowe summary in ACLU MSS, reel 209, v. 2422, 14–15.

48. *Daily Oklahoman,* June 19, 1941.

49. Minutes, June 20, 1941, ILD MSS, reel 1; *Daily Worker,* June 20, 1941. Telegram in Wood MSS.

50. *Daily Worker,* June 21, 1941. Pictures of Ina can be found in *Clearfield* (Pa.) *Progress,* July 1, 1941; *Coshocton* (Ohio) *Tribune,* July 1, 1941; *Helena* (Mont.) *Independent,* July 3, 1941; *Dunkirk* (N.Y.) *Evening Observer,* July 2, 1941; *Burlington* (N.C.) *Daily Times-News,* July 3, 1941; and *Wisconsin Rapids Daily Tribune,* July 9, 1941.

51. This was a reference to Iowa v. Sentner, 298 N.W. 813 (June 1941).

52. *St. Louis Post-Dispatch,* June 20, 1942; *Springfield* (Ohio) *News-Sun,* June 20, 1941; *Los Angeles Times,* July 9, 1941. See also *Christian Science Monitor,* June 28, 1941; *Brainerd* (Minn.) *Daily Dispatch,* July 1, 1941; *Indiana Evening Gazette,* July 8, 1941; *Clearfield* (Pa.) *Progress,* June 30, 1941; *Wisconsin Rapids Daily Tribune,* June 30, 1941; *Iowa City Press Citizen,* July 1, 1941; and *Panama City* (Fla.) *News Herald,* July 3, 1941.

53. For background information, see Morgan, *Reds,* chapter 9. The ILD also quickly recognized the international situation would have a direct bearing on the outcome of the trials. See Letter, Special Agent in Charge H.G. Bannister to J. Edgar Hoover, January 19, 1942, Shaw FOIA File.

54. *Enid Morning News,* June 26, 1941; *Daily Worker,* June 24, 1941; June 26, 1941; and editorial, June 28, 1941.

55. *Daily Worker,* June 23, 1941.

56. *United States Week,* July 12, 1941. See also "Memorandum for Members of the National Committee," September 26, 1941, ILD MSS, reel 1.

57. *Proceedings of the Eighth Annual Convention of the American Newspaper Guild Detroit, June 23–27, 1941,* 284; *St. Louis Star-Times,* June 26, 1941.

58. *Daily Oklahoman,* June 29, 1941. See also *Christian Science Monitor,* July 12, 1941.

59. *Duncan Banner,* July 18, 1941; *Chelsea Reporter,* July 17, 1941; *Payne County News,* July 17, 1941; *Okmulgee Times,* July 15, 1941; *Okmulgee Daily Record,* July 17, 1941; *Tulsa World,* July 17, 1941.

60. "Oklahoma Trials Important to Books and Booksellers," *Publishers Weekly* 140 (July 5, 1941): 21–22.

61. Irene Paul, "An American Girl Goes to Jail for 'Dangerous Thoughts,' " *Midwest Labor,* June 27, 1941; "Flouting Americanism to Defend America," *Christian Century* 58 (July 2, 1941): 852–53.

62. *The Christian Evangelist* 79 (July 3, 1941): 775; *New York Herald Tribune,* July 14, 1941. See also "Halt Hysteria," *Midwest Labor,* July 25, 1941. The *Herald Tribne's* editorial was reprinted in several other newspapers. See, for example, *Salamanca* (N.Y.) *Republican,* July 15, 1941.

63. Richard O. Boyer, "If This Be Reason," *United States Week,* July 12, 1941; *Dayton Herald,* July 16, 1941.

64. *Beacon Journal,* July 27, 1941; "Oklahoma Terrorism," *New Republic* 105 (August 18, 1941): 205. See also *In Fact* 3 (July 14, 1941): 3; Greensboro *Daily News,* July 22, 1941.

65. "Special Oklahoma Issue," *Equal Justice* 14 (Spring 1941), found in Jaffe MSS, Box 1.

66. Copy of this pamphlet found in McCoy MSS.

67. *PM,* July 29, 1941.

68. *Norman Transcript,* July 17, 1941. See also *Oklahoma Daily,* July 17, 1941.

69. *Norman Transcript,* July 23, 1941; *Oklahoma City Times,* July 23, 1941. See also *Oklahoma Daily,* July 24, 1941. The *Times* carried a large picture on page one.

70. *Oklahoma City Times,* July 23, 1941; July 25, 1941; *Oklahoma Daily,* July 24, 1941; *Norman Transcript,* July 24, 1941. See Press Release, August 22, 1941, ILD MSS, reel 2.

71. *Tulsa Tribune,* July 25, 1941.

72. Eli Jaffe, "Hooded KKK Fascists Ride in Oklahoma, Threaten Liberal Professors, Communists," *People's World,* July 26, 1941; *Daily Worker,* July 28, 1941; August 20, 1941.

73. Pearl M. Hart to "Dear Friend," July 29, 1941, copy found in OSR MSS, Box IV.

74. Minutes, ILD National Board, August 17, 1941, ILD MSS, reel 1; Anna Damon to "Dear Sirs and Brothers," September 5, 1941, copy found in ACLU MSS, reel 209, v. 2422.

75. *Daily Oklahoman,* August 18, 1941; August 19, 1941.

76. *Stigler News-Sentinel,* July 24, 1941; August 7, 1941; August 21, 1941.

77. Frederic G. Melcher, "Radical Books In Oklahoma," *Publishers Weekly* 140 (August 23, 1941): 521. See also Zachariah Chafee, *Freedom of Speech* (New York: Harcourt, Brace and Howe, 1920).

78. *Milwaukee Journal,* August 28, 1941; *PM,* August 29, 1941; *New York Evening Sun,* August 29, 1941; *Christian Science Monitor,* August 29, 1941; *Troy* (N.Y.) *Morning Record,* September 1, 1941; *Emporia* (Kans.) *Gazette,* September 5, 1941. White column quoted in *Daily Oklahoman,* September 8, 1941.

79. *Daily Oklahoman,* August 30, 1941; *New York Times,* August 27, 1941; Knights of Pythias Brief, Robert Wood, 1.

80. *Oklahoma City Times,* August 26, 1941; *Daily Oklahoman,* August 28, 1941; October 3, 1941.

81. Green, "I Face an Oklahoma Prison," 32–33. See also Elizabeth Green,

"Oklahoma — Battleground Against Home-Grown Hitlerism," *Daily Worker,* August 24, 1941.

82. Green, "God Made Oklahoma Rich — I," 13; "II," 19.

83. Cunningham, *Red Dust,* 207.

84. Belden to Baldwin, April 14, 1941, ACLU MSS, reel 209, v. 2422; Baldwin to Belden, August 6, 1941, ACLU MSS, reel 201, v. 2340.

85. *Daily Oklahoman,* September 4, 1941.

Chapter Six

1. "Protests Seen Cause of Oklahoma Trials Delay," *Daily Worker,* September 10, 1941.

2. "Publishers Protest Against Censorship in Oklahoma," *Publishers Weekly* 140 (September 13, 1941): 921. The *Daily Worker* welcomed these "vigorous protests" from the nation's "leading publishers." See *Daily Worker,* September 23, 1941.

3. Sinclair, Dawson's Book Shop, and Harry W. Schwartz, Inc. quoted in NFCL Brief, Robert Wood, 26–28; Levin, North, and Duell quoted in *People's Weekly,* September 25, 1941; "Witch Hunting in Oklahoma," *Survey Midmonthly* 77 (October 1941): 296–97. Kerr and *Booksellers' Bulletin* quoted in "October Bulletin," Oklahoma Committee to Defend Political Prisoners, 2, copy found in ILD MSS, reel 22.

4. See National Board, League of American Writers, October 20, 1941, copy found in ILD MSS, reel 22. See also Franklin Folson to Governor Leon Phillips, LAW National Executive Secretary, October 20, 1941, copy found in ILD MSS, reel 22.

5. *Dallas Morning News,* September 14, 1941; "Promoting Disunity," *New York Herald,* September 9, 1941.

6. Minutes, September 26, 1941, ILD MSS, reel 1.

7. "Memorandum for Members of the National Committee," September 26, 1941, ILD MSS, reel 1. See also Friessen, *Oklahoma Witch Hunt;* and "October Bulletin," Oklahoma Committee to Defend Political Prisoners, 6, copy found in OSR MSS, Box IV.

8. *Daily Oklahoman,* October 10, 1941; *Oklahoma Daily* quoted in "October Bulletin," Oklahoma Committee to Defend Political Prisoners, 1, 3, copy found in ILD MSS, reel 22; and in OSR MSS, Box IV.

9. *Daily Oklahoman,* October 1, 1941; October 2, 1941. See also *Oklahoma Daily,* September 30, 1941; *Norman Transcript,* September 30, 1941.

10. See Women's League for Democratic Rights to "Dear Friend," October 3, 1941; and flyer announcing Midland Hotel meeting for October 13, ILD MSS, reel 22.

11. See *Chicago Daily News,* October 29, 1941.

12. Ina to Bob, October 21, 1941, Wood MSS.

13. *Washington New-Dealer,* November 20, 1941, copy found in ACLU MSS, reel 198, v. 2315; *Portland Oregonian,* November 26, 1941. Oregon had its own syndicalism law upon which the Oklahoma law had been patterned. See also Letter, Bob Wood to Nena Beth Stapp, October 12, 1941, quoted in Report, P. E. Foxworth, Assistant Director, FBI, to Special Agent in Charge, February 21, 1942, Shaw FOIA File.

14. See "Resolution in the Oklahoma Case," August 21, 1941, ILD MSS, reel 22, and Report, P. E. Foxworth, Assistant Director, FBI, to Special Agent in Charge, February 21, 1943, Shaw FOIA File. For more detailed accounts of ALA's slowly evolving policy toward censorship, see Evelyn Geller, *Forbidden Books in American Public Libraries, 1876–1939: A Study in Cultural Change* (Westport, Conn.: Greenwood Press, 1984); and Louise S. Robbins, *Censorship and the American Library: The American Library Association's Response to Threats to Intellectual Freedom, 1939–1969* (Westport, Conn.: Greenwood Press, 1996).

15. *Daily Oklahoman,* September 4, 1941; *Oklahoma City Times,* September 3, 1941. Attorney General Williamson quoted in Report, P. E. Foxworth, Assistant Director, FBI, to Special Agent in Charge, Oklahoma City, February 21, 1942, Shaw FOIA File.

16. Alexander Laing, "Friend of the Court," *Library Bulletin* 3 (December 1941): 148–50.

17. Ralph T. Esterquest, "Books Stand Trial in Oklahoma," *P.L.C. Bulletin* 3 (December 1941): n.p.

18. Green, "Oklahoma Ordeal," 19–20.

19. "January Bulletin," Oklahoma Committee to Defend Political Prisoners, copy found in ILD MSS, reel 22; "Keep America Free," *Woman's Home Companion* 68 (December 1941): 2.

20. "Scholars Protest," *Survey Midmonthly* 78 (January 1942): 21. For the AP story, see *Long Beach* (Calif.) *Independent,* January 9, 1942.

21. The discussion was later quoted in "January Bulletin," Oklahoma Committee to Defend Political Prisoners, copy found in ILD MSS, reel 22.

22. *Tulsa Tribune,* November 10, 1941, and quoted in "January Bulletin," Oklahoma Committee to Defend Political Prisoners, copy found in ILD MSS, reel 22.

23. "January Bulletin," Oklahoma Committee to Defend Political Prisoners, copy found in ILD MSS, reel 22, 4.

24. *Tulsa Tribune,* January 8, 1942; Ex Parte W. L. Winnett, 121 P.2d 312 (Okla. Crim. App., January 7, 1942).

25. See *Survey Midmonthly* 78 (October 42): 50; Minutes, December 19, 1941, National Board, ILD MSS, reel 1. See also Green, "God Made Oklahoma Rich — I," 12–14; "II," 17–19; *Daily Oklahoman,* January 19, 1942; "Interest High in Oklahoma Sedition Case," *Publishers Weekly* 141 (January 24, 1942): 262; and "Petitions Annoy Oklahoma Governor," *Publishers Weekly* 141 (February 7, 1942): 665. See also letter from H. E. Anderson to N.Y. City Special Agent in Charge, January 27,

1941, Robert Wood FOIA Files. Scores of the protest letters Phillips received are cited in Report, P. E. Foxworth, Assistant Director, FBI, to Special Agent in Charge, Oklahoma City, February 21, 1942, Shaw FOIA File.

26. Taken from unidentified transcript of news story, found in ILD MSS, reel 22, and possibly dated February 1, 1942.

27. Nena Beth to "Limey," January 26, 1942, ILD MSS, reel 22; *Oklahoma City Times,* January 24, 1942.

28. See "A Message to the Booksellers of America," *Publishers Weekly* 141 (May 9, 1942): 1739.

29. Unidentified news clipping, dated February 28, 1942, in Jaffe MSS, Box 1. A copy of the 21-page catalog, with prices each item brought penciled into the margins, can be found in LAW MSS, Box 2. See also "Sale of Books and Mss. To Fight Against Book Burning in Oklahoma," *Bulletin of the League of American Writers,* January 19, 1942, 11, copy found in LAW MSS, Box 1. See also [unknown] to Erskine Caldwell and Vito Marcantonio, February 26, 1942, ILD MSS, reel 22. The *Daily Oklahoman* carried a story about the second sale in its March 7, 1942, issue.

30. *Daily Oklahoman,* May 4, 1942; Minutes, National Board Meeting, ILD, June 1, 1942, ILD MSS, reel 1. Sometime during the winter of 1942 Bob had taken ill and had secreted himself away to the New York apartment of his brother, Joe Sherin, where his sister-in-law Ruth nursed him back to health with a homemade remedy of hot milk, butter, and rice traditional with Russian Jews. Nephew Ed Sherin remembers giving up his bed to his "Uncle Charlie." Telephone interview with Ed Sherin, March 21, 2005.

31. National Executive Board of the State, County and Municipal Workers of America, "Resolution on Oklahoma Criminal Prosecutions," April 25, 1942; Atlantic District Local Two, American Communications Association of the CIO, "Resolution on Oklahoma Criminal Prosecutions," May 5, 1942; both copies found in ILD MSS, reel 22.

32. See ILD Press Release, September 25, 1942; Circular, "Labor and the Oklahoma Cases," ILD MSS, reel 22.

33. See circular, "Draft Resolution on Oklahoma Cases," ILD MSS, reel 22, especially those sections headed "Some of the Labor Organizations That Have Acted on Behalf of the Oklahoma Defendants" and "What Union Leaders Say."

34. Plaintiff's Brief, Robert Wood; "Oklahoma News," *Equal Justice* 15 (Autumn 1942): 7–8. See also Defendant's Brief, Robert Wood; *600 Prominent Americans Ask President to Rescind Biddle Decision: An Open Letter Sponsored by the National Federation for Constitutional Liberties* (Washington, D.C.: National Federation for Constitutional Liberties, 1942), 7–8; and www.oac.cdlib.org, which also contains a register of the Harry Denton Bridges Papers. Bridges was never deported; the U.S. Supreme Court vacated the deportation order in 1945. Bridges v. Wixon, 326 U.S. 135 (1945).

35. Defendant's Brief, Robert Wood.

36. American Legion Brief, Robert Wood.

37. *Daily Oklahoman*, July 25, 1942; ILD Press Release, "August 17 Marks Two Years of Fight for Freedom in Oklahoma," August 14, 1942, found in ILD MSS, reel 2. See also two press releases dated August 21, 1942, ILD MSS, reel 2.

38. "Oklahoma Case Against Booksellers up For Appeal," *Publishers Weekly* 142 (August 22, 1942): 545.

39. *Daily Oklahoman*, September 9, 1942; September 10, 1942. See also "Oklahoma Book Trial Appeals Heard — State Proves It Has No Case," ILD Press Release, September 12, 1942, ILD MSS, reel 2.

40. "Oklahoma Book Trial Appeals Heard," ILD Press Release, September 12, 1942, ILD MSS, reel 2; Defendant's Brief, Eli Jaffe; Defendant's Reply Brief, Robert Wood. See also *600 Prominent Americans Ask to Rescind Biddle Decision*.

41. "Oklahoma Book Trial Appeals Heard," ILD Press Release, September 12, 1942, ILD MSS, reel 2. See also *Black Dispatch*, September 12, 1942; *Daily Oklahoman*, September 10, 1942; FBI Report by Jack H. Dillard, November 25, 1942, Robert Wood FOIA File.

42. *Black Dispatch*, September 12, 1942.

43. Quoted from "Oklahoma Book Trials Appeals Heard," ILD Press Release, September 12, 1942, ILD MSS, reel 2; *Black Dispatch*, September 12, 1942.

44. Herndon v. Lowry, 301 U.S. 242, 256, 263–64 (1937). See also Schenck v. U.S., 249 U.S. 47 (1919); DeJonge v. Oregon, 299 U.S. 353 (1937). See also Charles H. Martin, *The Angelo Herndon Case and Southern Justice* (Baton Rouge: Louisiana State University Press, 1976), 148; Rabban, *Free Speech in Its Forgotten Years*, 373–76.

45. *Black Dispatch*, September 12, 1942.

46. Quoted in "Oklahoma Dislikes Protests Over Bookstore Sedition Cases," *Publishers Weekly* 142 (September 12, 1942): 924–25. See also *Daily Oklahoman*, September 13, 1942; *Christian Science Monitor*, September 9, 1942; September 11, 1942; *Chicago Tribune*, September 10, 1942; *Washington Post*, September 10, 1942.

47. Minutes, September 14, 1942, ILD National Board meeting, ILD MSS, reel 1. See also Press Release, "Nation-Wide Letter Writing Campaign to Oklahoma Urged by ILD," September 18, 1942, ILD MSS, reel 2.

48. ILD Press Release, October 2, 1942, ILD MSS, reel 2.

49. Adams to Williamson, quoted in ILD Press Release, October 2, 1942, ILD MSS, reel 2;. Copy of "Open Letter to the Attorney General" can be found in Report, W. H. Erwin, Special Agent in Charge, Little Rock, Arkansas, to FBI Headquarters, January September 43, Shaw FOIA File.

50. Letters quoted in ILD Press Release, October 10, 1942, ILD MSS, reel 2.

51. ILD Press Release, October 17, 1942; October 1, 1942; December 13, 1942, ILD MSS reel 2; Minutes, ILD National Board, November 30, 1941, ILD MSS reel 1. See also *Chicago Defender* (national edition), November 21, 1942. Ellis County At-

torney letter to Williamson quoted in Report, Jack H. Dillard (Oklahoma City Agent) to FBI Headquarters, February 1, 1943, Shaw FOIA File.

52. Jaffe, *Odyssey*, 156; e-mail from Wilma Jaffe, August 12, 2004; letter, Eli Jaffe to Arthur Miller, March 14, 1992, in Jaffe MSS, Box 2; *Daily Oklahoman*, September 27, 1942; interview with Wilma Jaffe, January 9, 2004.

53. *PM*, October 18, 1942.

54. ILD Press Releases, October 24, 1942; December 13, 1942, ILD MSS, reel 2; Minutes, November 30, 1942, ILD National Board meeting, ILD MSS, reel 1.

55. Eli Jaffe, "Freedom on Trial," *Weekly Review*, December 15, 1942.

56. *St. Louis Post-Dispatch*, November 27, 1942.

57. *Daily Oklahoman*, December 2, 1942.

58. [Unknown Informant] to Major Brasfield, December 17, 1942, Shaw FOIA File. See also Report, Jack H. Dillard (Oklahoma City Agent), to FBI Headquarters, January 13, 1943, Shaw FOIA File.

59. FBI Report by Ralph T. Hood, March 22, 1941, Shaw FOIA Files; H. M. Caldwell (Superintendent of Mails, Oklahoma City) to Wesley Williams (Superintendent, Northwest Station, Oklahoma City), November 18, 1942, Shaw FOIA File; Transcript of telephone conversation with Nena Beth Stapp, May 24, 1943, Shaw FOIA File; Memorandum from E. A. Donahoe, September 7, 1942, Shaw FOIA File; Memorandum from John Edgar Hoover, September 8, 1942, Shaw FOIA File; FBI Report of Jack H. Dillard, September 8, 1942, Shaw FOIA File; Memorandum from Special Agent J. F. Callaghan, April 16, 1942, Shaw FOIA File; FBI Report by Willard K. White, April 3, 1943, Robert Wood FOIA File; FBI Report by Ralph Joseph Gregg, May 6, 1943, Robert Wood FOIA File; FBI Report to Jack H. Dillard, May 26, 1943, Robert Wood FOIA File. See also numerous copies of letters sent to the defendants in their FOIA File.

60. Information about Bob's employment found in letter to FBI Director from Special Agent W. G. Banister, April 13, 1943; Report by Jack H. Dillard, May 26, 1943, Robert Wood FOIA File; telephone interview with Gandy, August 21, 2005; "memorandum for the File," Special Agent Edwin P. Park, Tulsa, Oklahoma, January 23, 1943, Shaw FOIA File.

61. Shaw v. State, 134 P. 2d 999; Jaffe v. State, 134 P 2d 1027; Wood v. State, 134 P 2d. 1021 (Okla. Crim. App. 1943). Doyle told the *Daily Oklahoman* he intended to file a dissenting opinion "when he had time to prepare it." He never did. See *Daily Oklahoman*, December 19, 1943.

62. Shaw v. State, 134 P. 2d 999, 1012.

63. Shaw v. State, 134 P.2d at 1014, quoting Herndon v. Lowry, 301 U.S. 242 (1937).

64. 134 P.2d at 1016, quoting *Life and Writings of Jefferson* (Foreman), 296–97; 134 P.2d at 1019–20.

65. *Daily Oklahoman*, February 18, 1943. See also *Norman Transcript*, February 18, 1943.

66. "Interviewing Eli Jaffe," *Weekly Review,* March 23, 1943, clipping found in Jaffe MSS, Box 1.

67. *Daily Oklahoman,* February 18, 1943. See also *Miami Daily News-Record,* February 18, 1943; Letter to Hoover from W. G. Bannister, February 12, 1943; February 22, 1943, Shaw FOIA File.

68. Lorren Williams, "Reversal Ends 'Red Hunt' in State," *Tulsa World,* February 21, 1943. In its "Service Edition" published that same Sunday, the *Daily Oklahoman* framed the decision carefully. "Outcome of Oklahoma's spectacular 'Red' trials was reversed this week in a criminal court of appeals decision," it said. "The cases flamed into nationwide prominence more than two years ago after Oklahoma's hot-blooded 'Red Hunt,' bookstore raids, and the subsequent arrests and sensational prosecutions." See "Service Edition," *Daily Oklahoman,* February 21, 1943. The paper admitted to no role in any of this.

69. *Daily Worker,* February 19, 1943.

70. "Three Oklahoma Cases Reversed," *Publishers Weekly* 143 (March 6, 1943): 1096; *Washington Post,* February 18, 1943; *Wall Street Journal,* February 1, 1943; *Chicago Tribune,* February 18, 1943; *Daily Worker,* February 19, 1943.

71. *New Masses* 44 (March 2, 1943): 7; (March 9, 1943): 8; *Daily Oklahoman,* March 2, 1943. The FBI described the March 2 rally in Report, Jack H. Dillard (Oklahoma City FBI Agent) to FBI Headquarters, April 13, 1943, Shaw FOIA File. Intervention by Barefoot discussed in Letter, Special Agent W. G. Bannister to J. Edgar Hoover, April 10, 1943; and "Memorandum for the File, March 4, 1943, Shaw FOIA File.

72. Shaw v. State, 138 P. 2d 136 (Okla. Crim. App. 1943).

73. See *Daily Worker,* May 21, 1943; May 22, 1943; May 24, 1943; *Christian Science Monitor,* May 21, 1943; *Daily Oklahoman,* May 20, 1943; Report of ILD National Secretary, June 12, 1943, 2–3, ILD MSS, reel 1. See also *Chicago Tribune,* May 21, 1943.

74. Wood v. State, 141 P. 2d 309 (Okla. Crim. App. 1943).

75. Wood v. State, at 316, quoting *Schneiderman v. U.S.,* 320 U.S. 118 (1943).

76. Wood v. State. See also ILD Press Release, September 21, 1943, ILD MSS, reel 2; FBI report by Frank L. Dougherty, September 3, 1943, Robert Wood FOIA File; FBI report by Edwin P. Park, October 2, 1943, Shaw FOIA File.

77. Beth McHenry, "The Woods — Ina, Bob and Timothy," *Daily Worker,* September 20, 1943.

78. *Daily Oklahoman,* September 16, 1943; *Norman Transcript,* September 16, 1943; *Daily Worker,* September 17, 1943; September 29, 1943; ILD Press Release, September 16, 1943, ILD MSS, reel 2.

79. *Daily Oklahoman,* September 17, 1943.

80. *Daily Oklahoman,* September 19, 1943.

81. *Daily Oklahoman,* October 6, 1943. Although we were never able to determine the ultimate disposition of these materials, we suspect Alan Shaw eventually

retrieved them. He loved to read and was proud of his book collection. Interviews with Jo Biddle, June 14, 2004, and Peggy Rose, September 14, 2004. There is some evidence in FBI files that some of the books may have been sent to the Abraham Lincoln School in Chicago, but because so much information has been redacted, we cannot be sure. See F. Lewis Ingraham, Memorandum to File, September 30, 1943, Shaw FOIA File.

82. ILD Press Release, October 9, 1943; October 16, 1943, ILD MSS, reel 2; *Daily Oklahoman,* December 15, 1943. See also *Daily Worker,* October 9, 1943; October 19, 1943.

Chapter Seven

1. Because coauthor Shirley Wiegand conducted most oral interviews, all references in this chapter to "I" refer to her only.

2. Interview with Wilma Jaffe, January 10, 2004; letter from Caroline Henderson to her daughter, January [?], 1960, in Henderson, *Letters from the Dust Bowl,* 227. Eli's notes provided by Wilma. See also Veterans for Peace Tribute, www.veterans forpeace.org/EliJafffe.htm [*sic*].

3. "For Hyde Park's Jaffes . . . Peace Is Still the Best Solution," *Hyde Park Townsman,* January 3, 1991. See also newspaper clippings, Jaffe MSS, Box 2.

4. Letter, Miller to Jaffe, March 21, 1947, Jaffe MSS, Box 2. Miller's career suffered when he was held in contempt for refusing to "name names" before the House Un-American Activities Committee.

5. Letter, Miller to Jaffe, September 22, 1992, Jaffe MSS, Box 2.

6. Letter, Jaffe to Miller, October 2, 1992, Jaffe MSS, Box 2.

7. "Eli Jaffe a Strong Advocate for Peace," *Poughkeepsie Journal,* September 28, 2001.

8. Interview with Wilma Jaffe, January 9, 2004; January 10, 2004; January 11, 2004.

9. John Edgar Hoover to Major General George V. Strong, November 29, 1943, Shaw FOIA File.

10. See, e.g., FBI Report of Frank L. Dougherty, October 14, 1943, Shaw FOIA File, which quotes extensively from letters between Alan and Nena Beth.

11. Jim Jackson, "Tomorrow's Commissar? He Lives in a Frame House," *Daily Oklahoman,* July 23, 1950; interview with Jo Biddle, June 14, 2004; *Daily Oklahoman,* October 6, 1950.

12. Information about Alan Shaw and his family from interviews with family friends Jo Biddle, June 14, 2004, John Eklund, August 24, 2004, and Peggy Rose, September 14, 2004 and e-mail exchange with Judith Wheeldon, March 21, 2006. See also Alan Shaw's "Obituary," *Milwaukee Journal Sentinel,* September 19, 1999. Information about Nena Beth's early drinking habits in FBI Report by Jack H. Dillard, February 3, 1943, Shaw FOIA File.

13. See, e.g., FBI Report by L. E. Kingman, January 26, 1940, Robert Wood FOIA File.

14. FBI report by William E. Ward, October 26, 1943; FBI Report by Frank L. Dougherty, November 25, 1943, Ina Wood FOIA File.

15. Interview with Timothy Wood, January 11, 2004.

16. "Robert Wood Expelled by Communist Party," *Daily Worker,* March 23, 1951. See also "Comrade, Be Gone," *Time Magazine* 57 (April 2, 1951): 19.

17. Telephone interview with Ed Sherin, March 21, 2005; letter from Timothy Wood, May 7, 2005. See also telegram "Scheidt" to FBI Headquarters, December 22, 1950; and Office Memorandum from "SAC, New York" to FBI Director, June 19, 1951, Robert Wood FOIA File.

18. See, e.g., *New York Times,* December 5, 1959, for an account of Wood's activism on behalf of the Chelsea Tenants Center he directed.

19. Interviews with Timothy Wood, January 11, 2004, March 11, 2005; telephone interview with Ed Sherin, March 21, 2005; David W. Chen, "Jane Wood, 96, Tenant Activist and Advocate for Poor People," *New York Times,* March 19, 2004; and "Mojo's June Hellraiser," *Mother Jones* 21 (May/June 1996): 14.

20. Interview with Wilma Jaffe, January 10, 2004; interview with Timothy Wood, January 11, 2004; letter from Timothy Wood, April 28, 2005.

21. *Tulsa Tribune,* February 19, 1952; *Tulsa Daily World,* February 20, 1952; *Richmond Independent,* February 19, 1952; telephone interview with Bobby Gene Croom, April 20, 2005, and Margaret Croom Gandy, August 21, 2005.

22. Belden to Baldwin, April 14, 1941, ACLU MSS, reel 209, v. 2422; telephone interview with Candy Wilcott (Belden's daughter), January 27, 2005, October 22, 2005.

23. Telephone interview with Candy Wilcott, Stanley Belden's daughter, January 27, 2005. See also *USA Today,* February 6, 1987.

24. *Daily Oklahoman,* January 13, 1990; David Zizzo, "Signs of the Times Lean to the Right," *Daily Oklahoman,* December 24, 1993.

25. "Judge Morris' Rites Incomplete," *Daily Oklahoman,* January 5, 1949; untitled article in *Sooner Magazine,* February 1939 (no page no.).

Epilogue

1. Robinson, *Loyalty Investigations and Legislation in Oklahoma,* 84–85.

2. *Wieman et al. v. Updegraff et al.,* 344 U.S. 183 (1952).

3. 21 Okla. St. 1266.2 (2004).

4. David B. Kopel and Joseph Olson, "Preventing a Reign of Terror: Civil Liberties Implications of Terrorism Legislation," 21 *Okla. City U.L. Rev.* 247, 248 (1996); Bill Walsh, "Senators Stamp OK on Anti-Terrorism Laws: Morial Pledges Support of Ashcroft's Campaign," *Times-Picayune,* October 6, 2001; Chris Casteel, "Keating Urges Caution with Tribunals; Governor Disapproves of Use for Legal

Aliens," *Daily Oklahoman*, November 17, 2001; James Risen & Eric Lichtblau, "Bush Lets U.S. Spy on Callers Without Courts," *New York Times*, December 16, 2005, 1. See also Military Order issued November 13, 2001, by President George W. Bush, 66 Fed. Reg. 222 (Nov. 26, 2001).

5. Geoffrey R. Stone, *Perilous Times: Free Speech in Wartime From the Sedition Act of 1798 to the War on Terrorism* (New York: Norton, 2004).

6. See Rabban, *Free Speech in Its Forgotten Years*, 379; Belknap, *Cold War Political Justice*, 137, 152–57.

7. Letter to Hoover from P. E. Foxworth, Assistant Director, November 6, 1942; Report by Jack H. Dillard, April 22, 1943, Jaffe FOIA File.

8. See letter from J. Edgar Hoover to Special Agent in Charge, October 31, 1941, Jaffe FOIA File; Memorandum for Hugh B. Cox, assistant attorney general and J. Edgar Hoover, Director, FBI, from office of the attorney general, July 16, 1943, Robert Wood FOIA File.

Index